Awakening the Divine Within:
Kundalini— the Gateway to Freedom

by: Jim and Anne Armstrong

iUniverse, Inc.
Bloomington

Awakening the Divine Within
Kundalini—The Gateway to Freedom

iUniverse books may be ordered through booksellers or by contacting:

iUniverse
1663 Liberty Drive
Bloomington, IN 47403
www.iuniverse.com
1-800-Authors (1-800-288-4677)

Because of the dynamic nature of the Internet, any Web addresses or links contained in this book may have changed since publication and may no longer be valid.

ISBN: 978-1-4502-5517-2 (sc)
ISBN: 978-1-4502-5518-9 (e)

Printed in the United States of America

iUniverse rev. date: 12/10/2010

Table of Contents

Foreward

Only in retrospect can most of us spot major turning points in a life. However, on rare occasions someone says, "If you do . . .your life will never be the same again."

In 1970, Charles Tart, Ph.D., then Professor of Psychology at the University of California, at Davis, asked Anne if she would be a major presenter at a university-sponsored conference on extrasensory perception (ESP) entitled *Extrasensory Perception in Laboratory and Life*. He said several scientists would be presenting laboratory data to substantiate the PSI function in humans, but he needed someone to present the practical aspects of ESP. He quipped that he and his scientific friends would represent the "laboratory aspect" if she would present the "life" side.

Up to this point in her "career," Anne's exposure to the public had been limited to some transpersonal counseling; a few months as a subject in a parapsychology laboratory, and leading or co-leading a few weekend workshops at Esalen Institute at Big Sur, California.

When Anne appeared about ready to accept Dr. Tart's proposal he added, "Anne, I hope you realize that if you accept my proposal your life will never be the same again."

Well, she accepted the assignment and we began preparing the material for her presentation. She was scheduled to be the first speaker of the second day of the conference.

The first day of the conference was held in a freshman chemistry lecture/demonstration hall—the ones with the steep theater seating and the long laboratory bench in front. At the 10 AM break, Anne and I went down front so she could get a feel for where she would be lecturing the next morning. She stood there, looked up at the tiers of seats and concluded that it wasn't going to be that bad. Then the TV news team arrived and talked with her about the Sunday program. Little did she realize the implications of that TV interview.

During the pre-conference meeting on Sunday morning, Dr. Tart informed Anne that there had been a slight change of plans. Because of the publicity the conference had received on the evening news, the chemistry hall would no longer hold the attendees. She would be making her presentation from the stage of the main auditorium of the University, which seated over one thousand people. She quipped to Dr. Tart that she preferred looking up at a couple hundred to looking down at a thousand.

As Anne walked up to the stage a friend in the front row handed her a slip of paper. It said, "Breathe, Anne, breathe." After being introduced, she took a deep breath and began to give that sea of faces a sketch of her background. A minute or two into her presentation, she decided to throw in a bit of impromptu humor to loosen up the audience as well as herself. Little did she know how humorous it was going to be as she blithely smiled and said, "And now I want to share a quote from my favorite philosopher—penis." She had meant to say "Peanuts." Needless to say, it loosened up this very serious audience. From that point on, she hit her stride, and as Charles Tart had predicted, Anne's life would "never be the same again."

Just to make the story complete, a year later we received a phone call from Washington, DC asking our permission to enter a tape of that lecture into the Library of Congress. I wonder if they ever listened to it?

Preface

I'm sure very few books have been written on a whim—certainly not this one. For twenty years we told ourselves that we were too busy to write a book, and besides anything we would write about had already been adequately covered. Then, in September of 1995, we started publishing a newsletter that became *The Azoth Journal of Esoteric Wisdom*. Sometime soon after the publication began, our dear friends Charlie and Judy Tart said, "Just keep this up and pretty soon you will have material for a book." Then, a year or so later, I wrote an "Open Letter to Alexander," our fourteen year-old grandson, giving him a bit of our history. When Charlie got that issue of the Journal he called and said, "You've got the first chapter of your book." For a month or two we pretended that we hadn't heard him. Then, the interview that Michael and Justine Toms of New Dimensions Radio had conducted six months earlier was aired on three hundred radio stations. The phone didn't stop ringing for a month. This is when we realized Charlie was right. The only answer was to write a book.

I must admit that a book had been floating through my mind for many years but Anne wouldn't even talk about it. I guess I have always been the pusher, but now she wholeheartedly agreed. The airing of the New Dimensions Radio interview finally convinced her that there was no other way to reach the people who were interested in our approach to the spiritual aspects of life.

But the question still remained, why did we want to write this book? Or, perhaps better phrased: Why did we believe there was need for another book about someone's search for the Divine Within?

For over twenty years, the catalog write-ups for our workshops contained the statement that one of the goals of the workshop was to demystify the psychic/intuitive realm. As far as we were concerned, that included the whole esoteric, spiritual aspect of mankind because a well-developed intuition is the outgrowth of a healthy spiritual development. For eons the priesthood of the prevailing religeion or religeons helped keep the search for God or Godlike qualities shrouded in mystery in an attempt to discourage the uninitiated from seeking and having their own experience of the Divine. Twenty-first century mankind, however, needs wisdom and knowledge, not mystery and ritual, in its search for enlightenment. The material advancements of our civilization outweigh the spiritual, and it is time—actually past time—to balance the scales. We hope that this book will help dispel some of the fog of mystery.

Another reason for the book is an attempt to reach people who have or are having Kundalini experiences, as well as those who diagnose and treat their condition. There is so little professional understanding of the spiritual-emergence process. Hopefully, Anne's own spiritual opening and her insights into the philosophy behind the process will enlighten both client and clinician. The number of people having Kundalini openings is increasing exponentially, so there is an increasing need for wise handling of these spiritual emergencies.

And finally, a research project (in this case two coincidental earthly adventures) is not complete until the final report is written. The research work for this project is about complete, so it is time to write the report, clean up the files, and get ready for the next project.

Jim Armstrong – July 2010

Acknowledgments

Most people looking at the dust cover of a newly-published book will, unless they have gone through the process of writing one themselves, have no idea what it takes to reach that point. All we see on that dust cover is the name or names of the author or authors. That tells only a small fraction of the story, for there are all these other people sitting at computers or desks in the middle of the night typing, editing and correcting copy, so someone else can see printed on that dust cover, "By _____."

Without knowing ahead of time that Marilyn Grow would be there for months of typing, typing, and typing, we never would have begun this project. As I look at this project in retrospect, it is the culmination of a bargain we made over twenty-five years ago. I told Marilyn that I would buy a state-of-the-art computer if she would learn to operate it. And learn she did---from DOS through MS Publisher. Marilyn was there from word one through the first rough draft. Then there was a several year hiatus. Mark Morton got the first CD off to the editor and publisher, then Judy Cochran and I got it ready for the dust-jacket. So, Marilyn Grow is at the top of our acknowledgment list. Without the hundreds of hours of grueling effort at her keyboard, this book would never have happened. Without your efforts, Marilyn, look at the fun all the rest of the crew would have missed!

Then there are Judith and Charles Tart, Ph.D., whose prodding over the years got the project off the ground in the first place. And without that chapter-by-chapter coaching, we surely would have missed the mark. Marilyn, just think of how much simpler your life would have been if Charlie hadn't pushed, but look at what you would have missed?

I never really acquired an understanding of English grammar until I began to study German in college. So we want to thank Susan Shuhert for bridging the gaps my English/German grammar created.

Then there are those beautiful people who provided the final impetus that launched this project—Michael and Justine Toms, of New Dimensions Radio. Their interview, and subsequent airing on over three hundred radio stations, finally convinced us there was no other way to reach the people who were interested in our approach to a fuller life.

Another coach and pusher has been our dear friend of over twenty years, Karen Turner. If you sense a psychological twinge in this book it is probably Karen's doings.

Last, but far from least, I want to thank my wonderful wife, Anne, who has put up with over a year of more neglect than usual while I have been assembling these one hundred thousand words into one bundle.

Jim Armstrong — 2010

Introduction

More than half a century of work in many areas of psychology, as well as my own personal experience, has shown me over and over again that we humans are "spiritual" creatures. No, I can't pin down "spiritual" in the clear, precise way we scientists like to define our terms. Indeed, most people think science is opposed to spirituality, that science has somehow proven that spirituality and religion— the social belief systems that start from spiritual experiences—are all a matter of superstition and neurotic attempts to avoid recognizing our limits and our mortality.

It is silly to ignore or deny the existence of something because you can't adequately capture it completely in words, although lots of people do that. More importantly, I've observed how the denial of any possible reality to our spiritual nature cuts us off from that higher nature and can create a lot of useless, avoidable suffering. This is particularly unfortunate, for properly used, essential science has given us striking evidence that humans sometimes show some of the qualities—telepathic communication with others, for example, or prayer affecting healing— that we would expect spiritual beings to have.

Scientism then, a rigid philosophy of materialism, pretending to be science, and all too often confused with it, denies and undermines our spiritual values and development. Individuals may have strong spiritual values or direct experiences, but then they pull back and deny their own inner experience because they believe science has shown the spiritual to be nothing but fantasy. As a psychologist, I can assure you that denying any aspects of your own nature is costly; realities don't disappear simply because you refuse to deal with them.

This book is about the initial struggle with success and then rich development of the spiritual in two of my oldest and closest friends, Anne and Jim Armstrong. Decades ago, long before my wife and I met and befriended them, they were living an ordinary American life, struggling to make ends meet and get ahead in the world, and not particularly interested in spiritual matters. They were, by prevailing social standards, "normal." Then Anne began having very painful and crippling headaches. They were not helped by available medical approaches.

As described in this book, they eventually tried hypnosis—and the headaches turned out to be caused by spiritual forces straining to express themselves through Anne. Flash forward many years from the initial struggle—the fascinating details are in this book—and we find that Anne and Jim accepted, worked with, and came to terms with these forces. Anne has been giving insightful and helpful readings to people—including me and many friends of mine—and together Anne and Jim have led many workshops worldwide, helping people understand aspects of the psychic and the spiritual, and how they can develop their own psychic and spiritual abilities.

This is a success story, but it makes you wonder how many other people today have, unfortunately, accepted the social/medical label that they are "neurotic" or "crazy" or "ill" when the spirit is actually trying to express itself through them? If you broaden your view to the wider anthropological study of human cultures, you will find there have been many societies—they are being slowly wiped out by "modernity"—in which some illnesses were recognized as possible signs of spiritual, rather than purely physical problems and led to people being trained as shamans, priests and healers, rather than left in the "crazy" or "ill" category.

Quite aside from all the fascinating stories and information in this book, I have encouraged Jim Armstrong to write it because of the story of hope it offers to many people confused or inhibited about their spiritual and psychic lives, as to broaden the audience that might be helped by the many, many inspiring teachings that have come through Anne. It is also inspiring to see how the Armstrong's were not just passive recipients of something more, but worked and negotiated with the spiritual for reasonable, rather than overwhelming, manifestations.

If even one person sees new possibilities in his or her life as a result of reading this, it has been well worth the work of writing and publishing, and adds another dimension to the many ways Anne and Jim have helped so many people over the years.

Charles T. Tart, Ph.D.
Professor of Psychology, Institute of Transpersonal Psychology, Palo Alto, California,
Professor Emeritus of Psychology, University of California at Davis.

PART ONE:

Living
with
Kundalini

CHAPTER I:

THE
AWAKENING

The scene is a cobblestone road on the outskirts of Ancient Rome, at about the time of Caesar. An impeccably uniformed young Centurion drives a chariot erratically at full speed for a hundred meters or so, then he stops, gets out and kicks the bloody body tied to the chariot. He again mounts the chariot, and whips the horses to a sudden start hoping to break the neck of the victim and bring this cruel ordeal to an end. Finally, the body fails to respond to the kicks.

Standing beside the once handsome body of a powerful athlete, but unseen to his executioner, is the indwelling spirit of Antonius giving thanks to the gods that his ordeal is finally over. He takes one last look at what had been his body, sadly turns his back on the world of flesh with all its pain and blends with the light of the unfamiliar realm of the gods.

For the past half-hour, Anne Armstrong, a petite young woman (my wife Anne Armstrong), affectionately known to her friends and husband as Eddie, had lain upon a couch in the suburbs of Sacramento, California nearly 2,000 years later, reliving every excruciating moment of the torture that began on a torturer's rack in what looked and felt like a dungeon. The ropes would be tightened until the victim passed out, only to be revived with a bucket of cold water then questioned again about confidential information he was believed to have. When he did not answer, the ropes would be tightened again and the process repeated. Finally, in frustration, the order was given to release the victim from the rack. He was then prodded up the stairs and tied by the neck to the back of a chariot, to be dragged on the cobblestones until his flesh was shredded and his powerful neck broken, releasing the indwelling spirit from the bloody carcass that lay behind the Centurion's chariot.

Following my suggestion, when I was an amateur hypnotist over forty years ago, my wife Eddie had been plunged into the past to "locate the source" of her migraine headaches—headaches, that plagued her for over thirty years. Moments after being given the suggestion that some part of her being "knew" the source of the headaches, she "awakened" in the body of a two hundred twenty pound, six-foot tall young Roman being tortured on a rack in a dungeon that she knew intuitively was near Rome. Nearby stood a Roman Centurion directing the torture and conducting the interrogation. The story line seemed to be that the man on the rack had information about Julius Caesar he refused to divulge to his captors.

The hypnotherapy that led up to this dramatic scene had been started a month earlier by Dr. Irene Hickman, a local hypnotherapist. Eddie and I had previously attended a hypnosis class taught by Dr. Hickman and, we were practicing the technique of regression with Eddie as the subject, when she, under hypnosis, began relating this story. For the next ten months, both Dr. Hickman and I continued to work as therapists with Eddie. During subsequent therapy sessions the events of Antonius' entire life unfolded from his birth to his untimely death behind a chariot. We both treated these traumatic events as if they were recollections from one of Eddie's previous existences on this earth plane. After all, the events that were transpiring were her reality and the scenario made a convenient and useful therapeutic vehicle.

Within six weeks after the therapy began, it became apparent that Eddie no longer needed to be hypnotized. She would merely lie down, close her eyes, take a few deeper-than-usual breaths and ease herself into the therapy session. Fortunately, tape recorders were becoming readily available, so it was possible to keep accurate records of everything that transpired. This proved to be invaluable at times, especially when the above scenes were being "re-run" to capture more detail and remove some of the emotional charge. Once, while Eddie "re-experienced" the scene behind the chariot, her breathing stopped. Soon her pulse became imperceptible and for two and a half minutes I fought to keep her alive. Only after resorting to mouth-to-mouth resuscitation did she begin to breathe as her pulse returned.

Eddie could describe these scenes in Ancient Rome with great detail, as if she were watching a movie. Yet, when asked to describe the Centurion directing the torture, she ignored his face. She would start at his feet, describe every strap and thong on his sandals, his short "skirt," sword and elaborate breast plate and then begin describing his fancy helmet with its crest and plumage, but never mentioning the face of the person. For weeks both Dr. Hickman and I tried to get Eddie to look at the face of her torturer. Eddie nicknamed him "fancy pants," brought in more and more detail of his uniform but never acknowledge that he even had a face. Then one evening when I was doing the therapy, I led her once more through a detailed description of her torturer. This time she looked at the face of the Centurion and screamed in agony, "It's you!"

This was a turning point in the therapy. But, was it allegory or reality? Eddie had grown up with a Greek step-father who still retained his old world views of girls being inferior to boys; so, to keep peace in the family, she totally deferred to his, and everyone else's, wishes. Then she married me. I have always tended to take charge if no one else would and she seldom did. So, was she being tortured in her present life? Yes. Did she want to be a strong male? Yes. Could she talk about it in the present? No. Perhaps, therefore, it would be easier to use this situation happening 2,000 years ago as a vehicle to take the charge off the present. Or did it all really happen 2,000 years ago—Eddie and I, settling old scores left over from Egypt or even Atlantis, and now in 1960, trying to level the playing field in a more civilized way?

Subsequent therapy sessions brought to Eddie's memory several other scenarios that appeared to be someone's life, perhaps hers. One evening, after listening to a half-hour description of life in Ancient Rome, I asked her, "Haven't you ever had a life where you were happy?" The response was immediate. "I'm dressed in this costume of gold brocade, performing madras, dressed in gowns with the fancy pointed shoulders, the elaborate headdress and the pointed slippers, doing a ritual dance in front of this huge, golden Buddha. My parents brought me to this temple when I was five or six years old and I was taught these rituals. They treated me well; I had good food, a nice place to live, and these beautiful clothes to wear. My name is Marija." She moved forward through that life, eventually finding herself in a harem-type arrangement having to sleep with a "fat, ugly man." During what seemed to be middle age, she found herself dying of some debilitating disease, like syphilis. After talking about the events of this life for sometime, I suggested she return to the temple scene and that she get up and demonstrate what she had learned there. For the next fifteen or twenty minutes she performed ritual dances, told stories with her hands (we later found that these movements were called mudras) and chanted in a voice with an incredible range, far greater than anything she could do in her normal consciousness.

One morning our next-door neighbor, who had originally convinced Eddie to try hypnosis for her headaches, came over for tea and a chat. She had been cured of headaches through hypnosis and was now learning a few techniques from the psychiatrist with whom she had worked. At some point Phyllis said, "I wonder if I could hypnotize you?" In a matter of minutes Eddie found herself in beautiful, plush surroundings, apparently in Ancient Egypt. She took on the identity of a dark-skinned woman who used psychic powers to maintain a position of authority and obvious wealth. As she continued to be identified with this unsavory person, Eddie realized that this woman's body had become deformed and frozen into grotesque shapes as a result of misusing psychic energy and that she "herself" was beginning to simulate that condition in her own body. Needless to say, our neighbor was terrified, but when Eddie returned to normal consciousness she assured Phyllis the energy would wear itself out in a half hour or so and she would return to her usual appearance. When I arrived home she gleefully announced she had discovered another personality, but this one seemed to be quite an evil person.

Eddie and Dr. Hickman did a lot of therapy around this apparent past life, getting Eddie to see that, if indeed she had been this evil person, she was now a totally different being; if she had had such abilities, there was no way she would misuse them now. In the last scene that Eddie observed, this evil woman ordered her servant to set fire to the apartment to destroy this grotesque body so no one would ever see it. Almost immediately, the soul passed into a condition that could only be described as hell. The space was dark, filled with what seemed like a never-ending series of grotesque monster-like creatures, snakes, and taunting, mocking voices. Although she experienced no sense of time as we know it, it could have been hundreds of earth years. Finally, a tiny light appeared in the eternal darkness and she was guided into a place of understanding and learning where she could begin to evaluate the past life and prepare for the approaching incarnation.

Although there were several vignettes during the course of the therapy, these three "lives" were quite symbolic of Eddie's present life: the beautifully developed Roman athlete represented her own competitive, masculine nature (in high school she had "letters" for every sport in which a girl could compete); the Siamese temple dancer was symbolic of her petite feminine aspect, a five foot, one hundred pound, beautiful young woman; the evil Egyptian woman with psychic abilities introduced her to the dark side of the abilities that lay hidden within her own psyche.

As noted earlier, within six weeks after Dr. Hickman began to work with Eddie, it became evident that hypnosis had simply been a temporary tool to get her back into the quiet, meditative state she had been avoiding for over sixteen years. A couple of years after Eddie and I were married, we enrolled in a course on esoteric Christianity, sponsored by The Rosicrucian Fellowship, at Oceanside, California. After a few months of study, exercises, and meditation, Eddie's psyche blew wide open. Years later, it became apparent that she had experienced a full-blown Kundalini opening, but no one in the Salt Lake City area in the 1940's had any idea what was happening to her. The doctors gave her shots and pills and told her she was psychotic. At some point she reasoned that before all this esoteric study and meditation she was at least functional in spite of dealing with migraine headaches, asthma and hay fever. She vowed therefore, to stop meditating, reading, or even discussing esoteric matters. Gradually, all the health problems she had, plus a few more, intensified. Sixteen years later she was desperate to find relief, especially from the migraines that came once or twice a week and lasted two or three days each time. So, when our neighbor suggested hypnosis, she reluctantly agreed to try it.

About the same time that Eddie noted hypnosis was no longer required to induce an altered state of consciousness, she became aware of an inner guidance that instructed her to set aside one to three hours a day for "instruction"—in what, she had no idea. But life was going so well that she reasoned it couldn't hurt to give it a try. Soon she became enrolled in what seemed like a "self-improvement course", for the soul. By now she had discovered that to enter the state necessary for therapy, or related activities, she needed merely to engage the meditative state she had avoided for over sixteen years.

The instruction began with simple breath awareness exercises, rapidly moving into complicated yogic breathing patterns. She simply relaxed into an altered state and the breathing patterns, no matter how complicated, would just start happening. Sometimes she knew ahead of time what was going to happen, but usually it was a spontaneous process. Consciously she knew the word yoga but that was about the extent of her knowledge of the subject. Soon intricate asanas (yoga body postures) were added. Eddie and I began to look for books on yoga, trying to identify what she was performing spontaneously. Soon, however, she was assuming postures that weren't in our books, so we began to search for books on more advanced yoga teachings. In one such posture, she rolled her tongue backwards forcing the tip down her throat and proceeded to "massage" the top of the throat cavity with the tip of her tongue, all the time wondering what on earth was going on. We found that the English translation of this yogic exercise was "moving in the void." It is an asana to encourage an elixir of the head chakra to be channeled to the heart chakra. This was just one of the obscure asanas that Eddie performed spontaneously. At some point, she ceased to wonder and just let it happen. One morning she invited me to join her and follow along so I could get a better idea of what she was experiencing. After an intricate breath routine, she opened her eyes and I was gone—really gone. To her amazement I had passed out, fallen backwards into an open closet full of clothes and sunk noiselessly to the floor. Apparently, I had skipped some preliminary training.

Along with the yogic breathing and asanas came detailed instruction on meditating, eating, sleeping, emotional control, and thought control—in short, how to live a more spiritually-oriented life. She appeared to be in a definite training program, but for what she still had no idea. Dr. Hickman was so intrigued with what was happening that several times she invited Eddie to come to her office for these training sessions so she could observe and take notes.

About two months into her "training program," Eddie awoke one morning with all the symptoms of an imminent migraine. Although I had never done this before, I called my secretary and said that I would not be coming into the office until the next day. Against Eddie's assurances that she had been handling headaches for thirty years by herself, I insisted upon staying home in case she needed me. About 10 AM, I came into the bedroom to see if there was anything I could do. We talked for a few minutes; she looked across the room to the open door into the hall then calmly announced that death was standing in the doorway and was here to take her. Trying to respect what seemed like a resignation to the inevitable, I asked her why she was so sure. With no emotion in her voice, she calmly stated that in a few minutes a blood vessel would rupture in her brain and that would be the end. Every minute or so she would announce that death had moved a little closer to the foot of the bed. I continued to talk to her, reminding her that she had a nine year-old daughter, a nice home, a relatively good life, and a husband and many other people who loved her very much. I urged her to consider this decision carefully, and emphasized that she was the only one who could make it. I finally raised her to a sitting position, got in behind her to prop her up and suggested that she send her uninvited guest away. Her childhood training as a Catholic emerged and she began very laboriously, as if her arms weighed one hundred pounds each, to make the sign of the cross in the face of death that now stood almost touching the foot of the bed. She couldn't make it with one arm so she held her right arm at the wrist with the left hand and with Herculean effort made the sign of the cross in death's face. She had made the decision to live. As Eddie described it, slowly, almost reluctantly, death backed up until he stood just outside the door in the hall. Within minutes her headache went away leaving no trace of soreness or other residual effects. Later, looking back upon the scene, she reasoned that this was probably her concept of the specter of death. She said it looked like a stereotypical cartoon image of death as a cadaver wrapped in a white cloak, or sheet—really quite corny.

A short time later, she got up, had a shower, and sat down with me to reflect upon the traumatic events of the morning. When Christine came home from school her mother was in the kitchen getting dinner so we could use the ballet tickets we had for that evening. There was, however, one residual effect of that day. The corny figure of death stayed about five steps behind her. He became her constant companion. I would call her from the office and ask her about her "new friend." She would look over her shoulder and say, "He's still standing there, I guess just waiting to see if I will change my mind." This specter of death remained week after week, but following our Easter morning meditation, Eddie became aware that "her friend" had left, never to return. Why he had chosen Easter morning to fade back into the astral, or wherever these thought forms reside, is anyone's guess.

Sometime during that eventful winter and spring, Eddie became aware of a personality or individuality attached to the daily instructions she had been receiving. Just about eighteen inches above her head, and a little to the right, she was aware of a beautiful Hindu face, his head wrapped in a white turban. She asked him for a name and when he didn't respond she just gave him the name, "Mister M," for Master. He was present whenever she looked up. Soon she found that if she had a question about the instruction, or even questions that other people had, she could hold out her hands, palms up, and instantly the answer was there. Talk about having the Genie-in-the-bottle, she had it—she thought. This went on for months, and then one evening I came home to find a sad, crestfallen wife sitting at the kitchen table. "He's gone! Mister M is gone! I put out my hands, looked up and he wasn't there. There are no answers and no energy in my hands!"

I considered the situation for a few moments, then reminded her that for months she had relied upon Mister M for everything she wanted to know, and in so doing had abdicated her own responsibility. I suggested that she go into the den and meditate upon the dependency that surrounded her relationship with Mister M.

She sat for a long time contemplating the events of the past several months and her growing dependency upon Mister M. Suddenly she felt that familiar charge of energy surge through her body and spontaneously looked up to see Mister M smiling approvingly. He raised his hand in a farewell gesture as if to say, "You got the message" and faded from sight, never to be seen again. Eddie has remarked several times since that it felt as if he had faded from sight and entered her heart.

Immediately following the disappearance of the specter of death and the withdrawal of Mister M from Eddie's life, the frequency of the migraine headaches went from once a week, lasting two or three days to once every other week and then to once a month; finally, stopping altogether. The goiter that the doctors wanted to remove became dormant, the hysterectomy that she had been threatened with for years became totally unnecessary, and the hay fever and asthma that had added such misery to her life for nearly thirty five years, failed to develop that spring. Psychologically and emotionally, she had never felt better.

There are some things in life for which there seems to be no logical explanation. The following events fit that category. Several years after Mister M's disappearance, Eddie and I were visiting some friends near Seattle, Washington. One morning our host suggested we go into Seattle to attend a seance. Since neither Eddie nor I had ever experienced that kind of psychic demonstration we were delighted with this opportunity. When we arrived the seance was already in process. The medium was on the stage of this small auditorium already in trance. As was the custom, we were told he had an assistant tape his mouth closed before going into trance. It is difficult to understand how this would prevent fraud in an auditorium situation, but our friends said this was standard procedure.

The séance room was totally dark. The audience was warned that a trumpet would float over their heads and discarnate relatives or whatever would speak to some people. Being the "scientist," I sat there in the dark smiling (or smirking) thinking what a bunch of baloney this is. In other parts of the auditorium a voice would suddenly be heard making an inane pronouncement that there is a spirit present who says she was Joe's grandmother and she has something she wishes to say to him, followed by some drivel about how well she feels now, and is he taking good care of the cats she had to leave. Then suddenly there was a swishing sound in the dark above our heads as if something were moving very rapidly. It was all I could do to resist reaching up in the dark to see what was up there. Then a booming voice thundered in our ears, " I am Mahando, I was your teacher ages ago in India. For a few months I worked with you in this life, but the day came when it was deemed expedient for you to be on your own." We were all so totally stunned by what had happened that no one remembered even the gist of the profound discourse that followed. These are the bare facts—but what does one do with them?

About a year after Eddie began therapy, Dr. Hickman asked Eddie to work as her assistant; her rationale being that since Eddie had turned her life completely around in ten or twelve months, healing all her own illnesses after telling the therapist why the particular problem existed and what needed to be done, surely she could do it for other people. Eddie was stunned and would have no part of it.

However, just as an experiment, Dr. Hickman handed Eddie a case folder and instructed her to just hold it, not open or read it. Immediately after closing her eyes she became aware of the client connected to the case folder, and began to "feel" as if she had several discreet compartments in her head, each mutually exclusive and seemingly unknown to the client until the personality associated with that compartment made its appearance in her daily life. When the client was functioning from one of these compartments she was a dowdy housewife, had several kids, a no-good husband, a miserable home life, everything in her life a mess, and had no self-esteem. When her consciousness switched to another compartment she was almost a society debutante with no husband or kids, a carefree life with no problems, fancy clothes and not a serious thought in her head. Eddie was experiencing all this as if she were the client, so she was effectively talking from inside this very confused person. She then switched to a third compartment and immediately her head was filled with sexual images. She saw herself in a psychiatrist's office using every ploy known to woman to seduce the doctor. There were other compartments, but at that point Dr. Hickman asked Eddie to return to herself and open the case folder. She soon found that this person had been in counseling with several doctors in the city, and what she had just experienced was almost a verbatim description of this woman's actions and attitudes as a multiple personality. She had tried to seduce every male therapist with whom she had worked. When her husband came home in the evening he had no idea which personality his wife would be, whether she would even recognize him as her husband, or if perhaps as the social debutante, she would have gone on a wild shopping spree at the most expensive stores in town and the bed would be covered with new clothes.

Eddie agreed to try out Dr. Hickman's proposal, but only if the doctor would sit with her during her sessions with the client, and if she could keep her eyes closed so she wouldn't be distracted by the client's reaction. The proposal was that the client would have a session with Eddie, then armed with that inside information, Dr. Hickman would be in a much better position to begin the therapy. As all therapists know, weeks or months can be spent digging out the roots of mental and emotional problems, so having access to a process where this information could be recovered in less than an hour was very intriguing. Within a year after beginning her own therapy Eddie was working in the doctor's office as her assistant. This arrangement continued for a year or two until Dr. Hickman became interested in politics and was elected as the county assessor.

During the time Eddie worked in Dr. Hickman's office she had an opportunity to meet some quite interesting people. Hugh Lynn Cayce was presenting a seminar at Asilomar based upon his famous father's work as a psychic consultant and healer. Many of the people in the hypnosis group, as well as Eddie and I, had read books about Edgar Cayce's well-documented psychic activities. So Eddie, Dr. Hickman, and I decided to attend. During the conference we heard about a parapsychologist named Dr. Andrija Puharich who had a laboratory in Carmel Valley Village, California. During an afternoon break, Hugh Lynn Cayce, Dr. Hickman, and Eddie and I visited Dr. Puharich's parapsychology laboratory. After giving the four of us a tour of the lab, Dr. Puharich invited us to a gathering at his home in Carmel that evening. Soon after the party got started, Dr. Puharich announced to the group that they had a "celebrity" with them that evening, and perhaps she could be persuaded to give them a sample of her talents. We all looked around to see who this person might be, until he said, "Anne Armstrong." When Eddie started to work with Dr. Hickman she began using her legal name, "Anne," as it sounded more "professional." Anne nearly fainted, and when her protests were overruled, she decided that the simplest way to demonstrate intuitive ability was through psychometry. She asked the host if he had some old object that might have had an interesting history, preferably a history of which he had some knowledge. He thought for a few moments, then took a ring from his finger. Anne looked at it and remarked that it looked quite new. He brushed the remark aside and as much as said, just hold it and see what you get. She did what she was told; after all, there were twenty people watching and she was the guest of a person whom she had only met hours before. So what if it wasn't old? The worst that would happen was that she wouldn't get anything.

She held the ring, first one hand then the other, then held it up to her forehead, closed her eyes and allowed her energy to merge with the energy of this "new" ring. In seconds she found herself in a steaming jungle getting hotter and more agitated by the moment. She described her feelings and surroundings and then made some blood curdling, unearthly sounds, a kind of primitive chanting, after which she opened her eyes and looked around the circle of people watching her. Her expression turned to one of pure evil, as if she hated everyone there and would kill in an instant if she had the means. For a moment she had the look of a wild, tormented animal, but soon resumed the evil look. Dr. Hickman and I looked at each other for a moment, then rushed into the center of the room and grabbed her. At that moment Anne was one hundred and two pounds of seething evil with the strength of a python. Dr. Hickman was a large, rather muscular woman and with her help I was able to drag this demonized person toward the kitchen. All attempts to wrest the ring from her grip failed. The two of us finally got this clawing, screaming, kicking mass of dynamic evil to the kitchen sink. Some evil intelligence within her knew what was about to happen and she was fighting to prevent having her hands and arms immersed in cold running water. Both Dr. Hickman and I were sufficiently versed in black and white magic ritual to know the effectiveness of cold running water in breaking a magic spell, and this was obviously what Anne had succumbed to when she tuned into that "new" ring. With all the force we could muster we finally subdued her enough to get her hands and forearms under the running water. Her grip relaxed, the ring dropped into the sink and she looked at the two of us and asked, "What is going on, what happened?"

The three of us returned to the stunned group of people, some who had come to the kitchen to see what was happening. I handed the ring to Dr. Puharich while Anne, looking disheveled and badly shaken, asked the Doctor what he knew about the history of the ring. He said Daddy Bray, a Kahuna leader on the Big Island of Hawaii, following his fire ceremony initiation into the organization, had just recently presented him the ring. Daddy Bray gave him the ring with the admonition never to take it off. The rest he "neglected" to tell the group. True, the gold setting was new, but the several, uncut rubies were from the "crown jewels" of centuries of Kahuna royalty. Later, close examination revealed that each jewel was set with five bezels, or chisel cuts, with the fifth bezel in each case offset and pointing downward. It didn't take an expert in black magic to recognize the forces represented and contained within that ring.

God only knows what those jewels had been exposed to during hundreds of years of war, treachery, intrigue, hatred, and murder in the steaming jungles of Hawaii.

This, however, is not even near the end of the saga. Andrija was intrigued by Anne's remarkable abilities and invited her to spend as much time as she could at this emerging parapsychological research laboratory, in Carmel Valley, California.

During the next year or so, Anne and I spent nearly every weekend and vacation at the lab. We came to the lab whenever I could get away from my job as a research engineer in the defense industry. Anne worked with Andrija doing research into the possible mechanisms of intuition, and I assisted Andrija in developing test programs, and designing and building test equipment.

A few months after we started going to the laboratory, Anne had an opportunity to meet Daddy Bray in Hawaii. His first greeting when they met was, "I want to shake the hand of the psychic who held that ring and lived through it. It could have killed you. I told Andrija when I gave him the ring never to take it off, and if he did, never let a highly intuitive or psychic person hold it. The forces it contained could kill an uninitiated person." He invited her to a fire ceremony on the Big Island, but because of the superstition of the lady she was staying with in Honolulu, Anne was prevented from having the experience.

A month or so later Daddy Bray came to the laboratory and reprimanded Andrija for what he had done, and said, "Give me the ring and I'll fix it so it can never harm anyone again." He did some ritual with his hands and some incantations, then handed it back to

Andrija. Later, on a trip back east, Andrija and Peter Hurkos, a well-known, gifted, Dutch psychic, famous for his work with the police of both Europe and America, were traveling on a train together. Andrija, still being the skeptical, inquisitive, scientific researcher, again took the ring off, handed it to Peter, one of the best known psychometrists in the world, and asked him what kind of energy or pictures he could get from it. After being silent for several minutes he handed the ring back to Andrija saying, "I can't get a thing from it."

When Anne and I visited Andrija in New York City, he asked her if she could help him find his ring. It had slipped off his finger while he was burning leaves on his estate up the Hudson River at Ossining, New York. She simply said that it was a fitting end for a ring that had lost its power to have its beginning and end during a fire ritual.

Anne's intuitive abilities developed very rapidly after those first several months of therapy. In less than two years, she began to deliver spontaneous lectures with very profound esoteric content, many of which have been published as essays in the *Azoth Journal of Esoteric Wisdom*. The members of our Edgar Cayce Study Group became aware of Anne's abilities and suggested that we meet each Friday evening and see what Anne might have to teach us. For the next eighteen months, the Friday Night Group met regularly. The group consisted of three or four engineers, a doctor, bank manager and astrologer, a librarian, contractor, and a couple of housewives. The members would begin arriving about 7:30 PM, the discussion would continue until everyone's arrival around 8 PM. We would then meditate for ten or fifteen minutes giving Anne time to become "still" after a busy day and prepare herself to receive the evening instructions or a spontaneous lecture. The group members, in addition to their own professions, were well schooled in Eastern and Western religious philosophies, the arts, astrology, etc. They were a very stimulating group of people.

Sometimes the spontaneous lecture added clarity to the early discussion of the evening, but usually there seemed to be a totally independent teaching agenda set by some force or entity separate from the group. The lectures, covering many aspects of emotional, mental and spiritual growth, were all recorded on tape and are still being used as material for the Azoth Journal. The teachings were based upon the esoteric philosophy of Jesus, so were non-sectarian and eclectic.

In January 1963 Anne and I went to Europe on an assignment with NATO. The Friday Night Group sessions were interrupted for several months but resumed when we returned. Even after the group finally disbanded, however, Anne and I would usually record one or more spontaneous lectures a week up until the end of 1967. From then until mid 1994 Anne was very involved in private counseling, workshops, seminars and teaching. A great wealth of wisdom and information was made available to us during those several years and we are still trying to absorb its essence and pass it along to fellow students.

CHAPTER II:

THE CONVERGENCE

While Chapter One of this account related the highlights of a short, yet rather dramatic, period of our lives. up to the fall of 1959 our time together had been good, but rather ordinary.

Lead Character

Anne and I were born and raised in two quite different worlds. She was born into a middle class Mexican family in Ciudad Gusman, near Guadalajara. Her mother was living in the family home when Enedina, Anne's given name, made her appearance and began her current life on July 1, 1919. Enedina was the first of twin girls to see the light of day, but through a series of unfortunate circumstances associated with home births at that time, her twin sister lived only a few hours. Her father either left home to join a local revolution or was kicked out by her grandfather. Her mother was never very clear about what happened. In any case, her doting grandfather died shortly after her birth and his second wife made life so miserable for her mother that she married a big-talking Greek, James Georgelos, whom she met in the family owned general store. When Enedina was less than two years old this wild Greek took his new wife and child to Texas, which he convinced Enedina's mother was "the land of opportunity." Knowing James Georgelos, they no doubt crossed the Rio Grand during the dry season in the middle of the night, further complicating Enedina's life.

After arriving in Texas, her Greek stepfather took the family to Amarillo. Anne still has vague memories of their deplorable conditions, living in a railroad boxcar in the Amarillo, Texas rail yards where for the next year or two James, the stepfather, worked as a railroad laborer in this great "land of opportunity." Rosa, Anne's mother, had been raised in a large hacienda with servants and a degree of affluence and almost overnight, she was reduced to stark poverty. She didn't know how to cook or take care of a house and family under the best of conditions, much less as an illegal immigrant in a railroad yard boxcar. It got so bad that Anne remembers begging her mother to give her away. A lovely Jewish couple who came by the boxcar selling clothes to poor itinerants, and who had no children, begged Rosa to give Anne to them so she could have a decent upbringing. But, despite her family's despicable living conditions, Rosa, Anne's mother, refused.

Anne doesn't remember the family's transition out of Texas, but a few years later she recalls starting kindergarten in Pasadena, California, the first day was traumatic. Her mother, who spoke no English, took her to school. The teacher, feeling compassion for this little ethnic, wanted to make her feel special in the game of hide-and-seek so she put her out the door and told her to hide. Not understanding English or the game, she thought the teacher didn't like her and was sending her away, so she ran home in tears. In spite of this unfortunate beginning, she learned English and was soon well integrated and loved school. It was certainly better than the drab surroundings of home. Her mother, however, was miserable since she could remember what it was like to have servants and adequate money. Anne's stepfather was a hard worker and would do whatever it took to provide for his family, but being uneducated and with no particular skills, the family continued to struggle, especially as the general economy took a downturn at the end of the 20's.

During the depths of the 1930's depression the stepfather got a job cleaning and re-landscaping bank repossessed homes. Part of his wages was in the form of free rent in the homes he was rehabilitating. Anne remembers as a kid getting a home nicely cleaned and comfortable and then having to move again because someone bought it.

Some time during the course of this chaotic itinerant lifestyle, Anne's family moved near a Catholic Church. Her family wasn't particularly religious, but Anne became interested in religious activities and worked very hard to prepare for her first communion when she was twelve years old. She came to church for the communion ceremony in the best dress she had, only to be sent away by the priest because her dress wasn't white. She was heartbroken. This incident, coupled with being told by the priest that she asked too many (unanswerable or embarrassing) questions, caused her to part company with Catholicism at an early age. One of the frequent family moves brought Anne next door to what she described as a "Holy-roller Church." She enjoyed the singing and the informal, exuberant style of worship and found the congregation and the minister to be very down-to-earth people, so for the next few years she experienced the more informal side of the Christian religion.

The difficult life and a sickly mother caused Anne to grow up quickly. At eight years old she was running a home, taking care of her half brother and sister, helping in family projects like picking walnuts, and still excelling in school. Consequently, she grew up as a very serious, responsible, highly intelligent child. Within a few years after learning English she was an "A" student, reading books way beyond her years. The Arthurian Legends were among her favorites. However, at about thirteen, during the depths of the Great Depression, she suffered what appears to have been a nervous breakdown of some kind. Her parents had probably never heard of a psychiatrist much less have the means to engage one, so Anne dropped out of school for several months until she became stabilized. Apparently, her delicate nervous system could withstand just so much between the living conditions and her insensitive stepfather. He was just not a nice person, and her mother was too sick to offer much support. An example of his ignorance of social decency emerged when Anne was about 8 years old, and her mother had just given birth to James's second child. He informed her that, "I now have my boy, and I don't want you ever to ask me for anything again—you are not my daughter." This was quite a shock for a very insecure 8 year-old. She had always assumed that he was her father.

By fourteen, Anne was beginning to look and act like a young woman which was "dangerous" in the ethnic neighborhood where they lived. Older men, twenty to thirty, began to be interested in her. One such was a young lawyer who began bringing her books and talk to her about the "outside world," but romantic overtones were not far beneath the gifts. Living in the conditions in which she found herself, made her vulnerable to their attention. Fortunately, a childless couple became aware of this overly responsible, intelligent young lady and began to help with her school expenses during the year. In the summer they invited her to live with them at the Venice Beach. Her new benefactor was a bank official in the repossession department that employed her stepfather.

In addition to being a straight "A" student, Anne was a first-rate athlete. An influencing factor here was probably that sports were an acceptable way to vent aggression that was not safe to express at home.

A circumstance that has always been a part of Anne's life is "luck," as if the Universe was always looking out for her. When she was quite young and the family was in the worst financial straits, she was forever finding money—quarters, dimes, even dollars. During those times a dime would buy a loaf of bread with perhaps a little change returned. By the time she was in high school she was taking jobs for 25 to 35 cents an hour cleaning houses or clerking in a local book and music store.

At the end of her junior year in high school, she again packed her suitcase and went with her benefactors to their home in Venice, just west of Los Angeles. It was pleasant to get away from her stepfather even though things at home were getting better. Her stepfather had a steady job with the repossession department of the bank, a nice home in Glendale (owned by the bank) and in general the economy was slowly picking up.

Her benefactors at Venice Beach however, had their own agenda. They had a twenty-one or twenty-two year-old nephew whom, they hoped, would be attracted to their summer houseguest. He had just graduated with a degree in education, so it looked like a win-win situation for everyone. In early August of 1937, the nephew was invited to his Aunt and Uncle's home in Venice to celebrate Mardi Gras in Venice, a trifle off-season, but California has always made its own rules. This nephew just happened to have a summer job where my motorcycle buddy, Don, worked, and here is where I entered the picture that August of '37. When I talked to Don during the middle of the week he said this new friend had asked if he would drive him to Venice that Friday after work. The enticement for Don was his Aunt and Uncle's well-stocked, liquor bar. This was too much for Don to resist. When I heard of the enticement, I became concerned because Don had a tendency, as do many young people, to drink too much, especially when it's free. Riding a motorcycle in Los Angeles was dangerous enough sober so I asked if I could tag along. I wanted to be sure Don got home safely.

Supporting Role

Since I just happen to be one of the major players in this seventy plus-year drama, it is only fitting that I give you, the reader, a glimpse into my heritage and life prior to August 1937. I wish I had been able to give you more of Anne's heritage, but I guess we are lucky to have anything of her personal history. It is interesting that not one picture exists of Anne's grandparents and that none of her mother's brothers or other relatives are known to exist. Her real father remains an enigma and her only "family" is a half-brother and sister and their immediate families. Don Juan said, "A shaman should have no personal history". Anne fills that criterion quite well.

I, on the other hand, according to members of the Armstrong family in New York, can trace my ancestors back to colonial days, maybe even the Mayflower itself. Genealogy has never interested me since I believe we should each stand on our own merits, not those of our ancestors. What counts is what we are today, this very moment, for that is the sum total of every previous existence that we have had since that spark of God began its apparent separate existence—whenever that may have been. But, just to establish a backdrop against which current family members can play out their roles, let's digress to the end of the nineteenth century when my grandfather, E.B. Miller, moved with his wife from Tennessee to western South Dakota where he became a very successful rancher, owning tens of thousands of acres of land and thousands of head of cattle. One of his eight children was my mother, Anna Miller. Anna grew up with all the advantages of a wealthy rancher's daughter. When it was time for college, she moved to Huron, South Dakota, and took room and board with the only family she and her family knew in town—the Armstrong's. When Anna was eight or nine years old, the only son of the Armstrong family, John, had already worked as a cowboy on her father's ranch for a short time. Then, several years later, Anna took room and board at the family home so she could attend college. A year or so later, college had been forgotten and Anna Miller became Mrs. John Armstrong. In less than a year, I became a new member of the Armstrong clan. Oh, yes, there was (is) an Armstrong clan, with their own family crest and tartan, in southern Scotland, next to the English border. From what I have read they were a band of patriotic cattle thieves who delighted in tormenting the English. The original Johnny Armstrong got himself hanged for his exploits by the King of England.

My father, John Armstrong, had a rather interesting, immediate heritage. Kitty Dearing and Nelson Armstrong met and fell in love in upstate New York, west of Albany, some years after the Civil War. The Armstrong family had a company that pulled barges along the Erie Canal with teams of horses. Apparently Nelson, a Civil War veteran, wanted a more exciting life so he and Kitty boarded a train for the Middle West.

They had seen ads that were part of a massive advertising campaign sponsored by the railroad through large posters and news stories circulated throughout the Eastern United States and even Europe. The enticement was two million farms on fertile prairie lands to be had free of cost in Central Dakota.

Kitty's background was quite unusual for a pioneer settler. At a very early age, she ran away from home and married a Shakespearean actor. Soon she was a Shakespearean actress with the troupe that was to be performing at the Ford Theater in Washington, DC, April 14, 1865 the night President Lincoln was assassinated. Since a contemporary play, "Our American Cousin", was being performed that night, Kitty was not in the cast, but backstage helping with makeup, when Lincoln was shot. Edwin Booth, brother of John Wilkes Booth, the assassin, was the troop's lead Shakespearean actor. Just a few days before the assassination, John Wilkes Booth bragged so everyone could hear, "Someday my name will be known where Edwin's will never be." At the time, Kitty was about eighteen years old.

Some twelve to fifteen years later Kitty became estranged from her actor husband. One night in Toronto, Canada a fire destroyed the large theater in which they were performing, along with her complete wardrobe and personal effects. Tired of the stage, she returned to her home near Albany, New York. It must have been very difficult to decide to make the transition from Shakespearean actress to becoming a pioneer wife on the prairies of Dakota. Obviously love and the excitement of the adventure masked the reality of the potential hardships. Kitty was probably about thirty years old when she and Nelson Armstrong came to the Dakota Territory.

The first thing they did when they arrived was sign up for adjoining homesteads and then get married. This way they received twice as much land in the fertile James River Valley.

I never doubted Grandma's stories about being an actress. I would sit at her feet for hours and listen to her recite Shakespeare, everyone's part. I asked her how she could memorize whole plays. She said she would read through the play in the evening, put the book under her pillow and the next morning she would have it memorized. Each winter, a week or so before Abraham Lincoln's birthday, at least one or two newspaper reporters from Chicago and/or Minneapolis would come to our home and interview and photograph my Grandma for their newspapers. The local Opera House would also send us tickets to special events, like a Shakespearean play. So I knew my Grandma was a very special person, especially to me.

John, the younger of two children, was born about 1885. Eventually, the Armstrong family moved from the farm into Huron, some thirteen miles to the north. This gave John an opportunity to attend a year or two of college before taking a job in a local bank. At some period during his early adulthood he found time to work as a cowboy on the E.B. Miller Ranch in western South Dakota. Another early adventure had him and a next-door neighbor driving a horse-drawn wagon from Huron, South Dakota to Yellowstone Park in northwest Wyoming, in 1912, a total round trip distance of about fourteen hundred fifty miles. In addition to the wagon team, they each had their own saddle horse. The "expedition" took from early May to October. There were no roads, only two ruts where other wagons had passed from town to town.

I grew up as a city boy in the big town of Huron, the third or fourth largest town in the state, with about twelve thousand people. The only long trips I recall when I was a kid were going with my Mother to western South Dakota to spend time on her siblings and father's ranches during summer vacation. Only once do I recall making that trip in the wintertime. My Dad was a local businessman, eventually owning his own furniture store until the 1930 depression hit. Prior to that, he had been a bank teller, insurance agent and furniture salesman, but his real love was fishing and hunting. When I was quite young, Dad would take Mom and me on fishing trips, but as I got older Mom stopped going and Dad and I and one of his fishing buddies would go. He always had the best equipment available, but no matter how good the equipment I hardly ever caught a fish.

When I was twelve years old, Dad bought me a hunting license, and although I was an excellent marksman for a kid, I didn't like the idea of killing things, even if they were for food. I never deliberately killed another animal after I was fifteen, not even a fish. My Dad never understood me. I didn't want to be a salesman or a sportsman—the things he enjoyed. I'm sure he felt rejected. When I left home for the last time he offered me guns and fishing equipment and I told him I didn't have the slightest idea what I would do with them. My real interest, after ten years of age, was building model airplanes. School to me was just one of those things everyone did; I had no feelings for educating myself one way or the other until the first year of high school. From then on, I was dedicated to learning the most I could in the time available.

Starting at an early age—eight or nine—I would pack my suitcase the day after school was out in early June, climb on the daily train and the next morning I would be in western South Dakota ready to spend three months on my grandfather and uncle's ranches that still covered tens of thousands of acres twenty five miles east of the Black Hills. So, one quarter of each year I became a young ranch hand: riding, hunting, stacking hay, milking cows, driving cattle, feeding the calves and hogs—the whole ranch scene. Then the day before school started, I would return to Huron. These summer pilgrimages to the ranches ended as I turned fourteen; when Mom wrote that we were moving to Virginia in time for me to start school in September. She had divorced my Dad so we were going to live with one of her sisters until she could get her life straightened out.

This was a major turning point in my life. My aunt Ethel with whom we went to live was my mother's youngest sister—the black sheep of the family. And now another one was joining her. Soon after World War I, about 1920, Aunt Ethel went to Belgium alone for training in the processing of synthetic fibers—rayon. When she returned she became an instructor in a processing plant in Hopewell, Virginia. Eventually she married a handsome southerner, Walter Le Bas, a supervisor at the plant where she worked. Mom and I lived with Ethel, Walter and their two children.

Soon after school started, my Aunt Ethel (she later adopted the name Geraldine) made her yearly pilgrimage to Richmond, twenty miles up the river. Once a year, a Hindu guru by the name of Singh came to Richmond for a week to lecture and teach classes on Hinduism. When my Aunt returned, she had a bag full of books and pamphlets on Hindu philosophy. I picked up one pamphlet and couldn't put it down. I read everything in the bag and every other book in the house on eastern philosophy. I was hooked. When I was younger the only disagreements my mother and I ever had were on Sunday mornings when she pressured me to go to Sunday School as a good Christian boy should, and now here I was, soaking up every word I could find about Eastern religious philosophy. However, I soon discovered that Christian mysticism was equally fascinating.

Besides sparking what has become a life-long interest in the religious philosophies of the world, our year in Virginia with Geraldine changed my life in another significant way.

I had always been a mediocre student in school, doing just enough to get from grade to grade. I never felt any drive to excel or compete. My reading speed had been on the slow side and up to then I had never been an avid reader, but my interest in Hindu philosophy changed that. Within a few months my grades had improved so significantly that I was looked upon as a superior student. I thought it was because those southern kids weren't as smart as we northern kids were. In any case, from then on, I always felt I let myself down if I received something other than an "A."

Another life changing event occurred during that year in Virginia. I had never heard the word "diphtheria" in South Dakota. I guess the dry/hot/cold climate didn't lend itself to incubating that kind of disease. In Virginia, all kids were inoculated against it—except me. Just before Christmas vacation I got deathly ill. In fact, they didn't expect me to live, but I fooled them. However, it left me with some kind of heart problem that the doctors, then, predicted would prove fatal in ten years or so unless I lived a very slow, sedentary life. I respected those restrictions for a couple of years and then forgot all about my heart and started living a normal teen life. When I tried to get into the Air Force ten years later, however, I had a lot of trouble passing one of the heart-related tests. If my weight hadn't been a problem, my heart might have been. As I look back, sixty-seven years later, I realize my path was slanted toward a more academic, sedentary life by that illness. No, there are no accidents in life. This Universe is too complex to be guided by random events. So the divorce, my aunt's philosophic choices, the diphtheria, my study/reading habits, etc., were all part of a plan that for good or ill has made me who I am. I'm sure that once I shed this physical body, with all its apparent limitations, I will find that I chose, or at least agreed to a particular path before I took on this physical body. The so-called unfortunate, uncomfortable events that influenced my life have just been prods to keep me on the path that I agreed to follow before I began this present trek through matter. There is a passage in the Christian Bible that speaks very eloquently, yet succinctly, on this subject. It says in effect, "not a sparrow falleth without the Father's knowledge"—it is all built into the plan. Life is too precious a commodity to be guided by happenstance. Many lives seem to be unguided, but how are we to judge what that soul is attempting to learn or what events it is scheduled to bring into manifestation? I seem to have digressed, or perhaps, this too, is also a part of the Divine Plan.

Oh, yes, another milestone that I glimpsed during my short stay in Hopewell, Virginia was that there were some different kinds of people out there, namely girls. It was a new awareness but, at least, it broke ground for future plantings.

I left Virginia almost exactly one year after I arrived. A few months earlier my Mom went to Los Angeles to help a friend start a bakery business, and the day school started I left for Los Angeles. Again, my school year was seriously interrupted. In March 1933, a violent earthquake hit Los Angeles and our school took a beating. For the rest of the school year, the high school students shared a junior high facility where we attended classes in the afternoons. My hobbies at this time of my life were building model airplanes and reading everything I could find on religious philosophy—mysticism in particular. I discovered the Theosophical Library, the Los Angeles Public Library and a great bookstore in Hollywood. I was embarrassed to ask for the location of the store's books on eastern philosophy and mysticism so I spent hours going from shelf to shelf. Finally, I found a shelf of books about four feet long, which held their total stock. There they were—Blavatsky, Heindel, Steiner, Bailey, Leadbeater, Besant and a few more. Once I found a book I wanted, the next problem was buying it so the clerk didn't see the title; heaven forbid that anyone should catch me reading a book on eastern religion or mysticism. I would carry it to the counter, quickly open the cover to where the price was written, then close the cover, and hand it upside down to the clerk, hoping he couldn't or wouldn't read the title.

I spent a rather uneventful school year in Los Angeles, except for the earthquake. The following summer I went to Chicago to attend the 1933 World Fair. Despite the worldwide depression it was the most elaborate educational display I could imagine. It was definitely instrumental in helping me choose some branch of science for a profession.

While there I met Ida Hagen Marshall, the first real clairvoyant I had ever known. Little did I realize that she would become an important mentor in my adult life. After the Fair, I returned to Huron for my last two years of high school. By graduation time, I had already applied and been accepted at the South Dakota School of Mines; getting there was just a matter of finding the money. My Mother worked a deal with a brother-in-law on some money he owed her, thus covering my expenses for the first year. At the end of the first year, we freshmen were told that unless we had full funding by some means other than working locally, we shouldn't come back. Rapid City, it seemed, had jobs enough to support only the juniors and seniors. Shortly after I returned to Huron that summer, I got a letter that Mom had remarried. There were no jobs in Huron, so I hitchhiked back to California. I realized when I grew up that it was a dirty trick to move in with a couple of newlyweds, but being the spoiled brat I had always been it never occurred to me at the time.

Since my real Dad was a member of the Masonic Order, the Los Angeles Chapter helped me find a job in a chemical sales company in East Los Angeles. After riding streetcars for a month or so I borrowed

$150 and bought a used, Los Angeles Police, Harley Davidson motorcycle. About the same time, my best friend from high school drove his motorcycle to Los Angeles, so I now had a friend in this big lonely city.

Late one evening, soon after Don arrived, we were both riding my bike down Figueroa Boulevard, when a car drove through an intersection in front of us. Don laid the bike down on its side and broadsided the car. He and the bike ended up on the hood of the car and I flew through the air and landed in its front seat on someone's lap. The bike was pretty bent up but we were unhurt. However, my head narrowly cleared the windshield during a trajectory that landed me in the front seat of this open roadster. The kids that we hit said, "Boy, were you lucky. We had our car parked in front of our house and when we came out a few minutes ago we saw that someone had just stolen the left, plate glass, wind wing. Before landing in our front seat, your head went through the space occupied, only minutes earlier, by that glass wind wing." When I look back on my teens and early twenties I realize I kept some guardian angel very busy. I sure hope I get a chance sometime to thank him (or her) for all the help. I rode motorcycles thousands of miles in southern California traffic, in all kinds of weather, and only got a few scratches and bruises.

The following summer Don and I bought two, new, red 1937, Harley Davidson 61 OHV motorcycles. It was the first time since I got my bicycle, at age ten, that I bought something brand new. What a thrill to watch my new motorcycle being removed from its crate, handlebars and battery installed, the engine filled with oil, and then that Harley sound as it started for the first time—yeah! What a thrill! Now all I had to do was pay for it—$550.

Then one Wednesday in mid-August, Don told me that on Friday evening he was driving a friend, Wes, to Venice. When I heard of the "well-stocked bar," he was planning to visit, I decided to wangle an invitation to go along to be sure Don stayed sober enough to drive home safely. I didn't have the remotest premonition that that Friday evening would change my life forever, and I mean forever. Little did I realize that I was on a collision course with destiny! At this moment, I know how true those words are, for as I write, my throat convulses and my eyes fill with tears, which is for me a positive confirmation of truth.

On Friday after work, the three of us headed for Venice on our motorcycles. We drove into the front yard of a home in Venice and were greeted by Wes's aunt and uncle and Eddie Georgelos, their summer time guest. They had found Enedina "too cumbersome" and too ethnic so they called her "Eddie," which was just another iteration of Enedina. Her family had shortened it to En. English-speaking friends usually called her "Anne," the name she adopted when she became an American Citizen. However, she is still known to many of our old friends as Eddie. "Anne" is her name in the world, but as far as I'm concerned, she is still "Eddie."

Our Relationship

I have no doubt that the convergence of the two paths that occurred that evening in mid-August 1937 had been well planned in some remote realm many years before. The intricate planning required to bring all the principles together in one place at one time boggles the mind. The plan worked flawlessly. The eyes of the three bike riders fell upon one scene—shoulder-length, straight, brownish-black hair; a flawless, tan complexion; small but shapely form in slacks and a loose fitting sweater and an almost Mona Lisa smile. She was introduced as Eddie.

We were invited in and offered a drink from the bar that had been the great enticement for my motorcycle buddy. The bartender was none other than the possessor of that provocative smile. Everyone except the bartender and I took an alcoholic drink. We were told about the Mardi Gras at the Venice Pier and asked if we had any preference as to where or what we wanted to eat. A Chinese restaurant on the Venice Pier was unanimously chosen so off the six of us went. I don't remember much about dinner except we ate at a round table and this very attractive young bartender sat right across from me. After the many Chinese dishes were consumed, the fortune cookies arrived. Amid gaiety and wisecracks, one by one we each read our fortune. When the fortune-cookie reading came around to our attractive bartender, her face reddened, she became visibly shaken, looked down at the table and finally read the "fortune" from her cookie. It said, "Tonight you have met the man you will marry." Everyone laughed uproariously, and after looking at the three motorcycle bums she said, under her breath, "No way."

After dinner the little party wound its way through the crowd, looking for the center of the activity. Four of the group decided they wanted an after-dinner drink, leaving me with the very lovely, olive-skinned, young lady with the long, dark hair. I suggested we worm our way through the crowd to where we could view the floats and the gaily-costumed entertainers. We finally arrived at a solid wall of bodies through which we could not even worm our way. I looked down at her and realized that at her eye level, there was nothing but backs to be seen. Being the rather straightforward, practical, young man that I was, I reached down, grabbed her at about knee level and unceremoniously picked her up so she could see over the crowd. She indignantly demanded that I put her down immediately. I smiled at her prudishness and obeyed. So we kept on moving until a passageway opened up and I drew her through to the front of that sea of bodies. The only other recollection I have of that evening was that I asked if she would like to go to a show early the next week. I found out later that my other two friends made the same request before the evening was over, but our date preceded theirs. Incidentally, Don stayed relatively sober and had no problem driving his bike home.

After the show on our first date, we walked out to the end of the pier. It was a beautiful clear and warm summer evening with millions of stars—no moon. We both remember my becoming quite philosophic about the vastness of the universe, the place of man in that vastness, the purpose that the Creator may have had in mind, but definitely nothing romantic—that just wasn't me. The response I got belied the coquettish, yet quiet exterior of my companion. I found that she understood what I was saying, and I felt encouraged to continue. Had I really found a girl who understood my serious, philosophic approach to life? When I dropped her off at her benefactor's front door, I suggested we go to the beach the next weekend. I did have a bit of a problem, however, as she would only let me drive my bike in low gear, about ten miles per hour. At the end of our next date, she informed me she would be returning to Glendale in a few days. My immediate internal response was that no female's company was worth driving across Los Angles and up to Glendale. Little did I know I was going to be driving that route three times a week for the next three years.

The week following our first trip to Venice, Don and I had a long, serious talk. We had lived our lives in small Midwestern towns where 99.9 percent of the population was descended from immigrants of north central Europe, the British Isles and the Scandinavian Peninsula. There was one Greek family in town that owned and operated a restaurant and candy store, but they always seemed to be very dark-skinned. Don and I agreed that Eddie was a beautifully proportioned young lady, but what would our hometown friends and relatives think if they saw us with someone with almost black hair and an olive/tan complexion? It was a serious problem that we never before had to consider. And sure enough, rumors reached South Dakota, via a cousin in Los Angeles, about this "dark-skinned young lady" with whom Jim was being seen. But, when members of my South Dakota family finally met her, they were as favorably impressed as Don and I had been.

Eddie, Don and I became a threesome with Don only occasionally inviting a young woman to accompany him. We rode together, attended motorcycle functions, shows, lectures and various meetings, but nearly always as a trio. I bought Eddie leather boots, jacket and helmet and she became a permanent fixture on the back of my Harley. It wasn't very long before she would sit behind me and sleep as we drove home at speeds of seventy to one hundred MPH. We had only one rather serious accident with no broken bones, only deep scuffs and bruises. It occurred one night, driving sixty-five or seventy MPH, when we hit some loose gravel on a turn. Among other maneuvers, the bike, with us as passengers, did a forward loop. Luckily, the bike was still drivable, as we were completely alone on a desert road east of Los Angeles. That was only the beginning. The next day we got separated in the desert, the bike became mired in sand, and I had a sunstroke. I was dehydrated, with a body temperature over one hundred and five degrees F, and a pulse in excess of one hundred fifty, I ended up in a small town, maternity hospital. Needless to say, I survived. My rescuers followed our tracks and found Eddie in a shallow cave where she had sought shelter from the sun. All of this in one weekend! Luckily, all my other accidents were "solo."

About a year or so into our relationship I bought a car so we could dress up on a date, but we continued to love the bike for weekend outings.

Even though our relationship moved along quite smoothly, my relationship with Eddie's family was not that good. My own family never tried to run my life, and I didn't think Eddie's family should try to run hers. My philosophy was also a problem—they saw the books I brought her to read, and by then, I made no effort to hide my beliefs. I was just not used to their approach to life and I hadn't yet learned tolerance. Soon after I started seeing Eddie at home, her mother told her she had met the devil himself and if she married me she never wanted to see her again. So we didn't spend much time at her home. My mother loved Eddie and even warned her that I was a spoiled brat and implied that she would be crazy to marry me. But after a year or so, we took several family diamonds and had a ring made in spite of family warnings and threats. The next two years were probably the best either of us had ever experienced. I had a good job, the national economy was slowly getting better and there was lots of good inexpensive entertainment in Los Angeles, but the world was getting closer and closer to all-out war.

The clairvoyant I'd met in Chicago in 1933, Ida Hagen Marshall, moved to Los Angeles, a year or so after I did and through my Aunt Geraldine we again made contact. This time Don, Eddie and I became good friends with Ida and I had an opportunity to experience her exceptional abilities first hand. As time went on, we got to know her as a highly developed spiritual being with incredible abilities.

One evening, Don, Eddie and I, and several other people, were invited to Ida's Hollywood apartment. After an evening of conversation, Ida began to address each of us personally. When she came to Don she said, "Don, there is going to be a war and the U.S. will be drawn into it. I see you in uniform flying airplanes. You are in the military, but you don't seem to be involved in the fighting." Then she went on to say, after a great deal of thought and deliberation, "I am aware of an airplane with a strange sound like a blow torch as it flies by. It goes very fast but it doesn't have a propeller."

When Ida came around to me she said, "Yes, Jim, there is going to be a war, but regardless of what you do, you will never get into the fighting. You have had your share of war. This time the war will not touch you no matter what you do to become involved." As soon as we left Ida's apartment that night we wholeheartedly agreed that the old gal had flipped her lid! We knew an airplane couldn't fly without a propeller.

I continued to work in the chemical retail business, but by 1939 I was becoming bored. It was time for me to quit and do something more creative. I immediately enrolled in an aircraft sheet metal school, and upon "graduation," I got a job in Lockheed's experimental division. My first assignment was fabricating parts by hand for the second experimental P-38 pursuit plane. Several months later, I took a job in another aircraft factory that was just starting to expand. I rapidly advanced from a sheet metal mechanic to tooling coordinator, to inspector, eventually becoming the last company inspector to check our production aircraft before they were turned over to the Air Force.

Eddie and I continued our relationship despite her step-dad chasing me through the neighborhood one night with a loaded 45 caliber automatic. He was a very dramatic fellow.

When Eddie and I met, she was between her junior and senior years of high school. Up to that time she'd been a model student with perfect attendance and straight A's. Now, however, if I had a day off she would skip school so we could take a long bike ride and our Thursday night date didn't bode well for Friday quizzes. Consequently, she got her first B in high school—a small price to pay for the fun we had.

During the spring of 1940, Eddie's family built a new home and was going to move ten or fifteen miles farther from Los Angeles. I guess this was the impetus we both needed. Within weeks after we met I think we both knew that we wanted to be together, but up until this latest move, there didn't seem to be an urgency to get married. Since I had a good job, getting married seemed the next logical step in our relationship. One day, near the end of June 1940, we went to the Los Angeles courthouse and got the license. On the afternoon of the Fourth of July—the only day off I'd had in months, Eddie and I got married during a very simple service. Not one member of Eddie's family attended. A couple of weeks later, I talked my boss into letting me take the weekend off so we could have a token honeymoon.

A couple of months after my marriage, Don and I bought an old airplane. I took the family car and all the cash we had and traded it for an airplane. I could never figure out why Eddie got so upset. After all, Don and I had always bought whatever we wanted, how was this any different? Shucks, we still had a motorcycle to go shopping. But, all joking aside, having our own airplane was a good experience. The only problem was we spent about four hours on ground maintenance for each hour in the air. We sold it about six weeks before the attack on Pearl Harbor. Little did we know that all civilian aircraft within one hundred fifty miles of the coast would be grounded if we got into a war.

After Pearl Harbor, the U.S. became an official member of the Allied forces. Within a few days after Pearl Harbor, Don had enlisted in the Air Force and started training as a military pilot—quite different from flying our Taylor Cub. Upon graduation from flight training, he was assigned to a P-39 fighter squadron. By the time the squadron was ready for combat, training accidents had killed or injured so many pilots that the remaining ones were assigned to another squadron. A few weeks later, a General whose duties kept him within the confines of the U.S. needed a personal pilot. Don was assigned to the General and remained with him for two or three years before becoming a test pilot at a Southern California repair base. After the war ended, Don was sent to Japan with the Army of Occupation.

I envied Don. I wanted to fly real airplanes, too! But the Air Force would not take married men for flight training. Four or five months later, I quit a good paying, civilian job near Los Angeles and we moved to an air base near Ogden, Utah where I took a job as an aircraft inspector for the handsome salary of $1860 per year. In a year or so, the Air Force began to take married men for flight training. After passing the written exam with "flying colors," I flunked the physical because I didn't weigh enough for my height. After several months of trying to gain weight, I gave up and tried for Naval Officers Training and various special service groups, but nothing worked out. I was not interested in being a buck private in the Army. In the meantime, we'd bought a house in a small Utah village, completely rebuilt it, planted a garden and I continued to work at the air base. Not long after, however, I quit my government job, we sold our house and drove to San Francisco and I joined the Navy. When the examining doctors weren't looking, I changed my weight from one hundred nineteen to one hundred twenty nine pounds on the form that I carried from doctor to doctor. A doctor said, "Hey, fellow you can't write on that sheet." I replied, "I'm just doodling," and moved on to the next doctor. The following day I was sworn into the Navy, given a First Class Petty Officer rating, Aircraft Metalsmith First Class, put on inactive duty, and assigned to the Naval Air Transport Service. I spent the balance of the war in San Francisco.

When Don, Eddie and I met after the war we talked about how accurate Ida Marshall's 1939 thumbnail sketches about the war had been. A few years later, Don retired from the Air Force as a Lieutenant Colonel and I took a job as a rocket research technician, and as Ida had predicted nearly seven years earlier, neither of us ever saw a minute of war. There seems to be something to destiny! Oh, and by the way, we began to hear about, and occasionally see, airplanes that sounded like huge blow torches and had no propellers—they called them jets.

CHAPTER III:

KUNDALINI'S FIRST APPEARANCE

The War and Post War Years

The preceding few pages covered the happenings in our outer world for the first five years of our marriage, but there were changes taking place in our inner life that were far more significant. With rationing, and other restrictions, life was not very exciting during the war in that small Utah village. However, my Aunt Geraldine, who had originally interested me in the spiritual side of life, had moved to Salt Lake City, where she'd met a fellow who lectured every Thursday evening on Rosicrucian philosophy. He was a member of an esoteric Christian organization founded by Max Heindel, a German clairvoyant who spent a lifetime researching the more subtle realms of the universe, commonly referred to as the spiritual realms. All the knowledge and wisdom gained in his endless research had been compiled in a five to six hundred page book plus several smaller ones. We bought the big book, The Rosicrucian Cosmo-Conception or Mystic Christianity, and enrolled in a study program based upon its contents. We studied the material together, though Eddie was more committed to the practice of the exercises and meditations than I was. I worked six or seven days a week and the old house always needed something.

After a couple months of intensive study and meditation she began to have spontaneous out-of-body experiences. From some other part of the room she could look back and see her own body. It was frightening, especially to a person who'd been sick most of her life. She wondered if she was dead, and if not, could she get back into her body? This would happen every time she got quiet, like meditating or getting ready to go to sleep. She constantly felt as if she and her body were not securely connected. There was the sense that her feet were not touching the ground; she would turn or move and the body didn't; she was frequently aware of the existence of another reality, and of beings that were not part of our physical world. I can recall going with her to a show or a lecture, any situation where she had to focus her attention, and seeing her look first to one side of her body and then the other. What she was doing was trying to figure out which body was really hers. She was aware of two Eddies. The pills and shots the doctors gave her only made the situation worse. Even our cat kept his distance from her, as if he could see things around her that we couldn't. Until I got into a higher management position, I sometimes worked night shifts, but Eddie would stay awake until I got home, even if she had to wait until eight in the morning.

It was several years before we fully realized that the spiritual opening that began in October of 1959 was a second attempt by Kundalini to complete the opening process that had begun in the fall of 1942. At that time Eddie was too immature to handle what was being thrust upon her at 23 years of age. As we look back we realize she did a lot of maturing in those 17 years. My return to college for three more years was a very maturing experience for both of us; then several years as Brownie and Girl Scout Leader and finally Summer Camp Director, helped prepare her to work with adults seeking a spiritual path. Having worked as Anne's co-leader for over 30 years I know that what she called deep level psychological counseling was really spiritual counseling of the highest order. It was right down to earth none of that New Age spiritual fluff.

After many months of intense discomfort and worry about her sanity, she concluded that the esoteric studies and practices were the cause of her problems and she vowed never to meditate again, or ever read about or discuss, esoteric philosophy. She vowed to stop the study and work in her garden. We had a great garden that next year despite the area having been used as a dump for the past 50 years. Perhaps the iron and tin from the cans had helped the soil.

One of the faculties Eddie retained for a few years was the ability to see auras around people. Many sensitive people throughout the ages have been aware of light patterns around people, especially around or near the head. After I joined the Navy, Eddie and I settled down in the San Francisco area. We rented a room in our home to a young Navy man, Carl, who was interested in auras. Carl and I decided to build an electronic instrument that would prove, that the aura did exist. Eddie could see auras, but we wanted to verify scientifically what she was able to see intuitively.

Eddie and I did experiments that proved to our satisfaction that she could "see" the aura. I would sit in front of a color-neutral wall and perform a number of mental gymnastics. She would record what she was aware of. Later, we would compare notes to see if what she observed matched what I had done mentally. For instance, I might sit and meditate for a few minutes, keeping my mind very still, then work an intricate mathematical problem in my head, followed by a period of mental agitation.

There was no doubt that she could correctly and repeatedly sense my state of mind by the colors and shapes of the auric field around and above my head. When I was in a meditative state, she would report a pastel glow distributed quite evenly around the head. If I shifted to mentally performing intricate mathematical computations she would report green streaks rising erratically from the head. Periods of emotional agitation always appeared as undefined clouds of red, orange, or gray energy, no definite shape or color, just a confused, pulsating mass of energy. Carl and I wanted to demonstrate electronically that those energy clouds or streaks that Eddie could sense so accurately did actually exist. We designed and constructed a piece of equipment that we thought might do it, but we needed to run some tests using equipment located in the instrument shop where Carl worked. So we wouldn't forget in the morning to take the equipment we were testing, we put it in the car the night before. During the night someone stole our car—and our aura-detecting instrument. We never built another. I got busy with FAA (Federal Aviation Authority) Certification so I could work on civilian aircraft when I left the Navy, and esoteric research was forgotten. After five years of war and nearly ten years of an economic depression, all those esoteric research ideas got lost in our effort to re-establish our lives. I was 29 years old with no money, no profession and no advanced education.

Immediately after the war ended, Eddie and I returned to Los Angeles. After several unsuccessful attempts to find a good business opportunity, my mother and her second husband, and Eddie and I left Los Angeles and bought a small piece of land just south of Kanab, Utah, near the Arizona border. The goal was to build a motel. By the time our house was built, Eddie's hay fever and asthma were so bad we had to return to the Los Angeles smog. I'm sure living with my family was the major cause of her nasal irritation.

I had become interested in rocket research and finally obtained a job as a research technician at California Institute of Technology's Jet Propulsion Laboratory in Pasadena. This was fascinating work, and I immediately enrolled in night courses at the Los Angeles Junior College. Now, more than ever, I wanted that engineering degree.

As I look back at that period I realize that our interest in the spiritual aspects of life had been almost completely obscured by the physical. We had become typical young Americans. My career was all-important. Between work and night school there was no time for pondering philosophic and esoteric verities. We were still vegetarians, but that was basically because of our respect for life and because we had lost our taste for animal flesh.

In August of 1949, our Daughter Christine was born. Now, it seemed more important than ever to become professional. I could clearly see my limitations without a college degree. At the end of the spring semester I told my school pals goodbye—I wouldn't be seeing them in the fall. From then on every move was aimed toward entering college full time in the fall.

I chose the South Dakota School of Mines and Technology for four basic reasons: l) It had a very high rating as an engineering college; 2) it was a small college, good for undergraduate studies; 3) I had taken my freshman year there in 1936-37; and 4) my Dad still lived in Huron, where I was born, and by stretching the facts I was a South Dakota resident so my tuition would be minimal, a necessity with our financial condition.

I still wake up in a cold sweat from dreams spawned by the events of that first year back in college. I had jumped right into the sophomore curriculum. My classmates were literally the "cream-of-the-crop." Almost all had been straight "A" students in high school (or they wouldn't be at "The Mines") and had just finished their freshman year three months before. I had finished my freshman year 13 years before. Even the basic theories of chemistry and physics had changed during that time—the atomic bomb research brought in a whole new era of science. So during the next nine months, I effectively took two years of college at the same time and ended up on the dean's list at the end of the third quarter. I never paid tuition again. From then until I graduated, an Armco Steel Scholarship paid all my school expenses.

Before school ended that first June, Eddie and I had found a position as managers of a run-down thirteen-unit motel on the edge of town. The contract we were asked to sign with the motel owner was beyond belief for a nearly starving student family. To make a long story short, two years later we left college with no debt and over $5,000 in the bank—a lot of money for a graduating student in 1952. Incidentally, I didn't graduate as an engineer. At the beginning of my junior year I switched to chemistry because I preferred the chemistry curriculum and the department head. I could take economics, psychology, philosophy and even some Shakespeare.

After graduation we had two choices: Carnegie Institute's School of Industrial Management for a MA in management (I had been accepted and had sufficient funds) or Eastman Kodak's Industrial Engineering Division where I would get similar management training on the job). For better or worse, we chose the latter and spent the next two and a half years in Rochester, New York, at Kodak Park. Then one, cold, February evening we received a phone call from the previous director of our research project at the Jet Propulsion Laboratory in Southern California, offering me a position on a high priority, top-secret rocket program. In five minutes we gave up all the Eastman job security and training. A few weeks later, we drove back to California to join a group of eager young engineers and chemists committed to designing and making operational the first atomic warhead air-to-air missile, in military history—and we had less than two years to do it.

I worked on the project for nearly two years before another chemist's wife told Eddie what we were developing. She had never asked me what we were making because she knew it was highly classified, so she was surprised to hear about it from one of the wives at a dinner party. The project was successful and I became well established as a research and development engineer, despite the fact that I was a chemist by education. As was customary, one of the senior engineers of the project would follow the unit into production for a year or so. I accepted the assignment and became a production engineer until the process was running smoothly.

One of the contracts for the development of the largest solid rocket motor ever attempted up to that time—the Minute Man, First Stage—was awarded to our company and I soon found myself as senior engineer over a group of new recruits. I stayed with that project for a year or two before being asked to return to a management position in production—first Production Control and then manager of the Igniter Division.

The Beginning Internship

I had never known Eddie when she was even close to being healthy. She suffered from hay fever and asthma every spring or anytime we drove into the country and migraine headaches could strike at any moment from innumerable possible causes. I believe it's conservative to say she had migraine headaches a minimum of two or three days every week since she was a little girl. And just for variety she had back problems, typical female problems, a goiter, and things we have both forgotten. In spite of all these problems, Eddie lived a full life, never allowing her poor health to interfere with getting things done.

As Christine, our daughter, was growing up, Eddie was working her way up from Brownie leader, to Girl Scout leader, to summer camp director. Meanwhile, her general physical condition was only getting worse. During the summer of 1959 the house next door to us was sold to a family about our age. The wives found they had something in common—migraine headaches. One day our new neighbor announced that her headaches were gone! She'd found a psychiatrist/hypnotist who regressed her back to some terrible confrontation she'd had with her mother, and after a series of sessions the headaches were gone.

Naturally, she insisted that Eddie must get an appointment with her doctor. The problem was that about every esoteric text we'd ever read said to stay away from hypnotists. To assure her that it was perfectly safe the neighbor gave her a little do-it-yourself book on hypnosis. Eddie never looked at it, but one rainy Sunday afternoon in late October she asked me to hypnotize her to find the cause of her headaches. I thought she had finally gone over the edge—me hypnotize someone? I hadn't even seen a stage hypnotist perform. But she assured me that didn't matter because her next-door neighbor had given her a book on hypnosis and if I read it I would know what to do. With tongue-in-cheek I took the book, looked at the table of contents, then opened the book to the section entitled "Techniques." I read a couple of pages until I found the first technique, and then suggested we go into the bedroom and try it.

I was convinced that whether I read a page or the whole book, I wouldn't be able to hypnotize anyone. Once she got comfortable on the bed, I started to do and say what I'd read. The technique was to have her look at two fingers held above her normal line of vision so she had to strain her eyes to see them, and then suggest that her eyes would become tired and would close. To prove that she was hypnotized I was to tell her that she couldn't open her eyes. I knew that as soon as I said that, her eyes would pop wide open and I could say, "See it doesn't work," allowing me to return to the book I was reading when all this nonsense got started. But guess what? Try as hard as she could, her eyes wouldn't open. No one was more surprised than I. But I figured that as long as she thought she was hypnotized I might as well carry this silly business one step further and see if we could learn what caused her headaches. I reasoned that the logical way to find something like that was to proceed backwards sequentially from her current age until something caught her attention. I asked that she scan her 39th year, then 38th, etc., back until we reached her 18th year. As we moved through the years she didn't say a word nor did the expression on her face ever change.

When we reached the 17th year and still no response I felt prompted to ask her how she felt about her step-dad. The reaction was immediate. She began to scream and cry hysterically. I got concerned and tried to return her to her normal state of consciousness, but to no avail. Finally, after a few minutes of this hysteria she stopped, opened her eyes and said, "Wow, that was great, let's do it again" I agreed but not until I read a few more pages of that book to find out how to return the subject to a normal state of awareness. Then we tried it again. In a few minutes, she was back in the same condition—totally hysterical. I tried to return her to a rational state using the methods suggested in the book, but again it didn't work. After a few minutes, the energy expended itself and she came out smiling—no thanks to my skill as a hypnotist. I later learned that if left alone the hypnotic condition wears off and the subject returns to a normal state of consciousness. But this time I insisted that we stop this foolishness since we really didn't know what we were doing.

As so often happened in our life, the Universe seemed to have other plans. Two or three days later, while at work, I took my morning break in the hall near the coffee machine. Over the din of dozens of conversations, I heard the word "hypnosis". I turned to the two engineers behind me and inquired about their conversation. They told me that a Dr. Hickman, the wife of an engineer in another building, was teaching a class on hypnosis and most of her students were engineers from our company. Eddie and I went to the next meeting and sat in the front row. After a short lecture on hypnosis, Dr. Hickman asked for a volunteer. I don't think Eddie had ever volunteered for anything before, but her hand shot up, and being in the front row, how could she be refused? The Doctor asked her if she had ever been hypnotized. She wasn't sure what had happened in our first attempt at hypnosis, so she answered no. After using a standard induction, she gave Eddie a few suggestions resulting in the same hysterical condition that we observed less than a week earlier. Dr. Hickman knew how to handle the situation. When Eddie returned to her normal state, the Doctor told her she had a problem that could not be solved there in front of twenty people, and that she should come to her office the next week so they could work privately. Eddie and I joined the class that night and the next week she had her first private session with Dr. Hickman.

Immediately after the first class we began to practice hypnosis techniques on each other. Eddie was a good subject and I was a poor one. But, I had become a good hypnotist and Eddie soon became the designated subject since she was the one with the headaches. We learned that what we had inadvertently done that first afternoon was called regression and that it was a standard technique for discovering the cause of psychological and physiological problems. During the next few weeks, we tried all the typical therapeutic approaches but didn't seem to be making much progress. I frequently regressed her to time zero looking for something traumatic enough to have caused the headaches, but always to no avail. This particular night, I induced a deep state of hypnosis and talked to her something like this, "I have regressed you many times from your current age, to birth and back up again without finding any event traumatic enough to have brought about your headaches. I know that some deep part of your being is aware of the cause of the headaches. In a few minutes I am going to regress you to time zero, then I will continue to count in minus numbers. Those numbers may represent seconds, minutes, years or centuries. Your deep inner being will know the significance of those minus numbers and will carry your awareness to the cause of your current headaches."

I had never heard of anyone giving such a suggestion to a subject, but to an engineer with an esoteric background it seemed quite logical. So with this suggestion firmly planted in her subconscious I started the regression. I have no recollection how far down I counted in minus numbers, but at some point she reached up and began to massage the left side of her neck and head, something I had seen her do many times when she was starting to get a headache. For an instant I was alarmed, thinking I might have caused her to get a headache, but my second thought was that perhaps the headache would lead us back to its cause. I didn't have long to wait. Eddie began to writhe with pain and screamed, "Someone is trying to break my neck." I suggested she become the observer so she would feel no pain and describe for me what was happening. She said she was aware of a huge male body, probably weighing well over two hundred twenty pounds, superimposed over her small, one hundred pound, female body, and that this huge body was being stretched by ropes across a rack in what appeared, as stated, to be a dungeon. Intuitively, she knew it was in the outskirts of Rome a long time ago. A young Roman Centurion, in his handsome uniform, stood nearby conducting a one-sided interrogation. When he got no answers to his questions he instructed the guards to tighten the ropes. The person on the rack passed out, was doused with a bucket of cold water and asked the question again, perhaps with a slightly different twist. The gist seemed to be that this big fellow had information that the Centurion wanted. At this point I determined we'd had enough drama for one evening and suggested that she would remember everything she had experienced, and that during the next session she would know why this man was being tortured.

During her next visit to Dr. Hickman, Eddie shared the events of our discovery and the unorthodox way we obtained it. Dr. Hickman worked with Eddie once or twice a week and I worked with her whenever we had an open evening, which I tried to arrange as often as possible. This was the beginning of the most exciting period of our lives.

Subsequent hypnosis sessions revealed that this big fellow, Antonius, whom Eddie identified as a personality she had been in a previous life, was apparently an athlete who performed in the Circus Maximus and the Coliseum, and had become closely associated with Julius Caesar. So close was the association that some of Caesar's enemies drugged Antonius, put him in a dungeon and tortured him on a rack, trying to extract confidential information from him.

During the next several weeks, Dr. Hickman and I, working independently yet sharing our results, obtained enough details about Antonius' life to have written a full-length novel. Eddie's ability to "see", or "sense", intricate details of Roman life, and Antonius' in particular, was nothing short of amazing. I still have boxes of 7-inch tape reels filled with therapy sessions recorded during the fall and winter of 1959-60. I'm sure Irene Hickman had nearly as many tapes or transcriptions from her sessions with Eddie.

Eddie has remarked many times in workshops that the really significant breakthroughs occurred when we worked together, in spite of my amateur status. There was probably a good reason for it and not one in anyway associated with the skills of the operators. After all, I was an amateur hypnotist and therapist. I knew nothing of hypnosis before reading those few pages of that do-it-yourself book a couple of weeks earlier. The reason for the breakthroughs was probably much more subtle, as would soon become clear.

As I stated earlier, Eddie had a penchant for detail. When Irene or I asked her to look at the Centurion who was giving the orders for the torture, she would start at his feet and describe every strap and clasp on his sandals, his short "skirt," his elaborate breastplate, and tunic, jump right over the face and describe the helmet with crest, plumes and all. This went on session after session whether the hypnotist was Irene or me. She would completely ignore the face and no amount of questioning or suggestions would help. Finally, I tried one more time to get her to look at his face. When she finished describing his breastplate and looked at his face she screamed in agony, "It's you!" I'm afraid I had known for some time that it was I, but she had to discover it for herself. From that moment forward, Eddie's headaches became less frequent and less severe. They dropped to once a week, then every other week, lasting only a day or perhaps hours. Within a few months, migraine headaches that had plagued her for over thirty years disappeared, never to return.

The torture and death of Antonius came at the outset of the therapy. The next month or more was spent in returning to the horrible torture and death scenes and in digging out the story line. Irene did a lot of that part of the therapy. However, Eddie and I continued to do hypnotherapy whenever we had a few spare hours. One weekend we decided to remove some more of the emotional charge from the torture scenes. I placed Eddie in a deep hypnotic trance and suggested she return to that dungeon in Rome, nearly 2,000 years ago. She re-experienced the torture on the rack, the prodding up the stairs, and being tied by the neck to the back of a military chariot.

After Antonius was dragged for some distance Eddie began to show physical signs of being choked to death. She stopped describing the scene and began living it. Her breathing stopped: her face became flushed and distorted—it was all there except the rope. I took her hand, ostensibly to comfort her, but actually so I could monitor her pulse. In less than thirty seconds after the final choking began her pulse stopped. I rolled her over and used the old Boy Scout method to restart her breathing—she didn't respond. Then I suddenly remembered her demonstrating mouth-to-mouth resuscitation, something she had learned two days before during a camp director training session. I rolled her over again and applied what she had taught me the day before. After several attempts she started to breathe again, her pulse picked up and she began to regain consciousness. The tape deck had recorded the entire near tragedy. From it we determined that her breath had stopped for at least three minutes. Exactly when her heart stopped and re-started will never be known. But from all outward appearances she was dead for at least three minutes—no breath, no pulse. I have heard and read that a person will not die from a hypnosis-induced trauma, however, I am firmly convinced that the resuscitation training she received a few days earlier saved her life.

Al, a physicist who had worked on the Manhattan Project (the atomic bomb) became fascinated by the events happening in our very "straight" home. Thank heavens our neighbors had no idea what was really going on, or they would have been horrified. Phyllis, the neighbor who was interested in hypnosis, knew that Eddie was getting better, but not all the details. However, Al was intrigued by Eddie's newly found abilities. Within six weeks after we started using hypnosis, we found that it had just been a way of getting her into the relaxed, meditative state that she had been avoiding for the last 16 years. By now, for Eddie to switch to the intuitive mode, she simply closed her eyes, took a few deep breaths, allowed her mind to become quiet and she was ready to go to work. She could do her own guidance, since she was completely conscious, or accept suggestions or guidance from outside. Al and I were fascinated by her ability to "see" such intricate detail in scenes that were two thousand years old. We wondered whether she just had a very vivid imagination or if she really could "see" all that detail.

One night while doing a regression with Al present, we ran into what appeared to be the life of a person in France. Eddie's description of the room she was in included mention of a silver vase. Without telling her why, I directed her to look inside the vase. I suggested she make her consciousness small enough to fit inside the vase. She described the inner wall of the vase as having tiny concentric circles or ridges. Al and I looked at each other in astonishment. She had no idea how a silver vase was made. For at least a hundred years, and no doubt much longer, silver and other malleable metals have been spun over a mandrel or form, leaving ridges inside the vessel. The outside would be machined and polished, removing telltale marks of the process.

This idea of asking her to make her consciousness smaller before looking at something had intriguing possibilities, especially to a physicist and a chemist. I directed her to make her consciousness even smaller. She then said the inner surface looked like a plowed field with huge ridges. When asked to make her consciousness smaller still, she said she was becoming aware of a three-dimensional latticework structure that seemed to be fixed in space, but she had a sense of movement or vibration within the structure itself. We were amazed. She was beginning to be aware of the crystalline structure of the metal, yet she knew little or nothing of classic atomic and crystalline structure theories. She was again instructed to make her consciousness even smaller and look at one of the corner units of that lattice. She said there were a lot of objects in circular orbits and their motion seemed to be controlled or confined. We were convinced that she was looking at atoms of silver in a crystalline structure.

Becoming yet smaller, we asked her to look at one of the objects that seemed to be in circular orbits around some stationary object. She said that they had no definite shape but, rather, appeared to be only energy. Then we suggested she make her consciousness even smaller and look at the more or less stationary object in the center. She said it seemed to be made up of even smaller objects she described as a bunch of basketballs floating around in a rather confined space. She said there appeared to be something there that was very bright.

We asked her if she could go inside it. She hesitated a few seconds, then physically recoiled and screamed, "I can't, I'll be destroyed!" She had been exploring atomic structure with her consciousness, and from what we knew she was being quite accurate. So when you read reports that the holy men of India knew the structure of matter, and even the atom, thousands of years ago, it now makes sense. Eddie had done it in our living room.

This crude experiment gave Al and me ideas for some slightly controlled experiments that might shed light on how Eddie's extended consciousness worked. She was just as curious as we were, and was willing to cooperate in any way she could.

We asked Eddie to stay in the living room until we set up the experiment. We divided the spare bedroom with a portable screen; on our side, we had a table with an array of bowls, spoons, water, flour and sugar. We had her come into the room from the other side of the screen so she had no idea what we were going to be using. We observed in the silver vase experiment that she had a mobile consciousness that could take on a variety of perspectives. It was just like checking out a new piece of laboratory equipment. We wanted to know what its capabilities were, what its limits were, how it worked, and how reliable it was. One of the many problems was that consciousness is infinitely more complex than any mechanical or electronic instrument. What we were going to do was far from scientific. All we hoped to do was establish some parameters and areas of further investigation.

I began by picking up a brass bowl and just holding it in my hands. I simply said, "I am holding something in my hands, can you describe it?"

She said, "I feel that I am round, concave, cold, smooth and hard." What we were immediately aware of was that she didn't describe the object as being separate from herself. Instead she said, "I feel... or I am..."

As soon as she finished talking, I slowly began to rock the brass bowl back and forth. She responded that she felt as if she were in a boat, and that if I continued to do whatever I was doing, she was going to get seasick. Incidentally, we gave her no feedback until we finished all the experiments.

Next, I quietly turned the bowl upside down onto a towel on the table. After a few seconds she said, "I don't know what you're doing, I can't see, it's dark." I now told her I had a brass bowl in my hands and I wanted her to make her consciousness so small that she could "walk" down the inside slope of the bowl, across the bottom and up the other side.

After a few seconds she said, "I can't, I will drown." I had very quietly filled the bowl about one quarter full of water.

Next, I dried the brass bowl and filled it with dry white sugar. Again I asked her to make her consciousness small enough to allow "walking" down the slope of the bowl and up the other side.

To this she reported, "I feel as if I am walking in very coarse gravel—it's difficult to walk but I can do it."

I then dumped out the sugar and replaced it with white flour and once more I asked her to make her consciousness small enough to walk across the bottom of the bowl.

After a few seconds she said, "I feel like I'm walking in very deep snow—no, it's more like very fine powder or dust." Then she physically sneezed, saying, "It's very dusty in here."

We did a few other experiments, but her accuracy began to drop off. It was getting late and, knowing her, she was also becoming bored. She really didn't like to do lab work but she would cooperate until she became tired or disinterested.

From these very simple experiments we concluded that the psychic sense she was using was similar to the physical sense of feeling. She did not "see" the way one sees with eyes, but she seemed to "know" the "feeling". The sneeze in response to the "dust" was interesting. She later reported that the fear of drowning in a half-inch of water was very real. We concluded that her consciousness was not only mobile but also could change size and could "sense" its environment.

Dr. Hickman's hypnosis group was very important in our lives during the early 1960's. When the group members heard about Eddie's psychic/intuitive opening, they began asking if they could come to our house and just observe. Many people find past life regression fascinating. We were never quite sure about its authenticity but in our therapy we assumed it was a fact.

One evening several of the members of the group showed up and wanted to observe a regression. This particular evening the question came up as to how far back in time one could be regressed, so we tried to find out. I suggested that Eddie continue to go back farther and farther in time. Finally, she began to describe an environment, and some primitive tools or weapons. Someone asked what sex she was. She stood up, looked down for a few seconds and then said, "I have so much hair, I can't tell."

In the next regression she said she was an American Indian male in a warm, swampy area. He was hunting deer with a bow and arrow, all of which she acted out. We jokingly accused Eddie of being a frustrated actress, because wherever appropriate she would act out the scenario. The part that cracked everyone up was Eddie's mimicking of her Indian's struggle to get the dead deer into the canoe so he could take it home. It was a difficult task for one person with a large deer and a relatively small canoe.

The bowl experiments were about the only physical experiments we ever did ourselves; however, about a year later Eddie began to work as a subject in Dr. Andrija Puharich's parapsychology lab in Carmel Valley. Here she engaged in many experiments. Andrija was an extremely interesting fellow who was involved in paranormal research for many years. His second wife wrote an interesting book about his long and varied career that some of you might find interesting.

A lovely lady in Carmel invited Dr. Puharich, Eddie and me to dinner one evening. The occasion was that Hans Bender, a noted German parapsychologist, was passing through from Asia on his way to a conference on the East Coast. Our hostess turned out to be one of Dr. Rhine's colleagues.

Dr. Rhine was one of the most published parapsychologist in the world during the post war (World War Two) period. He was a professor at Duke University for many years. Dr. Charles Tart worked in Dr. Rhine's laboratory until coming to the University of California, Davis, in the 1960's.

After dinner, and until 3 AM, these three Ph.D.s sat and swapped stories related to their field, stories that for lack of documentation they were unable to publish. Our hostess told of a trip she made to India at Dr. Rhine's behest to investigate some very controversial phenomena like materialization and psychokinesis, subjects in which it was not politically expedient for him to be involved. In the course of accomplishing her assignment she made friends with a Maharaja who had connections with various talented holy men back in the mountains. He agreed to bring one of these highly developed yogis to his palace and try to persuade him to perform a materialization. The meeting was arranged and a few local people were invited to attend. The demonstration was staged in a large, white, marble-lined enclosure. The holy man sat in the center under a slow turning tropical fan and the guests sat in a circle around him. Peering through the openings were servants and their children—a very informal affair that didn't lend itself to sophisticated scientific equipment or cameras.

The holy man meditated for a long time, then asked what someone would like to have materialized. A British Army officer said that on occasion he had obtained a very delicious bon-bon from a particular bakery in Calcutta. Could he materialize one or more of those bonbons? Without making a comment the holy man settled back into deep meditation. Quite some time later their attention was attracted to a space just below the blades of the tropical fan. There, settling down in front of each guest was a small box. The British officer picked up his box, opened it and exclaimed, "By Jove! This is the same box that I always get them in, and mine is still warm and it tastes just the same!" They each opened their box and ate the tasty morsel. The holy man asked if anyone

54

else had a request. This time another well-traveled gentleman named a rare grape that as far as he knew grew only in Italy, but this was not the season when they would be ripening. The holy man returned to a deep meditation for a period of time, long enough for everyone to surmise that nothing was going to happen. Then suddenly the space above the blades of the tropical fan was filled with ripe, red clusters of grapes. They hit the fan and were splattered all over the white marble walls and floor of this beautiful room. The servant's children came running in, picked up and ate the lush clusters of grapes. The gentleman who requested them said that indeed these were the grapes he had in mind.

Dr. Puharich related a similar story of a yogi who lived at his Maine laboratory one summer. After repeated requests the yogi agreed to try a materialization. Andrija said he really didn't expect anything to happen, but they did have him strip and wear a simple white robe furnished by the lab. There were no high-speed cameras or other sophisticated electronic equipment in the demonstration area. The yogi sat in the center and about twenty people associated with the laboratory sat in a circle around him. While the yogi was meditating, preparing himself for the demonstration, one of the observers left the room to take a phone call. A few minutes later, those who were aware said that suddenly many small objects appeared above the yogi's head, one falling in front of each person. The objects, which were small seashells, were counted immediately. A minute or so later the person who took the phone call returned to the room, and the next time the shells were counted, there was one more.

The evening continued with story after story. Considering the caliber of the people present, there was little reason to doubt the truth of the tales.

Anne and I spent many weekends and three or four weeks of my vacation at the Carmel Valley Laboratory. Andrija was a hard working, dedicated researcher and always had a number of projects in progress. One afternoon Anne and Andrija were working on an ESP project involving the use of the Faraday cage. I was acting as observer and technician. Andrija's cage was an eight-foot by eight-foot by eight-foot room covered on the outside with sheet copper. It could be either electrically grounded or be electrically insulated from its surroundings and a two hundred thousand volt, electrical charge applied to the exterior copper shell. The charge, of course, would be applied after the researchers entered the cage. The cage was basically to shield the researchers from the radio, TV, or other electromagnetic waves that fill our normal environment. One of the disadvantages of working in the cage was that research time was limited by the air (oxygen) available when the door was closed. There was no ventilation system.

We'd been in the cage about 15 minutes when Anne remarked that she was being distracted by some mischievous entity scurrying around under the table trying to divert her from the project that we were working on. Andrija asked her to describe the annoying little creature. Jokingly, she said it reminded her of Casper the Friendly Ghost in the cartoon strip. We were rapidly running out of oxygen, so we signaled to have the electrical charge removed and the door opened. When we came out we were surprised to see three young people sitting around a lab bench. They were Stanford students who periodically came down to the lab to work with Andrija on projects or just to hang out.

We were introduced, and after a few minutes of small talk, one of the students asked what we had been doing in the cage, and if the experiment was successful. Then he asked if there had been any distractions during the experiment. Andrija, Anne and I looked at each other and then said that, in fact, there had been a distraction just before we came out. The three of them began a very "knowing" laughter, and asked us to describe the distraction. Anne told them what her impression was, and I showed them the lab notes I had written down as Anne was describing the disturbance. After having a good laugh, they told us about a little "thought-form" that they admitted resembled the cartoon character Casper the Friendly Ghost. They said that among themselves, over the past several months, they had conjured up this little fellow and would "send" their creation to distract other members of the group. That person would then call the senders to see if he was perceiving correctly. To them it was just an esoteric joke. They had previously told the other lab assistant that they were all going to concentrate on this thought-form, cause it to go inside the cage, and see if anyone could detect it. They were delighted that Anne had been aware of their creation.

Apparently, what they had done was to consciously build a "thought-form" with enough force and intent that it could be "sensed" or "seen" by a sensitive person. Each time they worked with this "thought-form", it increased in strength, and became easier to detect.

A "thought-form" is just that—a mental form created either consciously or unconsciously by the human mind. It starts with an idea and is refined until it becomes visualization. Then, adding detail, energy and emotion increases the power of the creation. Does that sound familiar? It should because we do it everyday. Our lives, to a large extent, are the result of it. It is so true that as a man thinketh, so he is. Consciously and consistently aim to construct only useful "thought-forms" and you will have a healthy, creative, prosperous life. Most people in our world unconsciously build "unuseful" thought-forms: my life is a mess, no one likes me, I'm not pretty, I'll never have any money, I'll never find a husband, I'm so stupid, I'll never have a job I like, and on and on. Then, daily we reinforce those thought-forms until the whole monstrous creation envelops us and even though most people are not sensitive enough to see it, they at least sense it and react to it. So in effect these harmful thought-forms become a shield that keeps us from having the good, useful things of life.

Therefore, be aware of your persistent thoughts. If an unuseful harmful thought comes in, replace it with a "useful" one, or just say, "Cancel that thought, I don't need that condition in my life." Soon this will become a habit, and as it does, your life will slowly change for the better. You may have had that attitude for a lifetime (or several) so don't expect your life to change tomorrow. Your "attitude" toward life can change today, the results may take a little longer.

Just to give you an insight into the reality of thought-forms, about fifty years ago we took our daughter, Christine, to see Swan Lake Ballet at the old Sacramento Auditorium. At intermission we stayed in the auditorium rather than brave the smoke-filled halls. After all the people around us had left, Anne said to Chris and me, "You'll never guess what is in the middle of this auditorium." We were sitting in the front row of the side balcony about a third of the way back from the stage. Anne pointed nearly to the top of the auditorium and said, "Remember the wicked magician that has just turned all the girls into swans? Well, he is filling the whole center of this auditorium, from just below the ceiling down to the main floor, It looks like one of the balloon figures in Macy's Thanksgiving Day parade.

She went on to say, "As soon as I became aware of it I asked what I was seeing. The answer I got was that this is a "thought-form" that literally travels with the ballet from performance to performance. The "substance" that fills this gigantic form is all the anger and hatred that the patrons feel towards the wicked magician. It continues to be fed at each performance by thousands of attendees, growing fatter and more substantial—so substantial that I can see every detail just as clearly as you can see Macy's parade balloons."

You may be the only one feeding your thought forms (and there may be several), but if you have thought, lived and fed these unuseful thoughts for years you will have created a monstrous, negative thought-form beyond your belief. So stop feeding it and it will die of starvation. From this moment on, be aware of everything you feel, everything you think, every word you speak, and every act you perform and vow to make them the best, the most useful you can. This simple, though difficult, exercise in right living can, and in time, will change your life for the better. The negative shield that has kept goodness from coming into your life will change to a magnet attracting only the good, the useful; soon, your feet will become firmly planted on the path that leads to Home.

These Stanford University students would frequently play with a very sophisticated pinball machine Andrija had built for mind control experiments—psychokinesis. The device released steel balls at the top of an accurately machined sloping steel plate with a knife-edge at the bottom of the incline. When properly adjusted, the balls would hit the knife-edge and half would fall to one side and half to the other. A run of one thousand balls might result in five hundred five on one side and four hundred ninety five on the other.

The Stanford students could will the steel balls to go one way or the other, it was just incredible to watch. The balls would literally curve as they rolled down the incline. The count instead of being five hundred on a side would often be in the vicinity of three hundred to seven hundred. I don't think Andrija ever got around to doing any serious research with these three young minds.

The NATO Assignment

One Sunday afternoon, following a busy weekend at the lab, Anne and I went to the Carmel beach to relax before starting the drive back to Sacramento. We had been sitting in the sand, quietly watching the waves, when suddenly Anne began to tell me about a vision she was having, saying something like this, "I see you crisscrossing Europe from one country to the other for the next couple of years. You are dressed in a suit and carrying a briefcase, as if you are on business. You seem to be coordinating something." I listened but didn't have the slightest idea what she could be talking about. She said she saw me traveling by air with many trips from country to country. About three weeks later, my secretary said that the manager of the Solid Rocket Division wanted me to come to his office. When I entered his office he told me to close the door behind me. I wondered what I could have done to get fired. He motioned me towards a chair, then asked me what I knew about the Hawk Igniter.

Just in case you are not a rocket engineer, the Hawk Missile System delivers an explosive payload to great heights in seconds. The igniter for the missile is the "match" lighting the solid propellant charge that propels the missile.

At the time, I was manager of the Igniter Department, and The Hawk was just one of many solid rocket igniters that we built, both experimental and production models. It seemed like a strange question. After a few seconds I said, "Well, if you put all the parts on this table I could build you an igniter that would work." He then asked me who else in my department could do that. I responded, "For one, my shop superintendent." I still didn't have a clue where this was leading. He then said, "I have to assign a technical advisor to NATO to help France and Italy go into production on the Hawk Missile, and I need an igniter expert. Who do you think I should send?"

After a few moments of thought I told him that he should send me because this was as much a diplomatic assignment as it was a technical one. "I'm glad you agree with me," he replied. "You need to be in Paris the latter part of October. That will give us time to find another manager for your department and for you to get vaccinations, shots and briefings." Briefings? From then on I carried a U.S. Army ID and was issued a NATO Top Secret Clearance; and yes, I was briefed as any Army officer would be briefed before a mission in a foreign country.

On the first trip, I spent a little over a month in Europe flying between Paris, Rome and Bordeaux getting acquainted with the people and the project that would consume my attention for the next twenty months. Anne had been so accurate in her prediction a few months earlier.

Another interesting sidelight on this assignment took place at the California State Fair in Sacramento. About a week after I was told about the assignment, Anne and I came upon a crowd of people watching a blindfolded lady on a stage who was working with a man circulating through the crowd. He would ask people to show him the serial number on a piece of paper money, and thirty or forty feet away she would rattle off the number. She also seemed to be doing other psychic things that seemed quite amazing.

At one point, he announced that if anyone had a specific question, she would answer it for $5.00. We thought that just for fun we would ask her about the European assignment. I had been told that I would go to Europe for a month, return to California for another month or so, and then move with my family to Europe for a year or two. We were making plans accordingly. To us it was an academic question to which we thought we already knew the answer, but we thought it would be a good experiment; it would give us a chance to see how this clairvoyant functioned and how accurate she really was. When we asked the question we tried to convey the least possible information. The answer the psychic gave us was just what we had been told and what we were planning to do, so we concluded that she was really quite good. However, in a couple of months the plans were completely changed. When I returned from the one-month exploratory trip, NATO management decided it was costing too much to move whole families to Europe, so I stayed in California and the European entities sent engineers and various levels of management to California for training. A year later I was sent to Europe for about five months, and Anne accompanied me while Christine stayed with my mother in the Los Angeles area until we returned.

So how does one evaluate a psychic demonstration at the State Fair? Was this lady an excellent mind reader, or did she report the facts as they existed at that moment? It is incidents like this that have always made Anne and me very skeptical about psychic predictions. What is the sensitive really reporting? Is she reporting what she psychically sees happening at some future time, or is her report based upon the most likely occurrence given the current data? If the basic facts change, so might the outcome. Just being an excellent mind reader is no mean trick; and predicting the future based upon the current data known only to the other person, is no ordinary skill, but it is surely not something upon which one should base his future.

Anne has always avoided predicting the future unless it just pops in unbidden. It's the same thing when a client wants to make an appointment to explore "past lives." Neither Anne nor I believe the process of "rebirth" is as simplistic as most believers think. If that is what the person wants, she simply refuses to make an appointment. Would she be telling the person what they already believe, or perhaps relating a scenario that exists in the cosmos that fits what they believe? In either case, it probably would have nothing to do with truth.

A year later than originally planned, Anne and I went to Europe. We had our choice of making our primary residence in Paris, Bordeaux, or Rome. We chose Rome. I would spend a week or two in Rome, then fly to Bordeaux for a week or so. Paris was the site of our European headquarters but since most of my consultation was technical, I spent the bulk of my time at the manufacturing facilities near Rome and Bordeaux. An interesting little aside is that in France I was working at the same facility that had made black powder and cannon balls for Napoleon. They were now making rockets for NATO.

Anne and I lived at the Ritz Hotel in north Rome. We bought a new car in Italy so we could explore as much of Europe as time would permit. During the week while I was working, Anne would do research and reconnaissance toward a travel plan, so we could make the best use of our time on the weekends. The ruins of ancient Rome were of primary interest to us.

An Italian engineer with whom I worked gave us our first all-day tour of Rome. He was a student of ancient Roman history, as well as being well versed in East Indian philosophy. The first time we discussed Eastern philosophy I asked him his feelings about reincarnation. His response was, "But, of course, how else could it be? It is the only logical explanation." The next trip we took to the Roman Forum was on a wet Sunday in early February. We had the whole place to ourselves and we wanted to explore areas that Anne had talked about during her hypnotherapy three years earlier. The steps she talked about running up and down delivering or receiving messages were surely there, as anyone knows who has visited the Forum.

She wanted to visit the Roman Senate and while walking inside, she suddenly felt a strong urge to go outside in the rain, and walk among pieces of ancient buildings and damaged sculptures. As we walked, Anne dropped to her knees in front of a headless bust and cried out, "Master, Master!" Luckily there was no one around. Going inside again we found a guard, took him to the headless statue and asked what he knew about it. He said, "Oh, that is a bust of Julius Caesar that is being repaired." Next we walked over to the Circus Maximus, at the foot of Palatine Hill, where many competitive games had been performed. We wanted to walk across it to view Palatine Hill from that perspective. I was a little ahead of Anne, and suddenly realized she wasn't with me; rather she was standing just outside the curb that defined the edge of the arena, first picking up one foot and then the other trying to step over the curb and on to the arena floor. Her foot would get just to the edge of the curb and go no farther, as if there were a solid wall instead of the six-inch curb. Try as she might, in no way would that invisible barrier allow her to put a foot on the ground that had been one of the sites of the Roman games. About once a week Anne would come to the Circus Maximus and challenge the invisible force that would not allow her on the playing field. Finally, just a few days before we left Rome for the last time, we made another trip to the Forum, Palatine Hill and the Circus Maximus. We don't know what changed but this attempt was successful. We walked all the way around the large racetrack. Anne said that when she stood on the track, Palatine Hill came alive; she could hear the cheers from the spectators and felt a deep sense of fear in her middle, as if she were one of the performers. Was she sensing Antonius's anxiety when he performed there two thousand years ago, or was she sensing the general fear, pain, and anxiety associated with the activities that took place on that field so long ago? In any case, she finally made peace with the energy that nearly prevented her from ever again setting foot on that arena.

During the four or five months we spent in Rome, Anne had many experiences that seemed to confirm that she was on familiar ground.

One of our goals while in Italy was to see as many of Michelangelo's works of art and architecture as possible. Locating his creations was Anne's favorite "job" during the week. Before we left she knew Rome better than Sacramento; for months she either walked or used public transportation to explore the most famous points of interest in the city.

One lovely sunny, but cold, Sunday we drove to Hadrian's Villa, north of Rome. We walked around for a couple of hours and when it was time to eat our bread and cheese lunch we found a sunny place in the corner of a crumbling wall. At some point Anne said, "You will never believe what I am seeing. I'm seeing this Villa as it was nearly two thousand years ago. I see the people, the lavish parties, just as they were then. In fact, for many of these people nothing has changed; they are still at the party. The music, food, wine and entertainment are still happening—a two thousand year party! When you stop to think about it, in their state of consciousness, there is no time. Their awareness in that existence was probably pleasure centered, so why should they leave a good party?"

Another lovely, sunny weekend in March Anne and I drove to Pompeii. We got there early so we had several hours to explore the aftermath of Vesuvius' eruption in 79AD. Again, since it was still winter, we had a lot of freedom not possible during the tourist season. The guard took us into areas that were just being excavated and catalogued. Later we went in alone and had even more freedom to explore. Later in the morning, we were walking up a grassy hillside, I noticed Anne's strange behavior. She was slowly going up the hill, but her feet seemed trying to point in the opposite direction in a kind of push-pull situation. When we got to the crest we found we were at the top, back edge of a small circular arena. Anne had a terrible reaction to the site. She almost vomited. We just couldn't figure out what was causing this sense of repulsion. We located a guard and he told us the games had gotten so bloody in that arena that Rome ordered it permanently closed.

Later that afternoon, we came to a section of the city Anne said felt very familiar to her. She felt that if she tried, she could find the place where she had lived at some time, not necessarily during the eruption, and about this same time, she became aware of a severe discomfort in the lower parts of her torso. As we were leaving this rather well preserved area, we saw a placard that said this had been the red-light district of the city. By the time we reached our hotel about sundown, Anne's lower abdominal area was so sore she could hardly walk and her exhaustion was so intense she could hardly stay up long enough to have dinner. She said she felt as if she had been making love all day. By morning she felt fine but insisted that we return to the ruins on Sunday, especially the area that seemed so familiar to her. I jokingly accused her of just wanting to continue the experience and, sure enough, 15 minutes after we reached that part of the city it became very painful for her to walk. A half-hour after leaving the area she felt fine. What was she experiencing? Was it just the overall, residual, sexual energy of that immediate area, or was it something more personal? Another one of those questions that will remain unanswered.

The NATO assignment came to an end and we were free to return home, but not until we had seen more of southern Europe. It was spring, the weather beautiful, we had a new Alfa Romeo Coupe, it was an easy decision to just drive off the radar screen so my office couldn't find us. We headed north out of Rome, stopping when we were hungry or tired, no schedule. Just a few hours north of Rome, Anne was attracted to a small, strangely shaped, Catholic Church. We went inside, looked up the aisle toward the altar and started toward it. Suddenly, Anne gasped; she looked terrified, so I just watched. Again she had hit one of those invisible, impenetrable barriers, only this time she was fighting back. She was so determined to reach that altar that she got down on her hands and knees and literally crawled down the aisle. Luckily, it was in the middle of the week and no one was there. She acted as if she were doing battle with some dark, evil force or entity.

Finally, relying on what seemed to be superhuman effort, she reached the railing in front of the altar. On the way out we found a bronze plaque mounted in a large stone telling the history of the church. Originally, the structure had been a pagan temple and was, converted into a Catholic Church when Christianity became the official religion of the Roman Empire. But, what was it Anne had been battling? To me it looked very real and to her the opposing force was in deadly earnest. In those days, Anne was at the mercy of the psychic forces that are always present in "power spots." She could sense them but was yet unable to control the sensitivity that had just recently been awakened in her. Within a few years she became capable of choosing to investigate a psychic force or condition if she were so inclined or to ignore the energy emanating from them.

We got as far south and west as Portugal in our travels before we started north through Spain, up the Loire Valley in France on our way to Le Havre, where we put the Alfa on a freighter to San Francisco.

By late May 1963, I was finally back to work in California. I think I could have stayed another month without being missed. The defense buildup seemed to be peaking, yet no one wanted to believe it. Because of my top secret U.S. and NATO security clearances, which gave me access to all the data I needed, I was asked by our management to make a long-range business forecast in late 1963. The study concluded that in 6 or 7 years our company would be down to a fraction of its peak employment because the whole industry was shrinking. My immediate superior, the fellow who gave me the assignment, said the conclusion was totally unacceptable. He, however, stayed with the company long enough to realize the validity of the conclusion. When I resigned in 1970 our contractual base had been cut in half. It was time to leave.

CHAPTER IV:

SPIRITUAL INTUITION

The Workshop Scene

A couple of months after resigning from my position in the defense industry in January 1970, I entered a Zen monastery near Monterey, California as a working student. Our first meditation began at 5 AM and the last one finished at 9 PM. For about five hours a day I worked in the wood shop maintaining fixtures and furniture for Buddhist monastic worship. The directors even asked me to stay and accept an assignment to a Japanese monastery to learn traditional Japanese woodworking, then return to help in the construction of traditional Zen Buddhist structures and fixtures. The idea just sent shivers up my spine—I would have loved every moment of it but something kept me on the path Anne and I had begun years before. I didn't know the path we would follow, but when I strayed, something brought me back to that path that was just wide enough for two.

In June of that same year, 1970, I enrolled in a nine week, high fire, pottery workshop—another old love of mine. A couple of years later I found myself in my own high-fire pottery studio in the US Virgin Islands. It was an interesting but expensive foray into art and business.

After closing down the pottery studio in St. Thomas, Virgin Islands, I returned to Sacramento in June 1976. When I arrived home, Anne informed me that in a few weeks she had a workshop at the Mann Ranch in northern California, and she wanted me to help her put it together. I had always helped her plan her workshops but she would lead them, so this was going to be the same—I thought. I drove her to the Ranch, planning on a relaxed weekend for myself while she ran the workshop of a dozen or so people. As we walked through the dining area that afternoon, we noticed that there were table settings for a lot of people. When Anne asked how many people were signed up for the workshop she was told, "Oh, about 35 plus staff." She almost panicked, as she never wanted more than twelve or thirteen. I suggested that we go to our room and discuss it, but for her there was nothing to discuss; she just wanted to go home. I got out a sheet of paper and re-wrote the schedule with Anne facilitating one group while I worked with the other. From then until now she has had a co-leader.

In 1976, Anne's workshops consisted of a few exercises that sharpened intuitive skills we all have, but not much actual practice was included. Instead, Anne worked in a counseling mode with each participant in front of the group. That is why she limited the group to about 12 participants. So during this workshop, our first, I presented the exercises to rotating groups while Anne did counseling with the remaining participants.

Within less than a year, we were turning down offers to do workshops. Soon, we were working all over the United States and Canada, scheduling well over a hundred days of workshops, conferences and seminars a year, not including travel time. Esalen Institute, at Big Sur, California, became our "home base". We were listed in almost every Esalen Catalog for nearly twenty years doing weekend, five-day, and two and three-week workshops, conferences and seminars. In between Esalen workshops, we worked on the East Coast, in the Northwest, Florida, Canada, Mexico and Europe.

In case you have not been to the Esalen Institute, it is the original and still the finest human potential, growth center in the world. The site is the old Murphy Family summer residence on the Big Sur Coast, forty miles south of Carmel, California, reachable by Highway 1.

Originally, the Esalen Indian tribe occupied this remote, beautiful area. When the Spanish arrived, there were about five hundred of them living in villages along the Big Sur Coast. The good Fathers herded them into the missions of Carmel and Monterey where within a few generations they all perished. The Esalen Indian became the first native California tribe to become extinct. Then came the loggers and ranchers with sheep and cattle; finally, in the late 1930's a road connected this remote area with the towns to the north and south.

In the mid 1940's, Henry Miller returned to the United States from Paris and found his way into this California wilderness. Miller's books, Tropic of Cancer and Tropic of Capricorn had been banned in the United States. Probably this in itself was enough to create a national awareness of the Big Sur Area. This was the beginning of a loosely knit, West Coast Greenwich Village. From articles in "Harpers" by Mildred Edie Brady, the outside world began to hear about this Bohemian community of writers and artists that included people like Henry Miller, Emil White, Mildred Brady, and Anais Nin. In the 1940's and 50's, Big Sur was a beautiful, remote wilderness with a scattering of the original hippies and groupies. It wasn't until the very early 60's that Michael Murphy began to develop what has become the New Age culture center of the world, Esalen Institute.

Esalen Institute is built on a relatively level point of land jutting into the Pacific Ocean, with steep mountains to the east and a hundred-foot drop off to the sea on the west. Since the sunsets can be spectacular at this location, there is a platform and benches for meditation, or perhaps just to watch the sun go down. The grounds and facilities, as beautiful as they are, are always being improved. During many of the years that we worked at Esalen, we were living in the hot Sacramento Valley, so the month or two total that we spent by the ocean each year was like a paid vacation. Sure, it rains some, but that is what keeps the streams and springs in Big Sur running all year. The scenery is some of the most beautiful in the world.

The Esalen Hot Springs were also a favorite place for the Esalen Indians that inhabited the area centuries before the Murphy's and Miller's found it. The world famous Esalen Baths are a far cry from the hot spring, bathing pools used by the Esalen Indians, and later the whites, who ventured along this rugged coast, either by sea or land.

Even though Highway 1 now traverses this scenic coastline, there are frequently months at a time when it is impassible because of landslides and washouts. It is California's most difficult and expensive, highway maintenance project.

Nestled in this rugged beauty, is the Esalen Institute, accepted worldwide as a model for a new age growth center. In 1962, the Institute, conceived and developed by Michael Murphy and Richard Price, distributed its first catalog and began to establish a foothold in the Bohemian/hippie Community along the Big Sur Coast. During the next few years, succeeding Esalen Catalogs began to read like the Who's Who of the New Age Movement, with names like Abraham Maslow, Alan Watts, Gerald Herd, Charles Tart, Aldous Huxley, Willis Harman, Myron Stolaroff, Will Schutz, Joe Adams, Wilson Van Dusen, Gia-fu Feng, with Gregory Bateson and Fritz Pearls arriving a bit later.

In the early days, Esalen was quite spiritually oriented, but when I began working with Anne in 1976, nearly all the workshops were psychologically-based; there seemed to be no hint of spirituality. I believe if someone had mentioned God everyone would have walked out. Some of the leaders may have been spiritually inclined, but it was not overtly visible in the workshop presentations. Possible exceptions were the times when Lama Govinda gave workshops there. He was a German Buddhist who had spent most of his life following the teachings of Buddhism in Tibet. From time to time he gave workshops at Esalen.

After our first workshop there, I told Anne that if I were going to co-lead with her we had to find some way to introduce the spiritual element. We had been made privy to hundreds of hours of esoteric wisdom and it didn't seem fitting to ignore it. We started using guided imagery in our workshops where we could present disguised spiritual teachings without even hinting that there might be a Creator behind it all. We would suggest that the participants become aware of their feelings, thoughts, words and actions, and make them the best they could possibly be. This, of course, is the basis of all spiritual teaching whether it is Buddhist, Hindu, Christian, Hebrew or Islam, even though the followers don't necessarily practice these teachings. Over time we became bolder; until eventually, we began to speak of a Universal Force, the Creator, and finally, even God. I really believe we made it safe to speak of God in that psychologically-oriented environment of the 70's.

The founders of Esalen, Michael Murphy and Dick Price were very spiritual men. Dick, unfortunately, has taken up residence at an unknown address. It would seem that his soul led him to sit and meditate in the future path of a large boulder. We had dinner with Dick the evening before he failed to show up for his gestalt class on Monday afternoon. A thorough search of the valley where Dick frequently walked and meditated revealed his body, half in the stream where he had been thrown by a large boulder. The next morning the new Esalen Catalog was distributed. On the front cover of the catalog, which had been in printing for at least two months, was a picture of an empty, rocking chair in Michael Murphy's room; on the first page inside was a picture of a huge boulder. A lot of synchronicity, don't you think? There are no accidents.

Probably the best fallout from being a workshop leader at Esalen was the people you met, not only the other leaders but also the participants and the staff. You had no idea who that person might be sitting across the table from you during dinner or soaking beside you in the hot tub later that evening. Everyone went by their first name and wore their most casual clothes, to say the least. Your cabin maid or food server very likely had an M.D. or Ph.D. and the grounds keeper or maintenance man a Ph.D. in physics.

One of the highlights of our twenty plus years at Esalen (Anne worked there 34 years) was our on-going association with Stan and Christina Grof. Before coming to Esalen Dr. Grof was Chief of Psychiatric Research at the Maryland Psychiatric Research Center and Assistant Professor of Psychiatry at John Hopkins University School of Medicine. Stan and Christina singly and together have authored many books in addition to their pioneering work with Holotropic Breathwork. Along with their other activities, they led month-long workshops consisting of about thirty-five participants, and a staff of nearly equal number including Joseph Campbell, Ram Dass, Jack Kornfield, Brother David Steindl-Rast and Fritjof Capra, just to mention a few. We considered ourselves very fortunate to be part of that staff for about 10 years. During one of those workshops, we just happened to be the "scholar-in-residence" for the work scholars. The work scholar program gave its members the privilege of being a part of Esalen's work force, anything from making beds and cleaning rooms to working at the front desk or tending the garden. In their spare time the work scholars could sit in on workshops and enjoy many of the amenities of a paying guest. In addition, there was always a "scholar-in-residence" that gave a special workshop just for their groups. This particular month we were the "scholars-in-residence". Since our schedule with the work scholars was flexible, we had an opportunity not only to be part of the staff, but also to sit in on much of the month-long workshop. Just being around Stan and Christina for any length of time was a real privilege.

Anne had made her debut at Esalen in 1964 after someone introduced us to Claudio Naranjo, a Chilean psychiatrist. Claudio came to our home in Sacramento to meet Anne, and after dinner he asked her to co-lead an Esalen workshop with him later that year. Anne's response was quite short: "What is Esalen, and what does one do at a workshop?" He told her not to worry about those kinds of details. He would make the write-up for the catalog and all she had to do was show up in time for dinner on Friday night.

Since she really had no idea what Esalen was or what a workshop was, she promptly enrolled in one led by Red Thomas and Michael Murphy in the spring of 1964. Someone told the leaders who Anne was and they asked her to demonstrate the therapeutic application of her intuitive abilities with some members of the group. Part of the group saw her as a witch and the rest of the group saw her quite the opposite. A catholic priest turned out to be one of her strongest supporters. In those days if you got on the hot seat everyone in the group was encouraged to say whatever they thought, so it could be a very traumatic experience, especially for a Sacramento housewife on her first trip to Esalen. True to form, Anne survived, much the wiser.

The Friday evening of her first experience as an Esalen co-leader finally arrived. Being the cautious person she is (or was), she arrived well before dinner, got settled into her room, and around 6 PM went down for dinner—but no Claudio. She knew where the workroom was, so at 8:30 PM she showed up—but still no Claudio. After 5 or 10 minutes of sheer panic, she suggested to the group that they meditate, hoping Claudio would make his appearance. After all, he had said, "Don't worry, I'll take care of all the details." While she was "meditating" she prayed, "God, you got me into this, what do I do now?" To this day she can't remember what she did or how she got through her first Esalen workshop session. About 10 PM, Claudio walked into the room and explained that at dusk the fog had moved in as he was driving through Carmel and he had spent the last few hours on the road in the fog. He just looked the situation over and said, "Looks fine, carry on."

The next morning Claudio, who was a gestalt therapist, suggested that he and Anne each take a workshop room and do their own thing, and the group could flow between the two rooms. As soon as the afternoon session began, Claudio came to Anne's workroom and said, "May I join your group?" And then graciously added, "They find what you do more interesting." From that moment on Anne was securely ensconced at Esalen. For a time she and Claudio continued to co-lead workshops, then at some point Anne was asked to just do her 'thing' alone. And just what was her 'thing'?

Anne's spiritual breakthrough, less than five years earlier, had been a dynamic, energetic occurrence. As time went on and we learned more about the Kundalini process, we realized that she'd had a full-blown, Kundalini opening, and in less than a year had it under control. That was certainly a dynamic occurrence. So when she started to do workshops at Esalen, she found herself not only compelled to talk to people about their life situations but also to begin to work with their energy systems. This took the form of using her hands to stimulate their energy, especially using her own vital force to move the energy in their spine. Frequently, she would use sound to augment the process. Her sounds seemed to be a very primitive type of chanting, very difficult to identify. At times it sounded Hebrew, or Egyptian, or East Indian; yet, it was different from any of them. The effect on the recipient was usually profound. Frequently, the other participants were also visibly affected. The feedback was nearly always positive. The sounds seemed to break up crystallized, energy patterns in the body so their own vital force could begin to flow more smoothly, especially up and down the spine. Often, the recipient of Anne's energy work described it as a fifteen-minute psychedelic experience. As I noted earlier, therapy at Esalen at that time was psychologically and physiologically-oriented. So Anne's intuitive work fit right in because most people's problems have a psychological component. Even though Anne was not a degreed psychologist, it certainly was never an issue. Her intuitive work was basically deep level, soul psychology, eventually coming to be known as transpersonal psychology. In school, Anne had been academically oriented, and had she obtained her Masters or Ph.D. in psychology she would have become a great therapist; however, the transpersonal psychologist she has been for over forty years would never have evolved. She would be just one more competent psychologist among thousands, instead of the unique therapist that she is.

It should be made clear that all of Anne's therapy, whether talking, energy work, or chanting, is inspired by the needs of the person with whom she is working. True, we humans are much more alike than we are different from one another, but in the thousands of times I have seen her work with people, never have I been aware of her following an academic or planned script. Each piece of work is unique; where she places her hands or the sounds she makes are spontaneous and intuitively-guided acts. There is no way she can make those sounds on demand or when in a normal state of awareness.

Once Anne became a workshop leader, there were many other leaders, or would-be leaders, who wanted to co-lead with her. Probably one of the most successful team teaching situations was when she and Gabrielle Roth worked together. Gabrielle was just starting to develop her sound and movement work. Her music and movement would get people loosened up and relaxed, making it much easier for Anne to work with them. As a consequence, they had several, highly successful workshops.

Most of the people who attended Anne's workshops at Esalen, and other growth centers, were therapists. They would see Anne zero in on childhood traumas, or very subtle relationship problems in a few minutes, knowing it could take months of ordinary therapy to uncover the same events. Consequently, therapists soon besieged Anne with requests to teach them her techniques.

Anne's standard answer was, "I don't know how I do it, so how can I teach you? I don't know what causes me or allows me to do what I do. When I'm presented with a situation, I just seem to 'know' the answer." Thirty years earlier I had asked Ida Marshall, our clairvoyant friend in Hollywood, the same question, and I received the same answer. The reason, of course, was that both Anne and Ida were highly "intuitive." Webster's Dictionary defines intuition as, "The immediate knowing or learning of something without the conscious use of reasoning;

instantaneous apprehension." And what is the cause of these two people being intuitive? For one thing they both seemed to have come into this life with a high degree of spiritual development. I don't know much about Ida's history, but I do know Anne's. In summary, she had migraine headaches and other physical problems for over thirty years; she made a thorough study of a Christian, esoteric philosophy when she was about twenty three years old and this included a lot of meditation and spiritual exercises; she used hypnotherapy to find the cause of the headaches; she had some weird experiences that seemed to be past lives; she became the recipient of spontaneous breath work and yoga postures; she had a discarnate Hindu teacher who took her on as a student; and several months later she was working in a hypnotherapist's office helping her solve very difficult psychological cases.

So what combination of these situations caused or allowed Anne to be intuitive? Lots of people have illnesses but don't become intuitive. Many people have been repeatedly hypnotized during therapy and they aren't intuitive. However, many, if not all, highly evolved yogis have developed psychic and intuitive abilities as a natural fallout of their spiritual practice. Yogis look upon psychic abilities as a hindrance to their spiritual development and they truly are if one stays trapped at that level of development. In a nation ravaged with psychological problems, however, these abilities seem to serve a useful purpose. Highly developed yogis have sacrificed release from Samsara to be of service to humanity. But Anne was not a highly developed yogi or a guru. What right did she have to teach anyone? There didn't seem to be anything wrong, however, with telling people what she knew about spiritual development in general and then letting them find the path that suited them best. Anne and I knew every spiritual path had a form of meditation to quiet the mind. We knew that Buddhism, Judaism, Hinduism, Christianity, and Islam, among other religious philosophies, taught ethics, morality, right living and love. Surely if people followed these basic philosophic and spiritual principles, and some form of meditation, they would at least become better people; and, hopefully, some of them would develop intuition as a natural fallout of a healthy spiritual practice.

In hindsight we can now see that when Anne was about twenty-three she had an abortive, Kundalini opening. We, and everyone we consulted, were too ignorant to know what was happening to her. As a consequence, she tried to shut it down and the resulting Kundalini energy created more physical problems until the hypnosis got her back into the quiet-mind state that she had been avoiding for sixteen years. In the following few months her Kundalini again began to rise in the spine, only this time she had a discarnate Hindu guru as a teacher, a couple of good therapists, and an understanding husband, as well, to support and guide her. The stage was now set for a rapid spiritual development with a psychic/intuitive component that was brought under control within a seven-year period. During those seven years Anne's intuitive abilities give one access to an endless source of spiritual wisdom, much of which she incorporated into her way of life, which in turn gave her better control over the psychic/intuitive abilities.

By the time I joined Anne as co-leader in 1976, the requests for her to teach were becoming more numerous. Until then, her workshops had been mostly therapy, as were most Esalen workshops at that time. Soon, however, we consciously began to use guided imagery exercises (really a form of group hypnosis) that enhanced imagery and imagination, stimulated the emotions, and began to awaken the intuitive abilities latent in everyone; eventually, we taught many different forms of meditation. This way the person could choose the one that worked best for them. Gradually, we began to incorporate the esoteric/spiritual principles that Anne had obtained for her own spiritual development, as well as exercises she had been given during her seven-year "internship" from 1959 to 1966. Occasionally, we found or developed exercises that we incorporated into our program. Many times when we felt the need for new meditations and exercises, we would sit together in meditation and ask for the information we needed. Anne's "pipeline" nearly always delivered the raw material from which I could develop these new meditations and exercises. For over thirty-five years she has had the ability to receive guidance on spiritual matters, and in these instances the seed-thought behind our meditations and exercises came via that route. This source is still available on demand—just sit quietly and ask.

Between the summer of 1976 and the beginning of the new century, we reached tens of thousands of people through thousands of workshops, seminars and conferences, not to mention private sessions with thousands of clients that Anne has handled in her "spare time."

Compared to the exciting decade of the 60's, the rest of our life as a couple and as workshop leaders has been rather ordinary, but certainly never boring. We traveled to all the major growth centers in the U.S., Canada, and several in Europe and Mexico, presenting workshops and seminars and attending and/or presenting at conferences. I recall a conference in Prague, Czechoslovakia, where we led an intuition workshop with over eighty Czechs, practically none of whom spoke English. We exhausted three translators and ourselves, but at 5 PM the group was still going strong. Stan Grof's mother was one of the participants.

For many years, in addition to our domestic workshops, we spent four to six weeks each year traveling and presenting workshops in Ireland, Germany, Switzerland and Norway. We stopped going about ten years ago. Currently, we schedule eight one day workshops with participants we have worked with for up to thirty years.

Frequently, during or after a workshop I am asked if I am psychic/intuitive and if any of Anne's abilities have rubbed off on me. My casual answer is, no, because every act needs a straight man. A more serious and lengthy answer is that our partnership works because we each have our own area of expertise and responsibility, and we each operate effectively within that domain. Anne is the transpersonal psychologist, counselor, and intuitive. From her insights I develop and present the exercises and meditations for our workshops. I handle all the logistics: schedules, write-ups, brochures, transportation, housing, finances, and serve as scribe when necessary. We discuss general approaches but very seldom specifics; we respect each other's abilities and make allowance for shortcomings. The result is we have a good personal and working relationship—why change anything?

Up until 1976, Anne had many co-leaders. Almost without exception, they either thought they were highly intuitive or they wanted to be. It came across to the members of the group that they were trying to up-stage the leader. Anne wasn't threatened by their words or actions but members of the group would become highly incensed. Outside the workshop people would say, "Next time you come here to do a workshop why don't you just come alone." The message was loud and clear. Because of that, on the occasions when Anne had asked me to co-lead with her, my answer was to the effect that her public would not accept anyone as her co-leader. Then came that "fateful" day in the summer of 1976 when it became imperative that we join forces, each contributing their strong points.

People, especially couples, have asked us our secret in working together. There is really no secret. For years we didn't think it unusual for a married couple to work together. Then one day, I read an article in an in-flight magazine on the way to New York. The authors said their way of working together was for each to have their own area of expertise, neither jealous of the other person's successes nor meddling in the other's domain. I realized we had been doing just that for over twenty years.

I was a successful manager in the corporate world for years, so I'm not easily threatened, nor is Anne. I have no desire to do what she does and she has no desire to do the scheduling, editing and writing and other things I handle. It simply is no problem for either of us to stay out of the other person's domain. Jealousy is never a factor in our work relationship—neither of us envies the other's abilities, accolades, or compensations. I believe we both feel that there is enough of everything to go around. It is also possible that some of the essence of the hundreds of hours of spontaneous, esoteric, lecture material has soaked into our consciousness giving us a foundation of love and understanding on which to base our work relationship as well as our personal relationship.

Intuition

We have always told groups that it would be pretty presumptuous of us to say that we were going to "teach them" intuition. To begin with, everyone has intuition as an innate ability. It is an integral part of the mechanism that comes into play when there is no time to make logical, rational decisions; it is an attribute built into the system by the Creator. There is no way we would try to take credit for that, but we can help people recognize that built-in ability, then assist them in refining it. That is about all we do in the intuitive part of our workshops. The other thing we, quietly, sometimes almost surreptitiously do in our workshops is to allow the participants to start recognizing that they are Divine Beings with all the attributes of their Creator. By simply suggesting that, if during the day, they remain aware of their every feeling, every thought, every word and every action, they will rather rapidly become better people—that is what the spiritual path is all about. It has little to do with going to church or synagogue on the weekend. All we do in our workshops is attempt to convince the participants that they are already intuitive, and if they will accept that, we will give them some hints on how to be intuitive on "demand".

Our basic belief is that the conscious control of intuition comes as a natural fallout of a healthy spiritual practice. Anne has been told dozens of times in many different ways that all wisdom is to be found in the silence. Intuition is humanity's best connection to that place of all wisdom; intuition is enhanced by a quiet mind; and a quiet mind is the direct result of a healthy spiritual practice. Yes, there are unhealthy spiritual practices. They are out there.

Author's note: My editor put a note in the margin that I have repeated these thoughts about enlightenment several times during the writing of this manuscript. And he's absolutely right. I repeated these ideas because they are probably the most important bit of awareness that a seeker can practice if he/she is serious about troding the path to enlightenment.

I make no pretext of being an expert in unhealthy spiritual practices, but I believe there are a few easy ways of spotting them and their leaders. Very possibly the surest ways are statements or implications that there is only one path, one teaching, one religion, and that this leader or organization has that path or teaching. Be aware of bigots regardless of the size, age or general acceptance of the organization they represent. I tend to distrust the need for excessive ritual, hypnotic or brainwashing techniques. Be aware of people who have been "chosen to bring forth a message" that will save humanity. Humanity is probably no more lost than it has ever been. But if it were, do you really believe the job would be entrusted to this person? Be logical and perceptive. Be skeptical of those who believe they have a divine appointment to save us. Be aware of any teaching or doctrine that makes you feel special, or superior to others. Be especially aware of an organization or leader who attempts, subtly or otherwise, to separate you from your family or established friends, making him/her (and their followers) your new family and friends. So if it looks and feels like a cult, it probably is one; and if you feel unusually drawn to it you may find psychological counseling useful.

Intuition is not something you develop in a five-day seminar. However, many of the participants who have hung in there for ten years or so have developed considerable skill with their intuition—especially psychotherapists. Most therapists are already quite intuitive, so about all we can do is help them recognize their abilities and then give suggestions, exercises and practice to hone the skills they already have.

Meditation is probably the most useful practice we advocate because it leads to a quiet, controlled mind. We also suggest that one begin to work consciously toward a moral, ethical lifestyle. One "simple" way to do that, as noted above, is to start becoming aware—aware of every feeling, every thought, every word and every action, and making each one the best it can possibly be. Do this with some degree of devotion and you will begin getting insights into yourself that you would never have believed possible. A good adjunct to this practice is to review your day just before going to sleep. This review can be done as part of an evening meditation or in bed before going to sleep. You start with the last thing you just did—turned out the light, opened the window, brushed your teeth, took a shower, screamed at the kids to stop talking and go to sleep, yelled at your husband for not taking out the garbage, fixed dinner, gave a finger to the guy that cut you off in traffic, etc., right back to getting out of bed at 6:45 AM and cursing the alarm clock. As you are doing this reverse review of your day you evaluate every item—how did you feel? What thoughts did you have when you were doing it? Could you have used a better, kinder choice of words? Could you have done it differently? Was giving that smartass the finger really the proper thing to have done? Or, hey, I handled that situation at work in a really nice way.

The next logical step in this self-awareness exercise is to be aware, particularly of unuseful actions (or statements), immediately after they occur. Evaluate the situation while it is still fresh in your mind. Decide right there and then whether it was a useful action, and if not, resolve not to repeat it. If it was a useful action, be aware of it and compliment yourself for a job well done.

The next iteration is to be aware of the action while it is in progress. If it is deemed to be unuseful, attempt to terminate the action or reverse the impact as much as possible. If it is a useful action compliment yourself and smile inwardly.

The final step in this soul-growth program is to evaluate the situation while it is still in the thought phase, before one word has been spoken or a single action taken. If it is deemed to be useful, continue; if your evaluation indicates that it is an unuseful statement or action, terminate the thought before any more energy is expended on an unuseful endeavor.

Eventually, perhaps not in this lifetime, but eventually, the thought to commit an unuseful action will never even occur. When that day arrives you will be well on your way Home. I won't guarantee that you will be more intuitive tomorrow, but you will be a better person. These are not "New Age" exercises. The first time I read about these processes was in the writings of Ben Franklin. Then I ran into them in Rosicrucian teachings. Recently I found almost a word for word description by a Jewish Rabbi who lived in the 17th and 18th centuries. Manly P. Hall also notes similar exercises in his books on discipleship. No, these are not inventions of the New Age get-well-circuit. Rather, they are tried and tested techniques for spiritual development that have been around for centuries in all spiritual disciplines.

You've probably been aware that I have been using the terms "useful" and "unuseful" instead of the customary "good" and "evil," or "positive" and "negative," or just plain good and bad. So this seems to be as good a time as any to discuss those terms.

I'm sure Alan Watts must have written this someplace in one of his many books, but I recall him discussing it in a workshop held on his houseboat in Sausalito. California.

He began by saying, in effect, that polar opposites were usually quite "unuseful" terms because they were static, black or white, whereas nearly everything in our physical realm was dynamic and some shade of gray. Then he explained how the words, "good" and "evil" got into the English translation of the Old Testament and was carried over into the New Testament. When the translators were making the transition from Hebrew to Greek they encountered the two Hebrew words that Jewish craftsmen used when discussing processes involved in weaving a reed basket or throwing a clay jug on a potter's wheel. One of the words described a process that if employed would produce a fine basket or a utilitarian clay water jug. The other word inferred a process that if applied in one of their crafts would produce an inferior product. For the first term the translators chose the Greek word that means "good." For the opposite term they chose the Greek word for "evil." So the Hebrew craftsmen's terms for useful and not useful (unuseful) were translated in the King James Bible as good and evil. Now, let's go back to some more background on intuition and related subjects.

The Spiritual Intuitive Process

In esoteric or occult parlance, Anne would be referred to as a positive clairvoyant. A literal translation for clairvoyance is simply "clear seeing." Theoretically, it is looking at a situation from a perspective unencumbered by the body/brain/mind system. A trained clairvoyant hopefully can rise above or go beyond the frailties of the personality and give a clear view of a given situation. A positive clairvoyant is a person capable of "clear seeing" in full consciousness—full awareness—without an intermediate entity or guide. This process is the antithesis of much of the typical so-called "channeling" that is all the rage nowadays, where the channeler may invite a discarnate entity to take control of their physical body and then go into a deep trance, leaving the invited entity in charge. Actually there are all degrees of control, or lack of control, by the channeler in mediumship. In any case it is a form of negative clairvoyance. When the esotericist or occultist refers to the different processes as positive or negative he is not necessarily making a value judgment, but is simply distinguishing between the two.

Max Heindel in the Rosicrucian Cosmo-Conception uses the terms voluntary and involuntary to distinguish between the two types of clairvoyance. His theory is that during the very early development of the human race everyone had involuntary clairvoyance, but over the eons the ability has been lost. However, through certain practices the human race is beginning to develop voluntary clairvoyance. It is said that when psychic investigators view a medium, the chakras are rotating counterclockwise, whereas the chakras of a voluntary clairvoyant rotate clockwise, the same as a practicing yogi. In between the two extremes of positive and negative clairvoyance are many variations—psychism, intuition and various forms of what is termed channeling. Jon Klimo's book *Channeling, and Arthur Hastings' With Tongues of Men and Angels* discuss this whole area of paranormal transmission and reception. They are well worth reading if you are interested in the channeling process.

The method that Anne, as a positive clairvoyant, has used for over forty years is "spiritual intuition." The word intuition covers a broad spectrum of human awareness, from hunches or direct action at a purely survival level to a full understanding of the Universe—the wisdom of God. Some place along the path that leads to God Consciousness, the personality begins a conscious search for meaning, for answers to the age-old question—"Who am I?" Through physical, mental, and emotional disciplines, through meditation and contemplation, the seeker refines the physical, emotional and mental vehicles to the point where he/she starts to glimpse the inner workings of the Universe. In the beginning the insights may be involuntary, but eventually they come under the conscious control of the seeker. There are no intermediaries—just a direct knowing without any rational understanding of the source of the wisdom. The person finds that this wisdom is always available—there are no "off days." The range of knowledge and wisdom is inexhaustible, but the seeker soon realizes that the most useful knowledge is centered on becoming a better person, becoming aware of their relationship to the Universe, to God. At some point they lose their curiosity, seeking to know only that which will enhance their own spiritual growth and the spiritual growth of those whom they contact. They soon realize that spiritual growth and service to humanity are the major goals of being. Service to humanity can take many avenues, so there is no sense of a limitation of investigation or expression.

Willis Harman and Howard Rheingold in their book *Higher Creativity*, discuss this intuition spectrum in a very clear, informative way. They discuss the techniques consciously or unconsciously used by scientists, writers, composers, and poets—techniques used for accessing information from the universal archives. Alice Bailey has written at length about spiritual intuition and the many ways it operates through people on the spiritual path—automatic writing, directed writing, clairaudience, clairvoyance, clairsentients, direct knowing and various combinations of these. She herself published many books she'd written using some form of spiritual intuition. Max Heindel was a positive clairvoyant who spoke freely about using his spiritual intuition to explore other realms of consciousness—other realities—and from this he developed the cosmology of 20th century Rosicrucianism. Rudolf Steiner, Madam Blavatsky, Marie Montessori, Dr. R. Assagioli, Alice Bailey, and other late 19th and early 20th century esotericists all made use of their spiritual intuition in one way or another. Nevertheless, in their writings there are frequent warnings about the use of negative clairvoyance, the deep trance where a discarnate entity takes control of the medium's body and delivers a discourse while the medium in most cases is totally unaware of what is being said.

During the first several years of Anne's opening process she would experiment with almost any psychic/intuitive situation that presented itself. There were times when she got into some very compromising situations, but she always came through okay. I recall one evening when she had eased herself into a deep intuitive space and became aware of a discarnate entity that seemed to have something to say. The entity was quite insistent and soon Anne's voice and mannerisms became that of a hell-fire-and-damnation, Southern Baptist minister. He ranted on for forty minutes in that typical evangelistic syntax. Naturally, it was all being recorded. At some point his energy and enthusiasm were expended and a very limp Anne shook her head, opened her eyes, and said, "What has been going on? What happened to me?"

We replayed the tape only to learn she hadn't heard one word of what this evangelistic preacher had said using her vocal chords. Periodically, as she was listening, she would disgustingly interject, "I said that?" I don't believe there was one concept we agreed with, or at least not the way it was being said.

"Erase it!" I would hate to have anyone hear me say those things. I will never again allow my body to be taken over such that I don't know what I am saying. From this moment on, I will be present whenever I am in an altered state of awareness. That is the only way I can take responsibility for what I say in this state." For at least a week after the experience, each time she began to enter the intuitive state, her throat would tighten up as if some outside energy were trying to take control of her vocal chords and her body. After a period of resistance, the foreign energy would subside and she would end up in control. It has never happened since.

Again, speaking from an esoteric viewpoint, spiritual intuition is an inherent faculty of the human species. As we noted earlier, this faculty develops concurrently with the spiritual evolvement of the individual. Intuition is the Universe's way of making its wisdom available to the individual as he/she progresses along the spiritual path. Intuition operates constantly in our lives, being most conspicuous in those that excel in their chosen field. Successful people are creative, and creativity is mostly intuitively inspired. Intuition functions over a broad spectrum from the practical nuts and bolts of everyday living to an understanding of this creative force that we have given the name God. The level which an individual can reach with their intuition is commensurate with their own lifestyle, their spiritual development and their interests. All wisdom exists; the gestalt of every situation exists—it is only our individual and collective limitations that prevent us from accessing any or all wisdom.

Some of what follows may have been mentioned previously, but, if necessary for continuity, it will be repeated.

As a result of a series of synchronistic events in the early 1960's, Anne discovered that she could sit quietly in full waking consciousness, ask questions and get profound answers—answers from a source other than her own consciousness. Each of us had been interested in our own spiritual development since we were kids in high school, so the questions Anne posed to this seemingly endless source of wisdom usually had to do with matters of spiritual growth for herself or those of us who gravitated around her.

This information frequently came in the form of thirty to sixty-minute spontaneous lectures, most of which I tape-recorded. The content was always in general agreement with traditional esoteric or metaphysical teachings; the material was well organized, and it often left those who heard it with a profound sense of reverence. There was nothing kooky or cultish about the content, so Anne continued to make herself available several times a week for the instruction. We soon realized that this was a rather loosely organized training course designed to help her, and those around her, become better, more spiritually focused people. The subject matter covered about everything from eating, sleeping and thinking habits to the nature of God and the creation of universes. It didn't deal with flying saucers or other fringy material, just elaborations and explanations of esoteric cosmology. The content in no way conflicted with the accepted mystical traditions of Christianity, Judaism, Sufism, Buddhism or Hinduism, all of which we have studied to some degree.

So, we began to incorporate these principles into our daily lives. Meditation became a daily routine as did proper diet, self-watching, emotional control and other useful habits. Anne's transition to psychic/intuitive work with the general public came about in a very interesting way. One of the members of our Friday Night Group was president of the newly formed Rudolf Steiner School in Sacramento. Like any new organization, especially a school, they needed operating funds, so they organized a carnival to raise money. It was to be held at a lovely residence in Sacramento, and one of the booths was to be a Gypsy Fortune Teller. Someone looked at Anne and said, "Hum, long dark hair, olive complexion; with a scarf and the right dress you would make a good Gypsy fortune teller."

Even though Anne had been working in Dr. Hickman's office for some time, the thought of sitting across a table facing a different stranger every five minutes and being expected to tell them about their life was very frightening. They reassured her that this was just for fun to raise funds, and that no one would really expect to have their "fortune read." All she had to do was take their $5 for five minutes of her time, make up a good story and take the next client. Well, it didn't work out that way. When the first person sat in front of her, streams of pictures and words started to flow, and at some point she realized that the five minutes was up and someone else was waiting at the door. The stunned donator would inevitably say, "This has been too short; can you give me your office number so I can call for an appointment?" Anne was dumbfounded. She had no office, no card, no appointment times. Finally, they would produce a piece of paper and pencil and she would give them our home phone number. The next problem—could she charge them, and if so, how much should she charge? At some point she reasoned that if she was going to spend time talking to them she was not going to have time to do yard work and housework, so she would need money to pay a housekeeper and a gardener. Initially, she charged them $10 or $15 for an hour-long appointment. It soon became apparent that in an hour's time she could normally do what a psychiatrist or psychologist would accomplish in weeks or months of therapy, so it seemed a fair exchange.

During the early 1960's Anne also began counseling one-on-one with those of us in the Friday Night Group who needed help with our own individual spiritual growth. It was during this time that I became the self-appointed scribe. I recorded and edited all the spontaneous lecture material that Anne transmitted. As the editor I soon became aware that there was a vast difference in the literary quality of succeeding transmissions. Some lectures took two or three times as long to produce a readable manuscript. The quality of the syntax covered a broad range. At one end of the spectrum the syntax was loose, disjointed, as if Anne were describing a scene, process or concept, picking and choosing her words consciously, describing and repeating as necessary to convey some obscure aspect of reality. At the other end of the spectrum was a literary composition perfect in every detail of syntax, organization and cadence. All editorial attempts to improve the quality would fail, and the word I changed in one reading would be replaced when I read it the next day.

The lecture material fell between these two extremes. The discourses that were of a high literary quality were usually associated with some quite important spiritual process like an initiation or some other major step on the path. Another interesting aspect of these near perfect lectures was the quality of the vocal delivery. To deliver an inspired piece of literature effectively most of us need to read it through once or twice to get the correct voice inflections, accentuations and pauses. But here was a person delivering a spontaneous lecture that was not only perfectly organized and technically constructed, but also properly inflected with the pauses and accentuations correctly placed. It was as if the sentence or possibly the complete thought instantly appeared in her conscious mind, giving her time to process the meaning and come up with the perfect delivery. I never cease to marvel at the capabilities of our human mechanism, especially when operating in the realm of the paranormal.

And so you may wonder, what is the source of this material and how is it transmitted? Harman & Rheingold in their book *Higher Creativity* take a more or less scientific approach to this question. Klimo in his book *Channeling*, presents scientific, pseudo-scientific and esoteric explanations so that the reader can choose. I would like to take the more irrational, unscientific approach, based upon my observations, and tempered by my study of many other esoteric teachings. It appears that spiritual intuition is a direct transmission between Universal Mind and the conscious mind of the intuitive. The level at which contact is made with Universal Mind, and the clarity of the transmission, seems to be a function of the refinement of the human transmitter—the intuitive.

Let's then consider an esoterically logical rationale for this transmission. Most esoteric cosmologies agree that "Original Intelligence" divided Itself into many pieces or fragments so It could gain experience, and that each unit has the full potential of that Original Intelligence, or God. However, in humans layers and layers of conditioning cover it. Furthermore, most cosmologies agree that the connection between the Original Intelligence and Its fragments, and the fragments to each other, remains intact regardless of the earthly activities of the personalities. This may be the network that is sensed when one has that feeling of oneness with all creation during a transcendental experience. So, any single unit of humanity that can consciously make contact with this network can theoretically gain access to the knowledge and wisdom of the whole.

In actuality, having made contact with this network, you may be receiving information all the way from your own unconscious and higher Self to the wisdom of God. It is up to you to evaluate the content. Being able to make this momentary connection is the result of removing some of those layers of conditioning that overlay the "spark of divinity" at our core. At some point in this conditioning-removal-process, light begins to stream from a crack in these layers of conditioning and a connection is made to the network and to the source of all knowledge and wisdom. The more that the layers of conditioning are broken and washed away, the clearer and more secure becomes the connection to the Original Intelligence, until at some point one knows oneself to be one with God. At that point on the path, all the wisdom necessary for the next big step toward ultimate enlightenment is available to the personality. This is the purpose and the ultimate goal of spiritual intuition. Once the mainstream of science extends its limits to include God, it will probably find a better explanation.

The other aspect of the paranormal that we frequently hear about is psychism. Again from an esoteric viewpoint, psychic phenomena originate in the lower realms of the astral—the Cosmic dumping ground for mankind's less-than-useful "thought-forms." Consequently, referring to a person as a psychic is certainly not flattering. Unfortunately, common usage of the word psychic includes positive clairvoyance and spiritual intuition. A typical psychic works with thought-forms and telepathic information, neither of which leads to "clear seeing." Psychic phenomena are interim distractions that all serious, esoteric philosophies warn against. Psychism can be extremely glamorous, creating the ultimate distraction for the serious student on the spiritual path. Some get caught in the glamour and never escape during their lifetime. The best approach is to see psychism for what it is and move through it to spiritual intuition as quickly as possible.

Psychism includes many activities that became available to those who open the psychic door; and almost all have a heavy glamor factor. Just to mention a few, there are; various forms of magic, both white and black magic; witch craft; voodoo; many forms of channeling; mind reading; speaking in tongues; telepathic exercises and experiments; materalization; and psychokenisis, just to mention a few obvious examples. I'm not saying they are all bad, just that one should not get enamored by the glamor that goes with psychism. Experimenting with psychism is one thing, but getting hooked on its glamor is entirely different. Alice Baily has written a book on the glamor of psychism.

Getting a glimpse of one's own intuitive abilities is not as difficult as might be supposed. During our workshops over the past forty years, thousands of participants have discovered that access to that network of universal knowledge is easier than they thought. Everyone has the innate ability to make that connection—consciously. Developing one's own spiritual intuition is an essential step in personal and spiritual growth. It is essential for exploring other states of consciousness and one's own relationship to the whole—to God. At some point you no longer need depend upon what someone else says or writes. It may have worked for them but it may not work for you. If you can contact this universal wisdom, you can obtain that which is pertinent for your spiritual development at this particular point in time.

There are many indications that the human race has become sidetracked in materiality. Perhaps the current interest in channeling and the many other forms of intuition are an indication that the Original Intelligence of our Universe is reaching out to humanity, encouraging us to draw upon that limitless source of wisdom, and start making our way back to the Godhead.

Discrimination is essential in this entire psychic/channeling/intuitive realm. If you have access to psychic/intuitive information, you owe it to yourself to be logical before applying it. You need to ask yourself, "Can I apply this information to my daily life and spiritual practice? Does it leave me feeling happier, more loving, more reverent? Does it leave me feeling and thinking positively about life?" If the material is of a more mundane nature, check it against what you know about science, engineering or mechanics. Or, if it is highly esoteric, does the content in general agree with accepted spiritual and philosophic principles? Even if it just doesn't feel good to you, avoid it until you can do some investigation. If the material passes most of these tests the teachings probably contain a lot of truth and it doesn't matter a whole lot where it came from. Just don't be too gullible. Intuition can be your direct pipeline to the wisdom of the Universe—eventually to God.

CHAPTER V:

INTUITION
TRAINING

Can Intuition Be Taught?

I want to say again: Anne and I do not now, and never have, taught intuition. But, we have done everything possible to convince the participants of our workshops that they are already intuitive and need only recognize it, be aware of it, and practice using it at every opportunity. Just as they have eyes and ears to see and hear, and a digestive tract to process their food, they also have an innate personal intuition program that, if one stays tuned into it, will do everything from helping to prevent an accident on the freeway to providing access to all the wisdom necessary to complete this evolutionary path and return to the Godhead. The software for the intuition system is already on our individual hard drive; many just haven't learned to use it. All we can do is try to convince them that the program is already built into their basic structure as a human being; they just need to learn to make use of it, and that is where we enter.

Back in the '60s and '70s many—especially therapists—asked Anne how she did it. Her standard answer was, "I just know." That happens to be one of the short definitions for intuition—instantaneous apprehension. The next question from the inquirer was, "Can you teach me to do it?" That is about where I joined forces with Anne.

At that time there were books to help you develop your psychic powers and abilities, but we knew enough about esoterics to know that we didn't want to do that. It was too close to black magic. We knew that over the span of a few months Anne had become a reliable, positive clairvoyant, but we didn't know how to teach what she had been exposed to. During our search we realized that Anne, for some reason, had rapidly enhanced, and brought under control a standard human trait—intuition. The rapidity with which it blossomed was probably because of the activation in her of the Kundalini energy. Perhaps intuition could be cultivated, possibly more slowly, without stirring up the Kundalini. Through analyzing the process by which Anne's intuitive skills developed, we began to evolve a program that might work with a select segment of the population—those who were interested in personal and spiritual growth.

The necessary program components seemed to be:

- Ways to convince the participant that he or she already has a built-in intuitive system

- Meditation training to bring the mind under the control of the higher Self

- Various exercises to make the participant more aware of their five normal senses

- Make them aware of their feelings and emotions

- Develop the imagination

- Develop visualization

- Bring feelings and emotions under the control of the higher Self, so they could be turned on and off at will

- Exercises with feedback to give the participant practice using this newly discovered faculty

Practice with feedback to build up confidence seemed to be the crux of the program. Learning to use one's intuition at will is not a weekend project anymore than is becoming a concert pianist. However, participants who have hung in there for a number of years, especially therapists who use it everyday, have become quite proficient. Ten to twenty years may sound like a long time, but it is not so long when you consider that it is a skill you can use the rest of your life and each time you return to this earthly training ground. Do you believe Anne developed what she exhibited in 1962 in less than two years—hardly time to finish junior college? I believe that Anne, like anyone who exhibits unusual skills during his/her lifetime, brought that skill with her—from where, who knows?

A Typical Workshop

Leading a workshop at a growth center with 25 to 75 people who have responded to a catalog write-up is an interesting experience. The participants are all new people, each with their own unique background and expectations. And we are as much of an enigma to them as they are to us. Since we don't have much time we have to get to know each other as quickly as possible. We found that the best way to do that is to get them talking. Two or five days later (sometimes two or three weeks) we are amazed at how well it turned out. Nearly everyone has gone away happy and more aware.

You Are Already Intuitive

The first thing we do in a workshop of all new people, after a very short introduction, is to have them share paranormal experiences, things they don't feel comfortable discussing with the neighbors. This way they find that most people have had unexplainable things happen that they don't normally talk about. They soon find that being awakened by Aunt Tillie at 4 AM to say goodbye, even though they discover the next morning that she died a thousand miles away at that exact time, is not that unusual. People keep pouring out their untold stories, realizing that nearly everyone has had psychic/intuitive experiences. So they start to wonder, hmmm, perhaps I do have an undeveloped intuition program in there some place.

Workshop Introduction

Even though by this point in the book you have come to know us quite well, you have very little idea how we conduct a workshop unless you have taken one or more from us. Therefore, I'm going to turn the pen over to Anne and let her tell you how she motivates a room full of fresh recruits.

Anne: Welcome to our workshop on intuition. I'm Anne and this is Jim. I will take a few minutes to talk about intuition, and then we want to hear about your psychic/intuitive experiences.

One of the primary goals that Jim and I have for our workshops is to demystify this area so you can begin to trust the ability you already have in this psychic/intuitive arena. This is a faculty that we are all born with, but because of our programming and our own doubts, we have allowed it to atrophy. However, it is relatively easy to reactivate this faculty. One of our other goals for this workshop is to allow you to actually experience your own intuitive prowes, and learn to trust it. For you to feel more confident and trusting in this ability that you already have, I would like to talk about how I see psychic/intuitive skills.

We all have intuitive flashes but we tend to discount them as mere coincidence. So what we want to do is help you create a condition that we call being psychic on demand. But right now, let's talk about how this phenomenon is experienced spontaneously in our lives. If you happen to be a meditator, at some point you will begin to be aware of things or situations for which you didn't ask. When the mind becomes quiet for even a few seconds you can begin to hear that small voice that is always there, only we are usually making so much noise that we can't hear it. When the mind becomes quiet we start to become aware of its presence. In times of emergency, however, that small voice screams loud enough to be heard above all that mind chatter.

A psychic opening can be precipitated by a number of situations: a life threatening illness, the death of a loved one, childbirth, any severe trauma, as well as meditation or some other spiritual practice. These abilities are there to guide and assist us in time of need; though, I believe the most important reason to cultivate and refine this skill is to expand our awareness into other states of consciousness, states that otherwise are not available to us. We can read about them, dream about them, but until we have a personal experience of these other states of consciousness, we find it difficult to believe that this faculty is available to us.

The sixth sense is definitely part of our survival mechanism, and it often surfaces in childhood. If our environment is unsafe we develop other ways of being aware, of listening so we don't miss a clue. I know that is when I first developed this capability. I felt that if I could read everyone's mind, if I could know their desires and intentions, I could behave in ways that would make life safer.

Intuition is a gift we all have, but we have the mistaken idea that if we surrender to it, it might dictate what we are to do with our lives. I must confess that I, too, had these fears the first time it happened to me. If I had known then that indeed it was a benign energy, that it was there to assist me, that it simply wanted to give me access to deeper levels of my own being, and to cosmic wisdom, then I would have been more comfortable with that initial experience. When I look back upon that first opening I realize that my fears prompted me to shut down, which of course led to a number of complications. But, when I reconnected with these abilities the second time, I had matured, become more aware, more knowledgeable.

I believe that this energy makes contact with us in bizarre ways to get our attention. I discovered, however, that this energy, whatever it is, is willing to negotiate. What I mean is that I don't have to accept the initial form in which it presents itself. I found, for instance, that I could decide that the process was happening too fast for me to handle, that I could negotiate with it. I could simply tell "it" that I was willing to be open to the process, and what it might bring into my life, but please be more gentle, give me more time. I'm sure that if we all realized that we are simply re-awakening a part of us that has lain dormant, that has been waiting for us to beckon to it, to re-invite it to participate in our lives, we would feel more in control—hence, more powerful.

Once we learn the discipline of stillness and how to interact with that all-wise part of the self, we will realize that this is an ability we can use in any area of our lives. We can ask for and receive the guidance and information that is always available to us—once we learn the technique of being 'still'.

People in the helping professions are quite prone to psychic/intuitive breakthroughs. They have already learned to become extremely good listeners and to be aware of some of the cues. At some point in their work they realize they are picking up information that the client is not physically communicating to them. Without realizing what they are doing, they have identified so closely with the client that they are able to see the world through their client's eyes. A therapist, for one, would find this to be quite an advantage.

So, what we would like to do during this workshop is help you to trust, to risk, and to see that this is not a mysterious process. This is not an ability possessed only by special people; but, rather, an ability that we all possess, and is just waiting for us to invite it to participate in our lives. So take a risk, and when you do you will find your lives enriched with more creativity and clarity. This is an ability that can literally be used in any area of your lives, regardless of your profession. See it as a power just waiting to be unleashed. We will do our best to help you generate a sense of trust and faith so you can risk making the greatest decision in this lifetime—to begin to find out who and what you are. Generate enough trust in yourself to do the exercises, to ask questions, and perhaps to accept some things on faith until you can have your own experience of truth.

One way we have found to create a safe and open environment for learning and practice is to have you share experiences that defy logical explanation, that are too way out to share in most environments, experiences that you have never been able to talk about for fear of being labeled a kook. Trust me, I can't be shocked. I have come to believe that anything is possible, and there is no safer place to share your weirdest psychic, intuitive, mystic, spooky experiences. Once we start to share, you will find very rapidly that everyone has had these kinds of experience, they just haven't talked about them. So, put your "unexplainables" out there and find that you are not alone; you are not strange.

On the other hand, these don't need to be dramatic stories. They can be as simple as thinking of a friend you haven't seen in years and receiving a call or a letter from them the same day. There are strong psychic bonds between mother and children. There are many instances where mothers knew sons had been killed in Vietnam at almost the moment it happened, or simply that their baby in the next room was having trouble breathing.

Take a moment now to scan through your life and find the psychic event you would like to share:

> Group Member: A few years ago I was having a first date with a new lady. That afternoon, on a spur of the moment, she went to a flea market, and even though she had many bud vases, she bought another and brought it home. An hour or so later I walked into her home with a single white rose that was just looking for a bud vase. It really startled both of us. Even though this was very simplistic, it caused me to start becoming aware. And the more aware I became the more intense the situations became. For example, I frequently go into the upper Amazon area in South America to do medical work. I mentioned to a couple with whom I was working that I would like to go to Lake Winatocka, in another area. They said they had friends who were working in that area and that they would be happy to talk to them the next time they came down. They were scheduled to arrive two weeks after I was to leave for the States. I said, "Great, I'd love it if you could set something up." A few hours later we drove his brother, also a physician, to an airstrip in the jungle to meet an incoming plane. The two people from Lake Winatocka got off the plane— nearly two weeks earlier than planned. We discussed my wishes and they welcomed me with open arms. Two months later I was up there working.

> Anne: That is manifesting! Anybody else have another example?

> Group Member: I had an experience about six years ago with a blue light. I talked to a lot of people about it, and I read quite extensively about the blue light and the Blue Pearl. At that time I held the very pragmatic, atheistic viewpoint that if you don't see it you can't believe it. But I was seeing it, and I was quite aware of

it, and it was aware of me. It was very exciting. It really opened me up, and I started to accept that there was more—and the more can be very exciting. I felt curious about it although I didn't understand it, and it has never happened since. At the time, I was a being who was completely satisfied with herself, and that is when it happened. I appreciate how it opened me up.

Anne: What were the circumstances surrounding the event?

Group Member: I was alone in my home. I had just made love and my lover tucked me in and left. I was lying there feeling peaceful and loving, in total harmony. I felt totally safe, loved and in tune with the Universe— very much into my body. Suddenly it appeared in the doorway. I wasn't frightened, and I was surprised that I wasn't frightened. I felt that it was aware of me and that if I became frightened it would go away—all I needed to do was be aware of it. It started to move closer, the color began to change from a shimmering light-blue aqua to a royal blue. It was an airy ball, and as it moved closer it became larger and more nearly a royal blue. I kept thinking to myself, "Just be aware of this; it's very special, and if you become frightened it will go away." It came closer and closer and began to expand and become more purple. The dog didn't bark but he caught my attention for an instant. In a flash it was gone. I knew it was gone. I knew it had happened, whatever it was. I was cold sober and very aware. It was a wonderful experience, and it really did change my life. Since then other things have happened but nothing that exciting. I have read similar accounts in Native American books and in Judaism. I'm not particularly attached to it happening again, but it was very exciting.

Anne: True, you can't be attached to experiences like that. But that kind of experience just automatically makes us more open, more loving, more at peace with ourselves, which in turn creates conditions so new experiences can occur—not the same ones, of course. At least you know there is something out there—or in there. I am not sure whether it's in or out. Thank you, anybody else?

Group Member: I have one that happened about 5 years ago. I was doing some deep breathing work, and I got a really clear visualization of a beautiful place, with the smells, the whole thing, just as if I were there. It wasn't anyplace I'd ever been before. I didn't know where it was. I just thought it was a nice vision. Then, 2 months later, I came to Esalen for the first time, and Esalen was my vision.

Anne: That's precognition. Thank you.

Group Member: I've had a lot of strange experiences, but this is the one that has affected me the most. It still mystifies me. This was 23 years ago when I was in the French countryside. I was driving along in a car with three other people, and before I got to every town— towns I'd never seen before—I could visualize it and I knew what it was like, except I saw it in a war condition. There were bullets flying all around, noise and so on. It wasn't a short experience like my others have been; it went on for hours, and I was so hyper about it. Everyone else kept saying, "Shut up, Linda, we are sick of you." I didn't know what to do, I was so freaked out, and it just kept going on and on. I even knew there was a tower of bones coming up. I don't know what this all meant. It was like a rip in time.

Anne: Sometimes when that opening happens, it's as if we know everything. All of a sudden we feel omniscient. I've had those experiences where I just simply "knew" everything about that moment in time—everything was available. Everything that has ever happened is recorded someplace. So, if you are sensitive enough, or you just happen to create that psychic opening, you can pick up on it.

Group Member: I kept knowing what was coming, except that I was seeing it. I could see soldiers darting around corners and bullets flying, and then I'd come to the town and it would be the same buildings, but no soldiers and no bullets.

Anne: You were tuning into some war, probably, or a lot of wars. Thank you.

Group Member: I have had a lot of precognitive dreams and this one is quite interesting. When I was considering coming to Esalen, I had a dream about being here but having no place to sleep. Then when I called, they said, "It's no dream." I came anyway, and about 2 hours ago I got a room.

Anne: It was a very practical dream. At least you were forewarned. OK, anybody else?

Group Member: One night my mother was walking the floor and crying, "He's calling me, he needs me, and he's in trouble." Then we got word that my brother's submarine had been lost in the war. She'd heard him calling her.

Anne: That's the connection that I was talking about— Mother and child. That's very common. Thank you.

Group Member: This one didn't happen to me directly. We were living in New York and my marriage was breaking up. My daughter and I decided to take a trip up the California Coast, from San Diego to San Francisco on Route 1. My daughter is a very even-tempered person. When we got to Los Angeles and were planning the trip north, she became absolutely hysterical. I had never seen her this way. She cried, got very ill, and I had to stop at a hotel while driving through Los Angeles because she passed out. Finally, we got to a hotel in Malibu, and she refused to go any farther. She said, "I am going back home." Subsequently, she has grown, moved to Los Angeles, and has become involved in this sort of thing. She did a past-life regression, called me, and said, "You remember that incident?" It turned out that she'd had an unfortunate experience sometime in the 40's. She was born to a Nebraska farm family, went to Los Angeles to become a starlet, and was killed in a crash on the highway north of Malibu.

Anne: Those things happen. She didn't rest very much between incarnations, did she? I thought we got more rest than that! I'm going to ask for more time to relax. Thank you.

Group Member: Two or three years ago I did two different workshops with you, then started incorporating my intuition into my psychotherapy. I know all the theoretical psychological stuff, but when something off the wall pops in, I just put it out and it's always right on. And when I want to know something, I just ask and I almost always get some type of response, and it's nearly always right on. But, the difficulty I am having, usually in personal relationships, is staying separate. It is an on-going struggle with people I'm really close to. I recently had an incident with my 15-year old son who was involved in looking for a job, and I knew I was getting caught up in the situation.

One night, I had this knot in my belly. I knew I was in conflict with him, but I hadn't figured out what was happening. So I checked it out with him and found that he, who shows little emotion, was experiencing the same knot in his stomach. I was picking up his stuff without realizing it. This, however, helped me understand similar problems with clients.

Anne: When I first started my counseling work I would duplicate the client's symptoms in my own body, sometimes even the last moments before death. This gave me double assurance that I was correct, but it was sure hard on my body. One day I found myself complaining, "I'm doing fine work but I can't go on like this because at the end of the week I'm a basket case. I've got to quit this work—I can't handle it." Immediately, I heard this voice in my head saying, "If you are willing to just "know" about it—that takes a lot of risking and trusting—you can have it that way." I didn't know who or what I was answering, but I said, "I'll take that option." From that time on I seldom picked up symptoms in my body. Once in a great while if there is a lot of emotion involved in the situation, or if it is an area that I haven't quite resolved within myself, I'll resonate to it and pick up a semblance of it, but not to the extent that I did originally.

So you can negotiate. In the beginning it is reassuring, confirming to feel it in your body, but at some point you only need to "know". In your case you can say, "Can you please give me a scene, a symbol, a picture, or just a "knowing". I don't want to feel it in my body." It is ridiculous to go through a ten-minute asthmatic attack to find out someone has asthma. I'd rather just "know". I seldom get any body's sensations. I get some imagery, but actually, even that is just "knowing". True, it takes a lot of confidence to put it out when there is no confirmation. All I know is that I am in my psychic/intuitive mode and, therefore, it is OK to "just know". Remember, you can negotiate!

You mentioned picking up information or emotions from a family member—your son. I seldom pick up anything about my family because I have a contract with this part of myself that I will "see" or "know" nothing about anyone, especially a family member, unless they ask. But, if they have a stomach ache and ask me to see what is going on, I may see a lot of things—some that they may not have wanted me to see. But, I don't look until I'm asked. It is possible I overdo it to the point where I'm oblivious to what is happening around me. It's all a matter of negotiating. Are there any other examples?

Group Member: I've had many experiences, but one stands out in particular: I was sitting in my chair, and I felt very uncomfortable and was having some trouble breathing. I suddenly stood up and screamed that I was going to die, and I needed a lawyer. Three hours later I received a telephone call from Spain where my mother lived, and was told that she had gone into a coma after throwing a tantrum about finances. And, indeed, she did need a lawyer. The estate had been in a mess for years. I've had some nice psychic experiences, but this was quite unpleasant.

Anne: On occasion that happens—where the energy fields of two people blend. I have heard it called "Field Consciousness". It is where you can't distinguish your consciousness from someone else's. Worse than that, you don't even know that you've "become" someone else, because you so completely have his or her thoughts and feelings.

Group Member: I thought that I'd gone completely mad. What did you say you called it?

Anne: Field Consciousness, where the two energy fields merge. I've had that happen a significant number of times, and it's always exciting to me because I find out things that I can find out in no other way. True, it can be freaky the first time it happens to you. I've learned that no matter how far out I go or how much I feel like I'm somebody else, at some point I come back to Anne. But it's a matter of trusting that you are going to come back. You have a contract with life for "X" number of years, so you will get back. Anyone else want to share?

Group Member: I want to share a kind of casual one. I get my haircut at this place about twenty miles from my house. When I first started with these people, they weren't very busy, but now they are quite popular and there's a waiting list. I don't like to wait so I call up and make my appointment when I want to go, like the day before or when I have another appointment somewhere near there. Usually I say, "Do you have anything at 10:00 tomorrow because I will be in town."

The other day she said, "Oh yeah, someone just canceled five minutes ago. Do you meditate?"

I said, "Yes."

She said, "We have another client who does what you do, and she also meditates."

Anne: That's a very useful application. Jim does the same thing, he waits until his hair is clear down to his collar, then calls.

Jim: And I ask for a cancellation. Usually within 24 hours one comes just in the nick of time.

Anne: OK, can we have a couple more examples?

Group Member: About five years ago, I was working in the afternoon and all of a sudden I just walked off the job and didn't tell anybody. I started walking down the street. I'd never felt like that before. At the time I didn't know what I was picking up, but that night I got a call saying that my father had been seriously injured. I wasn't really surprised, as I knew that something had happened that day. I couldn't read it clearly, but I'd never felt like that before.

Anne: Well, it's hard for someone who is logical and practical to trust something that seems that irrational. The next time you have that kind of feeling just ask what is causing it. Then let your mind become as quiet as possible and just listen. Have no concepts; just be open to whatever pops in.

I think this discussion has indicated to you that you are not the only one who has had these weird experiences, and that in fact they aren't weird, they are quite normal; and the more you pay attention to this intuitive part of yourself, the more it will participate in your life. I wouldn't give up what I have for millions of dollars. It is the most wonderful thing that has ever happened to me. But there is the other side of it, and that is the fears that we have around it. So I would like you to put out your fears. What are the major fears or apprehensions that you have about this area? You need to take a look at them, see if they are valid, or see if they are something that you are simply making up and scaring yourself for no good reason.

Jim: Well, if you've watched many Hollywood movies, there are plenty of reasons—enough to scare anybody about being psychic or intuitive.

Anne: That's true...they really play up the negative aspects of the psychic. So, are there any fears that you would like to talk about?

Group Member: Even though I have never had such an experience, I have read and heard about becoming involved with the "dark forces." I find that possibility fearful.

Anne: I believe that most of the dark energy that people encounter psychically is from within themselves. One of the things that I discovered during the initial opening up process was that if I was to be strong enough and clear enough to handle what was happening to me (which I couldn't even describe at the time) I needed to know more about myself. I was insecure, extremely fragile, a real coward in a lot of ways. I still am in some cases, but not in this area. For some unexplained reason I have gained a tremendous amount of strength, confidence and trust in this area.

When I was just starting, I realized that I had to do something to stabilize my life. I had a therapist and a husband who more or less understood the process I was going through, but I also did a lot of bodywork and psychological clearing. I got to know myself quite well. Even then for the first couple of years I had some hair-raising experiences—ones I can't even talk about because no one would believe me. But since then I have never had a negative experience. I am thoroughly convinced that you attract the same kind of energy you contain. Like attracts like is a truism. Once I became stable and had cleaned out a lot of psychological garbage, the negative (dark force) experiences stopped happening. In the beginning, my energy was attracting problems. Sure the dark energy is "out there," but it only attacks you when you have similar energy within your system. If you have your act cleaned up you have nothing to fear. And speaking of fear, that is one of the most negative energies you can carry. For instance, I believe a negative, fearful person, full of hate and anger, would without a doubt attract that type of dark energy (entity) if they began to use the Ouija Board. Although I have no need for such a gadget, I believe I would contact a high level of information—or perhaps nothing.

Group Member: Well, I do a little automatic writing, because I do hypnosis, and I find it to be a wonderful experience. I have heard, however, that there are dangers.

Jim: My suggestion is that you evaluate each experience. If the material seems positive, logical, upbeat, and leaves you in a good place, fine. But if you don't feel good about what you write, if it leaves a yucky feeling in your gut, then you better take a second look at it before you do it again. When Anne and I were doing a lot of experimenting in those early days, neither of us wanted to miss anything. So, regardless of the possible dangers, we'd give it a try, but if it didn't feel good to her she wouldn't try it again.

Anne: There is something I want to comment on: There are getting to be a lot of people involved in "channeling." There are even workshops where you can learn how. This can be a great ego trap because many channelers have the concept that they have been singled out to bring this communication to the world from some lofty universal source, and that if they don't do it, humanity will be lost. Furthermore, since this "wisdom" is coming from some psychic realm, it is not to be challenged or questioned. They feel that they are privileged to be the communicator. Well, I realize that it is a privilege, but I also realize that if it's going to come through me, I want to be extremely sure of the source. Many people, the channeler and the recipients, feel it is blasphemous to challenge or question. I'm just the opposite. I feel that I must take responsibility for the source I am representing. At that moment the source is me, and I want to be fully conscious so I can assume that responsibility. If I were ever to doubt that the source was other than the Light, I would be the first to say so.

Group Member: If you have a hunch, how do you know it is a good hunch?

Anne: Lots of practice. Seriously, what I would say is that it is the "quality" of the feeling that goes with it. Lots of us have wish-fulfilling dreams or "hunches" about something we really want. This needs to be considered. If I feel the energy is up in my head I seriously question it. However, if I get a good solid feeling in my gut that persists, I'd give the hunch some serious consideration. But again it takes a lot of practice to recognize an accurate hunch from a wish-fulfilling desire.

Group Member: Would you buy a house on a hunch?

Anne: We have.

Group Member: Would you buy stock or bet on a horse?

Anne: For me there is something else involved here. It depends upon what you feel is right action for you. Me, I'm not a gambler, and I don't believe I could ever get a correct hunch if I were going to place a bet. I don't like to lose money, so that in itself would sabotage me. I don't feel I could get a clear enough indication to use it, most likely because I don't believe in using this ability in that way. I think you have to believe that it is right for you to do it. We have known people who I'm sure were unconsciously, but successfully, using their psychic/intuitive abilities to pick stocks. They said their investments were made on gut feelings.

Group Member: I operate something like that but I don't know how to develop it.

Anne: I believe the best way to develop these skills is to keep a log book in which you record what it felt like when you were right, and what it felt like when you were not. There may be a very subtle difference here, but if this part of you thinks you are serious, I believe it will make the difference between a right and wrong hunch more obvious.

Group Member: So the feeling is in the stomach, not the head?

Anne: For me it's in my stomach, but for you it might be in another part of your body. So pay attention to the trigger area of your body. Get a "sense" of what it feels like, keep records, and you will begin to see a pattern of growing intuition.

Jim: Another way to use a log is with your daily meditation. Let's say you meditate in the morning. Take the last three or four minutes of your meditation to scan the coming day. I used to be in industry management; so beforehand I would scan the meetings or other activities of importance I had scheduled for that day. Sometimes it was amazingly accurate and other times, probably because of desires, fears or anxiety, I would miss entirely. But, if I kept notes in a logbook, I could begin to get a better understanding of the hits and misses.

Group Member: Say you had nine hunches in a row that came in right, and the tenth was coming up——-

Anne: I'd be terrified!

Jim: Let me tell you a true story. The Carmel River ran through our backyard. The previous year I had planted about 15 small cedar trees in the flood plain beside the riverbed. To keep the gardener from hitting them with a weed-eater, or whatever, I randomly drove a stick into the ground near each little tree. The next spring the river flooded and covered the small trees with about 10 to 12 inches of sandy soil. The stakes, though still in the ground, were leaning badly and I had no idea on which side of the stake the seedling had been planted. With the first tree, I dug a hole three feet across before I finally found it. Anne was working nearby doing some other clean-up so when I got ready to liberate the next small tree, I asked her on which side of the stake I should dig to most easily find it. She paused a few seconds and confidently said to dig on the east side of the stake. I cautiously dug where she indicated and in a minute or so I found and liberated the seedling.

It worked so well I asked her again. This time she said it was located northwest of the stake. Sure enough, after a few shovels full of dirt I found it. And again I asked for her intuitive guidance. It was now two predictions and two hits. Her first words were, "I'm getting that anxious feeling in my middle; I'm not so sure on this one." Finally she said, "I feel that it's to the south of the stake, but I'm not as confident as on the first two." A few shovels full later the third tree surfaced. Again I asked for a prediction. It was now three and three. The anxiety level for Anne was rising—we all want to be right and she was no exception. She admitted the fear and anxiety over being wrong were building up, but timidly she made the fourth prediction. I ended up with a hole about three feet across before I finally found it. Her confidence had been shattered because of that human desire to be right. If she could have operated in a truly Zen mode of being totally indifferent to the outcome, she would have continued to locate the seedlings and would have suffered no anxiety. Do you see why she said she would be terrified?

Group Member: Then what good is intuition if you can't rely on it? A red light is red and a green light is green, and you go when it is green and stop when it's red. I'm looking for something like that.

Jim: In the case of the small trees, I don't think it was the intuition that was wrong, it was the static of the human vehicle that was keeping it from being heard. As for any hunch or psychic/intuitive prediction, in the end I believe you should fall back upon logic and reason—just plain common sense. After all, we have spent our whole bloody lives relying on and working with this rational mind of ours, and then to junk it totally in favor of intuition doesn't make sense. To me intuition is one more source of information. You take all sources of information, including intuition, put them together and run them through your logical mind, and then come up with a decision.

Another technique we found has merit is this: If you get a hunch or intuitive flash, try to change it. If it flips back, change it again and again and if it keeps coming back, you had better take a serious look at it. But on the other hand, if you can change it from this to that to that, there is a pretty good chance that it is just one of those wish-fulfillment thoughts, not a hunch.

Group Member: Mine don't change, and sometimes they are three years away.

Anne: When you get into a situation like that just ask where it fits in time. Time is a tricky area to work in—to know if it's past, future or now. This whole intuition field is operating outside of time and space. Let's say you intuitively become aware of an event, how do you learn to place it in time and space? Well, it's pretty tricky, but not impossible. Again it is a "feeling sense". For me, not necessarily you, I "sense" the past as over and behind my left shoulder, way back there someplace. The future "feels" like I have to look out in the distance in front of me, and if it's now it's right in front of my nose. The last several years I have been able to spot events in people's lives, like childhood traumas, right down to the age when it happened. With me it is simply a matter of knowing the age—no symbol. I just get the age when it happened to them.

Group Member: There are a lot of times when I know what to say.

Anne: Where does the knowing come from?

Group Member: I just say it. I had one where it said to reverse the order—instead of doing it by job, do it by people. It was a way of analyzing an operation. I tell you, just like that, it changed the whole way of operating. But this idea of feeling—I will have to check out the feelings.

Anne: Just dialogue with that part of the self. Ask it to give you a feeling as back up for the words or idea. Treat it as if it were another very real part of you, which of course it is. Ask it questions, and expect answers. If you don't understand, ask it to give you another example, another hint, symbol or feeling. It will do it. For instance, that reversing situation you talked about. It might have shown you moving people around, or a little skit it created for you, or some other kind of a visual aid. And, of course, it depends upon whether you are visual, kinesthetic or just knowing.

I do a lot of consultation work with business people. Sometimes they ask me how they should behave in relation to someone else, or how someone sees them. Or, I find that someone has been assigned to a job that they hate; they are just not suited for the position, so they are doing a lousy job. Then they put them in a position that is really an extension of them and it works out beautifully.

I used to do that for Jim when he was in management. He'd come home and say, "I have a vacancy and I have several resumes from people who seem to be qualified for the job. Which one would be best suited for the position and, hence, would be the happiest and do the best job?" He would simply give me the names and I would give him a rundown on each person. I could "see" who was the best match for the position. He would put the person in the job and it would work out fine. This ability is not just to do psychological counseling; it has a lot of very practical applications that can help us live a more effective life. Okay, what other fears, questions or concerns do you have?

Group Member: I have a fear of knowing things that I have no logical way of knowing, like calling a girlfriend at work—something I would never do, but I just felt compelled. The office told me she had gone home because her father had died. Another time she lost my phone number and was calling around to get it. An hour later I had a feeling of urgency to call her. It's scary.

Anne: Well, if you are really uncomfortable with that kind of "knowing", especially if it is knowing something you can't do anything about, then negotiate with it. Just tell it you prefer this energy to manifest in a different mode. This way you acknowledge it; it's just that you don't like the manner in which it tries to catch your attention.

Group Member: Well, I guess I also like to have the information; there is a conflict.

Anne: If you can accept that everything that happens is part of the continuum of life, that things are the way they should be, that death is an integral part of life; then what difference does it make if you see someone's death before it happens? But as I said, if you are uncomfortable with "knowing", ask to have it changed. Do you have these kinds of experiences in any other area of your life?

Group Member: Yes, at work, a lot. Yes, I am quite intuitive in lots of ways.

Anne: Well, then you do find it useful. Does anyone else have that kind of fear?

Group Member: Last year I got the information at the beginning of June that my ninety seven-year old grandmother, who had been dying for a year, was going to die on the 23rd of June. It just popped in and I dismissed it. Then I began thinking about it and wondered if I should share it with my parents. Was this an ego trip, was I sharing it just so I could be perceived to be right? Well, I reasoned that it would be helpful information for my father, and decided to share it. Ten days later on the 23rd, I called home in the afternoon and she was still alive. A few hours later, still on the 23rd, she died.

Anne: In this case I would ask the source, whatever you perceive that to be, if this person can handle the information and would it be useful for them to have the information. People frequently ask me how I handle "distressing" information when I'm working with a client. Actually, I don't have that problem. I am committed to putting out whatever I get. However, I have a contract with that part of myself that I am shown only information that the client can handle. I do not want to be put in the position of playing God. So with that commitment in place, I put out whatever I get. And death does come up. For instance, a client came to me bitching about her relationship with her husband, but was more interested in her aspect of the relationship. My attention, however, kept being diverted to her husband. She would say, "I don't want to talk about him, I want to talk about me." But I know that if something comes in I must honor it and stay with it until it runs its course, and then go to something else. It's part of my contract. So I cautiously kept asking her how his health was. She would say, fine and continue to put me off. Finally, I had to level with her, "Even though you feel that your husband's health is fine, he may die very suddenly." She said, "There is no possibility." About three months later she called and said, "Am I glad you talked about my husband, because I awakened to a dead man in my bed. If you had not warned me of that possibility I would have absolutely freaked out." So if something persists I always put it out, because I know it will serve a purpose.

Anne continued: I recall a situation where I talked to a psychiatrist in depth for over an hour, and a week later he committed suicide. I tell you, I searched my soul— why, oh why, didn't I see what was going to happen? When I calmed down, I was told that I would have put a whole rescue process in operation, and this man had a right to kill himself. He had tried it three times before and botched it or someone interfered. I had no right to interfere with his free will. Even God wouldn't do that. There are certain levels of privacy, I was told, where I am not to interfere. So I honor the laws of that level of the Universe. If I'm given information, I put it out; if I don't see it, I just have to accept that there is a good reason. So in your case, I'd ask each time if it would be beneficial to share the information with a given person.

What other fears do any of you have?

Group Member: This is not a fear, it's just that I was raised in an intellectual household that devaluated intuition. I was definitely taught not to trust my intuition. But in 1982 I was on a small island off the coast of Honduras and I mentioned to the person I was traveling with that there was no contact with the outside world from this island—my own father could die and I wouldn't be aware of it. The next day when I arrived on the mainland, a colleague and friend, Dr. Sandoval, met me at the airport and with tears in his eyes said, "Your father has died." I had completely discounted the intuitive prompting the day before when it was happening. I had been raised to distrust those things, so I have placed no value in them all these years, until recently.

Anne: Well, I hope this discussion has helped you realize that everyone is intuitive under the right circumstances. It is just that there is so much mind chatter going on all the time that the small voice of intuition is not usually heard, and even when it is, it is overridden by the intellect. Fear is also a deadly deterrent to the intuitive process. We will do everything we can this week to help you become comfortable with your intuition. It is now time for a short break.

I would now like to return to a general discussion of the material included in our workshops before presenting a transcript of an actual demonstration during a five-day workshop at the Esalen Institute in the Big Sur area of California. Let's start with the most important aspect—meditation.

CHAPTER VI:

MEDITATION

The keystone of spiritual development, and hence intuitive development, is meditation. Every spiritual philosophy worthy of the name has seen meditation as the most important, the most potent spiritual practice that has ever been devised. It is only organized Western religion, be it Christian or Hebrew, that warns the public against the practice of meditation. Just a few years ago the Vatican sent news releases throughout the civilized world warning its citizens that meditation was a dangerous practice.

All reference to meditation vanished from mainstream Jewish literature about 150 years ago. This was true even in Chasidic and Kabbalistic writings. In earlier Jewish writings, from biblical times forward, there are innumerable references to meditation but after over a century of silence on the subject, meditation is almost unknown in Orthodox Jewery. Only in the last twenty years or so have books begun to reappear on Jewish meditation.

Orthodox Christian teachings have suffered this lack of respect for meditation since a century or so after its inception. Most, if not all, early Christian and Hebrew sects that advocated any form of mysticism, of which meditation was a principle tool, were forcibly eradicated in the first century or so of the Christian era. So you can see that Western meditation has had a rocky path to travel. For anyone who is interested in the history of Jewish meditation I highly recommend Rabbi Kaplan's three books on this subject. A good one to start with is *Jewish Meditation*, Kaplan.

The basic objection of organized Western religion to meditation is that meditation provides a direct experience of realms beyond the physical and eventually a direct experience of the force referred to as God. As both the Jewish and Christian Orthodox Church leaders know, it is difficult to maintain a cohesive organization if each person has his or her own individual connection with the Godhead. So, financially and organizationally, it pays to discourage all forms of meditation and mysticism. And this is what mainstream Western religion has done.

However, a hundred years or so ago Hindu gurus began to come to the West to spread their philosophy that of course included meditation. Meditation has never been attacked by Eastern religions because individual enlightenment is the goal of their spiritual practice, not the preservation of an organization. In recent years freethinking Christians and Jews alike have sought out the Eastern philosophies for spiritual guidance, not realizing that their own religions were also founded on meditation/contemplation practice with individual enlightenment as the goal. Chasidism and Kabbalism kept Jewish meditation alive until about 1850 A.D., and the Rosicrucians, alchemists and Freemasons did the same for Christian mystical teachings. So what is this practice that has so threatened, and at times divided, Western religious philosophy?

Meditation is one of the simplest and yet the most difficult practices you will ever experience. It is simple because you get into a comfortable sitting position, close your eyes (unless you subscribe to a Zen school of meditation that recommends partially open eyes) and become aware of your breathing process to the exclusion of all thoughts. The difficult phase of the practice begins a minute or so later when the mind decides it wants to inject thoughts about everything else. Hundreds of volumes have been written about meditation so the best we can do here is just hint at the subject.

There are a number of basic forms of meditation—vipassana, watching the breath, Zen, mantra, simple visualizations and imagery, and then the very elaborate Tibetan and Jewish visualizations using the Sanskrit and Hebrew alphabets and Tibetan deities. If you are interested in these more intricate meditative techniques please refer to Rabbi Kaplan's book, *Jewish Meditation, or Tibetan Yoga* by Evans-Wentz.

In our one or two-week workshops we have presented several different types of meditation, avoiding the Tibetan and Jewish visualizations. This way the participants could choose the method that worked best for them. I have also found that it's useful to be proficient in two or three methods so if one doesn't work that particular day I can switch to another. This is particularly useful at a meditation retreat or "sesshin," where you meditate ten to twelve hours a day for several consecutive days.

Achieving Stillness

When studying Eastern, metaphysical, mystical or occult philosophies, you will eventually encounter a statement that says in effect that, "All wisdom is to be found in the silence." In the spontaneous lecture work that Anne has done for forty years or so, equivalent statements have occurred dozens of times. People who have been in this field for any length of time believe that those statements mean exactly what they say. There is no hidden, esoteric meaning. It simply says that if you can allow your mind to become still—stop thinking—eventually, You, the "Real Self", will gain access to the wisdom of the Universe, or if you wish, the wisdom of God.

I'm not saying that if you stop thinking for three minutes, volumes of esoteric wisdom will begin to flow through you. Life just doesn't work that way. But I do believe that at some point along the path when you are living a healthy spiritual life and the Kundalini energy is flowing smoothly through your chakra system, you will begin to gain access to the "inner wisdom" of the Universe. Whether it comes from the "outside" through the Thousand-Petaled Lotus just above the head, or it comes from "within", that is, the innate wisdom of the cells of the body, it doesn't really matter. All I know is that it happens—I saw it happen in Anne's life, beginning in 1960 and continuing to this day. And now, how does one achieve that state of silence?

Well, what is surprising is that it is much easier than you imagine. However, if you have tried to reach that state of stillness with inadequate or insufficient instruction, you have probably built some psychological blocks that may take a few hours to overcome. But we have seen so many successes in our workshops over the past 30 years that we have no doubt about the effectiveness of the training.

Environment

The first prerequisite of meditation is the environment. Have a quiet, comfortable, pleasant space where you can be undisturbed for up to an hour. You may want your own, small, sacred space—if you are into that sort of thing—with pictures and artifacts that you have collected. But this is in no way a requirement for successful meditation; it's just a nice touch for some people to have their own small altar.

Sitting

The next essential is a comfortable seating or sitting arrangement. During the 76 years that I have been practicing meditation, and I'm still practicing, I have sat in many different ways. I believe the proper way to sit is the most comfortable way you can devise, as long as the spine is vertical. In general, people in the Orient are more accustomed to sitting on a pillow on the floor than we Westerners. Oh, yes I know all the yoga rationale for the placement of the feet, heels and hands, but be that as it may, we Westerners have become used to chairs since Egyptian times, so maybe that should be given first consideration when meditating at home. A well-padded, straight-backed dining-room chair is a good place to start. The height of the seat should be so the feet rest comfortably on the floor. Use a pillow or pad for your feet if the chair seat is too high—make your feet and legs comfortable.

Back

Next, attend to your back. I believe it is the Taoists that say, think of your spine as a stack of golden coins with your head balanced comfortably on top. Having the back comfortably straight and vertical is important. I find a contoured foam support for my lower back to be quite useful.

Hands

Put your hands where they are most comfortable: on the thighs, palms up or down; in your lap, one cupped hand on top of the other; or perhaps laying on the cushion between your thighs. I sometimes find it comfortable to have my feet twenty four to thirty inches apart leaving space between the thighs for my cupped hands. But above all, find a position where the hands are comfortable. You should be comfortable enough to sit for 45 minutes with a minimum of movement.

Are you comfortable? If not, make whatever adjustments are necessary before you go any further.

Breath

If you are now comfortable, close your eyes and put your total awareness on the breath. I suggest eyes closed, but if you are comfortable with one of the Zen methods of partially open eyes, and you have a nondescript surface to look at, don't change. The important thing is to reduce visual input.

There are many ways of giving total awareness to the breath. One way is to put your awareness on the tip of your nose and be aware of the air as it passes in and out past that point. Sometimes it helps to think of the air as a fluid as it flows in and out through the nostrils. It was either Jack Kornfield or Ram Dass that said he was assigned to a space and given one admonition—follow your breath. He was told to be so aware that if anyone came to the door in the next week he would know at which point in the breath cycle he had been interrupted—on the in-breath, out-breath, or in between the breaths. That is real awareness of the breath.

Clear the Mind

Before you begin trying to reach a condition of stillness, you need to clear your mind of everyday concerns. So once you have reached a degree of awareness of the breath, clear your mind of any nagging problems. Bring the first situation into your awareness and make a decision as to what you are going to do about it. Or if it is too complex a situation to do that, then do a Scarlet O'Hara with it—"I'll think about it tomorrow," which in your case might be after meditation. In this way, make a decision on any item that could disturb your quest for stillness.

Awareness of the Breath

We can now get serious about meditation. Go back to an awareness of the breath. Know at any instant where you are in the breath cycle. Practice until you can maintain that degree of awareness for two or three minutes without breaking contact with the breath. Then you are ready to move on.

Moments of Stillness

Follow your next breath out until it stops naturally. Everything stops— the breath and all thoughts: only an awareness of the silence remains. When the body needs another breath just allow it to come in, then out until it stops. Again be aware of those few seconds of absolute silence between breaths. Then allow the breath to return, and again follow it out until it stops naturally. Again be aware of those few seconds of stillness, only this time when the breath returns allow the silence to follow it throughout the breath. The "stillness" is again reinforced at the end of the next breath and continues through the next breath cycle. At that point, just allow the process to continue, while you sit there aware, of the stillness.

Thinking and Awareness

Let us clarify the difference between thinking and awareness. Thinking is a dynamic process; awareness is a passive process. A dog barks; you become aware of it. You have a choice. You can think about it—"I wish he would stop barking," or you can simply be aware that a dog barked, period. This way there is awareness but no involvement, no thinking. In meditation, you are more aware than normal, but you simply do not become involved, so no thoughts.

The Thought Stopper

So now let's say you are human, and after a few breath cycles of silence, you think, "I hope the cat doesn't want to go out while I'm meditating." Oops, how do you handle that? The best way is take a short in-breath, like you were sniffing for smoke. It will stop a thought right in the middle of a word, and you are back in the stillness. The trick is to catch it before it becomes a whole scenario. That is where the habit of following the breath comes in handy. Usually, when you lose awareness of where you are in the breath cycle it is because a train of thoughts just got on your track. Or did that train of thoughts get on your track because you lost your awareness of the breath?

Breath Changes

Just remember that right from the start we are dealing with your normal breath—just whatever the body needs. After several minutes of meditation tending toward stillness, the breath becomes shallower, possibly even longer cycles. Just be aware of changes, don't initiate them.

Practice

Practice as indicated above as long as it stays productive. When thoughts get harder and harder to keep out, switch to a mantra or some other form of meditation. Perhaps just wait until your next meditation to again practice reaching that stillness. Next time just quickly review the following outline rather than this detailed text.

Instant Stillness

I believe what we are tending toward is where we can close our eyes, take a slightly deeper than usual breath, hold it in for 3 or 4 seconds while being aware of the normal tensions in the body, then let the breath flow out rapidly (don't force it out, let it out) while the shoulders settle down, indicative of the relaxation of the rest of the body. Leave just enough muscular tension to maintain an erect, vertical spine with the head balanced comfortably on the neck/shoulders. As the breath stops flowing so do the thoughts. After a short period of total stillness and silence the breath begins, but only awareness returns. It appears as a state of total rest, just awareness of the void. The sense of a body all but disappears in a thoughtless state of total awareness, of dreamless awareness, not sleep, just the achievement of instant meditation. Try it now. This may be all that is necessary for you to reach that place of stillness.

The state can be prolonged or reinitiated by a periodic slow, deep in-breath and a rapid outflow combined with muscular relaxation.

Outline for Achieving Stillness

Until you can reach a state of stillness in a breath or two, use the following outline as a quick reference.

- Get into a comfortable sitting position where your spine is comfortably straight and vertical.

- Close your eyes (unless you normally meditate with partially open eyes) and start becoming aware of your normal breath.

- Reach total awareness of the breath within one or two breaths.

- Take a few minutes to clear your mind of current life situations. Either make a decision about how to handle the situation or decide to put it on hold and consider it at a future time. Continue the process until all situations have been handled and the mind is clear.

- Return to an awareness of the breath cycle. Achieve continuous awareness of the breath cycle for periods of 2 or 3 minutes before moving toward the achievement of total stillness.

- Follow the next breath in and out until it stops naturally. Then enjoy the few seconds of stillness before the breath begins the next cycle.

- Repeat the above for two more breath cycles.

- Allow the stillness to continue throughout the next breath cycle. Reinforce the stillness at the end of that cycle and continue the stillness through successive breaths.

- Remember to use the short sniffs to squelch thoughts.

- Tend toward silent periods of one, two or three minutes with nothing but awareness.

The meditations that we have developed for use in our workshops usually incorporate esoteric wisdom obtained from Anne's esoteric lectures. These spontaneous lectures cover a vast array of topics, many of which are choice subjects for contemplation. After leading the participants into an altered state of consciousness using awareness of the breath, a mantra, or various more elaborate breathing techniques, we introduce esoteric truths that can serve as contemplation targets. We almost always use low-level, non-intrusive, background music and other superlearning techniques to enhance the retention of the truths being presented. We also leave spaces of just low-volume, background music to encourage total stillness of the mind, or at least one-pointedness. In her spontaneous lecture work Anne has said dozens of times that, "All wisdom is to be found in the stillness," so we have developed other meditations specifically designed to lead to a quiet mind. We assist the meditator in extending the stillness from a few seconds, to a few breaths and eventually to minutes. Thirteen of our most popular meditations have been put in an audiocassette album, and will soon be on CD's. It is a training aid that covers basic, advanced and highly esoteric meditations.

Intuition Practice

Asking someone to practice using a faculty they are not sure they really possess, can create a dilemma. We soon found that having people use intuition practice exercises or other academic approaches just wasn't working, so Anne asked if anyone in the group had a situation in their life where they could use some intuitive counseling. Someone in the back of the room timidly raised her hand and succinctly told the group the essential facts. Anne then told the group how she would use her intuition to explore a situation like that in a regular counseling session, and the questions she would pose to herself so she could dig deeper into the problem. At first we had people volunteer intuitive hits as they occurred to them. Some really got into it, while others became distracted and contributed little or nothing.

Then one day a middle-aged man spoke up and said he just wasn't getting anything. Anne asked him his name and what he did for a living. He said he was Milton Freedman and that he was a writer. We later learned that he was a presidential speech ghostwriter and had written for three or four previous U.S. presidents. So Anne said, "The next time we do this exercise, you write; in fact, why don't all of you take paper and pencil and we'll give you ten minutes to be still and make notes on the intuitive flashes that come into your awareness regarding this situation. Then use your notes for your report." What people needed was a real-life situation and a quiet period to listen to their intuition. It appeared that their intuition was not interested in hypothetical, meaningless situations. Right from the beginning the instruction has been that the practice exercise was not to be considered therapy, it was just practice. There was to be no psychological counseling or helpful advice, only intuitive input—no head stuff. There were unprintable phrases at Esalen for that kind of input. However, if the target person received some benefit from the group's intuitive input, that was a bonus.

After everyone had reported their insights, Anne would also intuitively look at the situation and report on any areas that had not been covered. So from then on nearly everyone wanted to be the target person of the practice exercise. And, by the way, Milton Freedman blossomed. Writing was his way of accessing intuitive information, whether it was writing a presidential speech or doing an intuitive scan. He had a ball! (Don't confuse him with Milton Freedman, the Washington economist.)

It was at this point that we began to make an audiotape for the target person. Frequently, there was some very useful information on the tape. In twenty-five years, we have never found a better practice exercise, and the group loves the personal interaction, especially Anne's input. We have always made it clear that this was simply a very useful exercise in intuition.

One of the qualms that we've had about this method of intuitive practice was that participants could get the impression we were training people to be "psychic readers." There was nothing further from our minds.

Over the years we have developed various other exercises to practice intuition, but they were designed to obtain information directly from Cosmic sources. Some of these have been our most popular exercises. For example, I have sold thousands of the cassette tape "Contacting the Cosmic Repository." It is popular because it really works. This exercise has been used to write books; re-write books that were in process; doctoral theses, creative projects such as painting and sculpting—anything creative.

We firmly believe that intuition should be the outgrowth of a healthy spiritual practice. So, underneath the intuitive awareness programming of our workshops is a firm esoteric foundation. However, we have no dogmatic religious views, we belong to no religious organization, and follow no particular religious philosophy to the exclusion of others. In our studies we have, as have all scholars of religious philosophy, found that all major religious teachings have come from one central source, or point of wisdom. Many religions today call that source God. In effect, there is only one religious philosophy, and we subscribe to it.

When appropriate, during a workshop, we will discuss what we believe to be the esoteric background or foundation of a process or principle. Most of our meditations have an esoteric, moral, ethical, and/or spiritual leaning that the participants are free to interpret any way they wish. We have always felt that our mission in life was to wake people up to the realization that they are Divine Beings with all the attributes, capabilities and potential of the Creator, and that they are on this earth having a physical experience for a few years—one of many such experiences they have had and will have. Once they are awake to who and what they are, we have no interest in their religious or philosophic affiliations. Personally, we feel just as comfortable in a Hindu Ashram, Buddhist Temple or Jewish Synagogue as a Catholic or Congregational Church—the same God energy is in them all.

Demonstration Exercise

As I stated previously, the best intuition training vehicle is what we have always referred to as a group scan—the group intuitively scans a real-life situation of one of the members of the group, or sometimes the group chooses a couple as the target for the scan.

Several years ago we were presenting a five-day workshop at Esalen Institute. After spending an evening together sharing psychic/intuitive experiences and fears, the group was ready to start some serious training. The next day began with a meditation; Anne talked about how she got involved in this intuition stuff; and then it was time to put the group to work proving to themselves that they really were intuitive. This first group scan is called an "intuition demonstration". For Anne to demonstrate that she is intuitive would be relatively meaningless, but for the group to prove to themselves that they are in fact intuitive is far more meaningful.

For this first demonstration scan three people and one couple volunteered. They each gave extremely meager information about their situations so as not to influence the group's intuitive reports if they were chosen. With enough information a good therapist can always come up with an answer, but it may not be the correct answer, so the volunteers are cautioned to be quite succinct when stating their situation. The group then voted to work on the situation presented by the couple.

> Jim: Tell us your situation. Try to state the question as succinctly as you can from both of your perspectives. Judith, why don't you start? Repeat what you said earlier.
>
> Judith: I'll just continue what Leslie began to talk about. It seems as if there is a block of energy between us, and there is a lot of fear. I have difficulty with the energy in my body stopping someplace right here (putting her hands over her lower abdominal area) and I simply, absolutely cannot have an orgasm when we make love. Although I am very aroused, I feel as if the top and the bottom of my body don't go together. I feel as if I want to scream and run away no matter what he does. We've

meditated together; we've prayed together; we've seen a therapist together. I've written, we've talked, we've done everything that we know to do, but there is a block. If Leslie gets too friendly I just head the other way, and he does the same if I get too close. He stays busy with his job and we both walk around with that knot in our gut, avoiding each other. It's really painful.

Anne: All that plus the fact that your kids don't understand what is going on between you. How many children do you have between you?

Judith: Four. I have three from a previous marriage.

Anne: A lot of misunderstanding. OK, do you have anything to add to that, Leslie?

Leslie: That's pretty accurate. I have a feeling that we don't deserve this in this life, especially after hearing your story today. Considering the way we've lived since our marriage, and the years preceding, we just don't deserve that kind of energy. It feels to me that it is something from the past.

Anne: We won't even consider that unless it comes up. We can't plant those seeds; we must look at what is actually going on now. OK, how long have you been married?

Leslie: A year and a half.

Anne: Do you have any children, Leslie?

Leslie: I have one from a previous marriage.

Anne: What kind of work do you do?

Leslie: I have a bachelor's degree in psychology, but I make more money selling.

Anne: And, Judith, you work with AA people. Does anyone need to ask any other question before I tell you how to set this thing up so we can look at it?

Group Member: Was this a pattern repeated from other relationships?

Judith: No.

Anne: OK, any other questions?

Group Member: How long has it been going on?

Judith: From the beginning—even before we were married.

Leslie: One of the things that I've discovered is that Judith is very honest in what she brings to me. We've made a commitment to total honesty with each other. My suspicion is that perhaps in my past this problem existed and no one told me about it, or that this problem exists in many relationships and no one talks about it. It's a really charged subject for me, perhaps everyone, and it's so easy to avoid, to gloss over, because we can play the role and no one knows.

Anne: OK, Any other questions?

Group Member: I have one. From what Judith has said it appears that she has the problem of disconnectedness and you react to that. Otherwise you don't have a problem?

Leslie: I've had an addiction to sex—along with everything else I'm addicted to—it's just one of the pieces. I have done some very dysfunctional things sexually—pimping, for instance—which I consider dysfunctional now. And, I don't know how this is affecting me. In terms of my own body functioning, it's working great.

Anne: We've got to go behind the scenes and to the best of our ability find out what is really going on. OK, if you don't have any further questions, let me give you some instructions as to how one goes about obtaining intuitive information. The information comes in a variety of ways; each person may obtain it differently. If you happen to be quite visual, you might get all of your information in pictures. They might be very clear images. If you happen to be kinesthetically inclined, you might actually feel things in your body. You might just know information in your head; you might just have a gut feeling about it, without any imagery at all. It doesn't make any difference as long as you are tuning into the source of the information and a sense of what it is trying to communicate to you. Write it down as it comes in.

One thing that works quite well is to do what I call staging, which means that you create a stage in your mind's eye and then ask Leslie and Judith to come onto the stage and begin to dialogue about things of which they may not even be consciously aware. There are a lot of different parts to the personality, and it may be just one part that is doing this whole number. We don't know yet; we've got to go looking for it. While you have them on the stage, you might actually do an interview with the sexual dysfunction. What can it tell you that you can communicate to Judith? There are many creative ways of getting the actual information. You can also do the same thing with Leslie. Ask him what's going on that he may not even be aware of. Ask some part of him that is really clear to come forward and give you information of which he might not be consciously aware.

If you get into this process deeply enough you may even feel like Judith or Leslie. You may feel like you are in Judith's body, or inside her head; you may be getting a sense of the problem or dysfunction from a whole different perspective, not from the way she sees the experience. The same could happen when you are interviewing Leslie. Ask them when they are on the stage to come together and talk to one another about this problem. Staging can be very informative. If they both have their arms open, extended to one another, they are in love and they want to work things out. Or, one may be stubborn, cross their arms and even walk off the stage. In the beginning one or both of them may refuse even to get on the stage. That in itself is a lot of information, but still you can ask why they are unwilling to cooperate.

You may feel various conditions in your own body—heat, coolness, anxiety, a change in your breathing, a pain in your stomach, frustration, any sensation is possible. Someone's face may keep coming into your awareness. Don't push it away. Perhaps something you know about that person applies to this situation. Everything that is in your data bank can be used to give you information. This is not a difficult process; it's a matter of learning to pay attention and listen. You pose a clear question such as: I need to know what's going on between these two people. What can be of help to them? Then you have to disconnect from your thinking—no more thinking—just witnessing whatever is bubbling up in your consciousness. Or you create the stage and just watch it, not letting your mind get in the way with a bunch of fantasizing—just allow the information to create itself while you watch. Ask if what you see or sense is childhood stuff; does it relate to their parents or to them? Do a lot of questioning, a lot of dialoging. The gestalt of every situation exists. It is just a matter of being creative in the questions you ask and the way you listen to the response.

OK, I think that is enough to get you started. We will talk more after you get some practice. Now take the next ten minutes to make notes on whatever you get.

I'm just going to sit here and do nothing because I want to share everything that happens to me as I work on Judith and Leslie's situation. (Ten minutes of silence)

Anne: It has been ten minutes. As I said, I just sat here and did nothing so you might get an idea how the information comes in, how I work with it, the questions I ask, etc.

I still prefer to close my eyes to avoid outside distractions, after which I turn my attention inward and experience myself as being centered. Next, I review the question: I need to know what is going on between these two people; what would be useful for them to know at this time so they can get on with their relationship? Now I will wait, making sure that the mind is quiet, absolutely still, simply watching, witnessing. At this moment I have no idea where it's going to start itself, so I will simply wait and watch until the information begins to volunteer itself. (Silence for twenty to thirty seconds.) I am noticing a tightness in my chest and a bit of agitation—I don't know what it means yet.

OK, the first impression that I am getting is that I am becoming very small, as if I am shrinking inside myself. As yet, I have no idea what this means, but I'll continue to go with the feeling of getting smaller and smaller, tighter and tighter. Now it is beginning to happen; I'm getting the sense that I can't breathe—that my breath is being cut off—almost a sense of suffocation. The next feeling or image that I'm getting is inside Judith's mother's womb. I'm a fetus, perhaps four months old and I'm feeling extremely threatened. I'm aware of the penetration that occurs during sexual activity, and I'm terrified. I have the feeling I am fighting for my life, that this is not a safe place to be, and yet I have no place to go. The breath of my body is becoming deep and agitated. OK, Judith, give me your father's name. Cosmo? Fine. The next thing I am aware of is Cosmo blending with Leslie. It's as if I can't separate the two

133

energies—the two male energies coming together. I don't know what this means. I'm simply watching the scene. I continue to watch the two penises blend and become one and the same.

Now, I'm going to start asking questions: What do Judith and Leslie need to know about this situation? Immediately, I'm getting a sense of ancientness about the situation—I just feel it in my body—very old, very ancient. And then I am getting the words "human sacrifice." I have no sense of location, just the fear that I have around that act. Now I am aware of Judith being on a stone slab. I'm still trying to find the location. I have a sense of confusion between your mother being pregnant and you being the fetus, and you on the stone slab being pregnant. And somehow being pregnant has made you particularly special—this I just "know".

Now I am aware of hearing a lot of voices around this figure on the stone slab which is you, Judith, in an altar-like setting. There are candles or torches, flowers, a lot of chanting in muffled tones.

My attention, or my energy is shifting over to you, Leslie. I have a "sense" that I have "become you" and that you are leading this ritual. You are making motions and chanting incantations. You are holding something, moving it up and down in a reverent way. I'm now in touch with both of you but primarily with your fear, Judith; yet, at the same time, you have been chosen in a very special way because you are pregnant. At the same time there was a need to offer yourself and go along with the ritual, in spite of the fear of what is about to happen to you. Now, Leslie, I am aware of you holding a knife with an interesting shape. It is like the knives that Turks carry, a kind of crescent-shaped cutting edge, extremely sharp. You are picking up the knife in two hands, holding it up for all to see. I'm aware of the flickering light from the torches or candles on the knife's sharp edge; I am aware of you, Judith, and the fear you are experiencing. But the die is cast; you must go through the ordeal.

I have very little knowledge of the cut made for a Caesarean birth, but the pattern that is going to be carved on the stomach of this pregnant woman, who happens to be you, Judith, is going to be quite different.

The prone body is being approached from the feet so the cut can be made in a specific way. I see the point of the knife—oh, my God—being used in a very skillful manner. The cut starts at the left, almost under the breastbone, and makes a semicircular pattern nearly down to the pubic bone.

The next thing I'm vividly aware of are all the layers of flesh popping up, one layer after the other—skin, fat, muscles, tissue. I see the folds of flesh open up behind the knife until it comes to the end of its course. All the time there are incantations, a kind of crying in the background, all part of the ritual. I don't hear pain, simply a kind of wailing incantation, as if it were part of a ceremony. All the time I am asking, where is Judith's consciousness? I get the sense that she is perfectly conscious—hands, feet and body bound so there can be no movement. To my horror I sense that this whole ritual has reverent, spiritual overtones, carefully choreographed and rehearsed.

Now I am aware of this figure that I experience as Leslie going around to the left side of the body, starting the cut just below the breastbone and again making a semicircular cut ending up at the pubic bone. Then the whole section of flesh is lifted, exposing the fetal sac. I have the sense that this was done so skillfully that the membrane enveloping the fetus has not been touched. Now I'm aware of the head rupturing the membrane, the fluid pouring out over the female body and the stone slab. There are tremendous sounds being made by the horde of male figures. The only female energy in the area is yours, Judith. I hear these husky male voices; naturally I can't understand what they are saying. But when the voices have quieted somewhat, Leslie reaches down and takes the tiny fetus from the womb, separating it from the mother. As he triumphantly raises it in his hands, the men again chant the wild incantations. Meanwhile, no attention is being paid to the woman. They have what they went after and what happens to the woman now makes no difference. What is important is that the fetus is alive. Now I am aware of the fetus being passed from hand to hand in a circle surrounding the body on the altar. The fetus is developed enough for me to "see" that it is a male. This part of the ritual is completed when the fetus returns to Leslie. The figure on the altar is suffering and bleeding profusely, but still alive. She raises her head slightly and for the last time, beholds the figure of her unborn child, takes a deep gasp of air, and the life is gone. As the life essence leaves her body I feel that I too must take a deep breath.

The next phase of this gruesome ritual is to see how long Leslie can keep the fetus alive. The singing and incantations continue as I probe for the reason behind this seemingly cruel and needless ritual. As I ask for clarity, I'm aware that you were chosen, Judith, and the sperm to impregnate you came from Leslie; you were carefully watched over until about four-to-four-and-a-half months into the gestation period. So it's his baby and it's your body. But what is the purpose? Please clarify.

As soon as I asked for clarification I became aware of a powerful voice wanting to speak to me—literally coming through me. My body is becoming extremely tense—my neck, shoulders, stomach—frankly, it is a bit painful; but for the sake of clarity I am willing to do whatever seems necessary. I have the feeling that I will be communicating with the male I identified as Leslie. I actually have a sense that I am holding the fetus in "my" hands because I feel the wetness and the movement. It is very much alive.

Now I am feeling like the most powerful male that you can imagine. I have had similar experiences but I believe this is the most powerful I have ever felt. It's a different kind of energy, perhaps it is the primitiveness that I'm experiencing. I am not experiencing it as benign. Nevertheless, I do have a sense of tremendous power, a sense of conviction about the truth of the belief, what is being done, and the necessity for what needs to be done. What I am being told telepathically by the male figure is that I have become him. "I must keep this fetus alive for three days. If I am successful in doing that, and I am determined that I will be, I will have been endowed with extreme power, power beyond my wildest dreams. I am taking something that is not fully manifested, and in a sense absorbing its energy, its essence, holding it in my hands unceasingly. In effect it is an initiation. Seen from my current perspective it was not a very spiritual initiation. It was devised by primitives, which we have all been, so it should not be that shocking. If at the end of three days the fetus is still alive, I will be endowed with tremendous power."

This male energy has stepped aside and I can see that the feat was accomplished, but I still sense that the power acquired was something less than benign, albeit extremely powerful.

My attention now goes back to the female who has succumbed due to the incisions. Candles are being lit; there are incantations over the body. She was a major participant in this; she gave up her unborn child. Now I have become Judith, for she has something to say. She is saying, "In this culture, one of the greatest gifts a woman can give to her man is to give up her unborn child so that he in turn can become complete within himself, according to our tradition. True, it is a very painful, fearful ordeal to go through, but it is a love offering. I am happy that the ritual was successful." I now see the body being washed and other rituals being performed preliminary to cremation, all being done with a tremendous amount of reverence. As the flames consume the body, I have a sense that the female is saying, "I care enough about you to give up my life that you may have this power." So there was mutual consent around this horrible ritual.

When I ask what this particular male went on to accomplish with the power gained from this unborn child, I feel my body becoming extremely powerful. "According to my tradition I have received the gift of vision, the psychic opening; I am revered by the males around me; I have been elevated to a position of great power; I have become a leader."

OK, what else do I need to know about this situation? I see you, Judith, and some aspect of Leslie facing each other. It is both now and in ancient times, and I feel that there is work that the two of you need to complete. That, of course, is the reason you are still having difficulties. It was a sexual act that led to the events I have been describing. Even though there was mutual consent, it was still a brutal act to inflict upon anyone. When I again "become you", Judith, I get a restless, unhappy, confused energy within me. Judith, you spoke earlier about fears you have around the psychic/intuitive abilities you exhibit from time-to-time. Some voice from a deep level of your being says you have had access to these energies before and have used them in many, many beautiful ways. You acknowledge this but there is still something that needs to be clarified. I'm aware of the words "equal" or "equality." It relates to you surrendering to sex with Leslie—going back in time and surrendering to this horrendous experience that I have just described. The memory is lodged in the pelvic area and the heart. There is still a sense of fear associated with it, as if you still can't trust that kind of a connection between the two of you.

Now my attention shifts to Leslie's mind where there is a very unsettled kind of energy, a confusion. I feel that you care very much about Judith, but there are times when you don't know how to relate to her—I almost want to say—"safely". It is as if you are busy defining your own strength to see if you can match hers, which is considerable. So I am perceiving areas that appear as weaknesses or lack of confidence. There are times you feel you may not be able to match her.

In an attempt to understand, I've "become" Leslie, and as such I'm picking up these thoughts: How can I find a safe way, a clear way, an equitable way to relate to Judith? What I sense about you, Leslie, is that (and this relates to your inner makeup) if you honor everything that Judith is now, it's as if you lose some part of yourself. This may be at a deep subconscious level that you are not even aware of. It is as if in the past she has given you her heart, her life, and she has given you her unborn child—the power to become a great leader—and you are not sure that this is going to happen again. I feel you are a very ethical, responsible person and there is still an area within you that is not quite comfortable with everything that happened in the remote past.

I'm asking myself what this means; what does Leslie need to know? There is something here that the two of them have yet to work out. Notice how I ask questions to get answers. If I don't ask the right questions the flow of information slows down or just stops. Then I have to prime it with more questions. I'm trying to demonstrate how I work, while at the same time I am obtaining useful information for these two people.

Now, back to you two. I feel this knowing welling up inside me that it is your turn, Judith, your time to possess your power and to use it; and it is your turn, Leslie, to support her. Her turn has come, and if you can take on the supportive role and really honor everything that has happened to Judith (and I don't know how far back that goes) she will bloom and you will have the opportunity to revel in her success. If this can happen, the power that you have known in the past will come forth again, manifesting itself in you and through you. Of course it will manifest in different ways than it did before; but, nevertheless, you will match her power in your own way. I "sense" that the two of you working together can accomplish tremendous feats, but only if there is acceptance of each other. However, when Judith offers herself sexually to you, all that old stuff gets triggered and at an unconscious level she is wondering, "Am I giving my power away again?" So it is almost death at an ego, or psychic level. If she gives you her power again, then who is she? In a sense, that imprint is so deeply embedded in the unconscious, it means death.

Now I'm asking, are there any further instructions around what needs to be done? The response I get to that is that you, Leslie, have your own brand of strength, you have your own clarity, you have your own intuitive abilities, all of which are quite different from Judith's. Now it is your turn to be supportive, to know that she is . . .I don't want to say the special one . . . but it's her turn to be honored by you, so the two of you can become equals. Now I see two thrones. If that can come about you will both ascend to a level of consciousness where you will be able to communicate with each other on all levels. This is a rare occurrence, indicating some deep level or ancient work that needs to be completed. But unfortunately, personalities get in the way and have to be dealt with. There is something fragile about your personality, Leslie, as if you are not quite sure of yourself, not quite confident, not quite aggressive enough. And, at the same time, you are a bit awed by what Judith does—a bit uncertain at times what it really means. So if you can accept these uncertainties in your life, I feel that the two of you will get it together.

I usually don't ask for a response when I report first because I want everyone else to have a clean field for their reports. However, some of these last words may have been of my own creation, even though I get a "realness" about them. So I would like to clear the situation up before we move on. Could you please respond?

Judith: Even though the symbolism has manifested itself differently on this plane, I feel it is right on. One time when I was working with John Heider in a group setting, he asked, "What will happen to you if you have an orgasm with Leslie?" I said, "I'll die."

Anne: Wow, that tells you something! And what were your impressions, Leslie?

Leslie: Before you began to talk I was drawing this picture. It was the middle of me and over to the side were these two round things—ovaries. I felt tremendous fear as I was making the drawing, but as you described the ritual, I felt sad about the whole process. However, as you describe the essence of that person, I could feel it—almost identify with him.

Anne: So you do identify with what has been said, making it possible for you to work on it? I believe these are some of your barriers.

Leslie: Part of what goes on between us is that she and I are quite different. We manifest ourselves in different ways. I have an intellectual desire to be supportive. I honor greatly what she does but I don't seem to say or do anything about it—as if there is some part of me that just doesn't want to let go. It's almost as; if I honor her, I'm diminished, so I haven't resolved how to honor her. I didn't feel diminished when we met. I feel that I have merged into a complete being—not anything I have done in this life. It's like I was complete before I met Judith. And yet, since we've been together, it feels that if I let go of that sense of completeness I will be back to feeling that I need her to make me complete again. I don't know if that makes any sense.

Anne: It makes a lot of sense. You were talking from many different levels. You still carry the imprint of your worth, the power you had and now suddenly you can't grasp it in the same form—you wouldn't want to. But still you need to know that it lies latent within you and that it can manifest itself in a form that you will feel good about, and in a way that will complement Judith. I feel that there is a lot of work that the two of you could do together, but you both have to get your acts together.

Leslie: Well, we were impelled to join forces. We didn't seem to have a choice.

Anne: Just like I was impelled to be with Jim, even though at times it has been difficult. I believe we had things to do together, so we just went ahead and did them.

Judith: Intellectually I resisted, I didn't want to get married. I have lots of money, I can go anywhere I want, and I don't need anything from anyone. I didn't want anyone telling me what I can and can't do—I just didn't need that aggravation. And yet there was this other part of me . . .I loved him so much. My head said, "Live with him, you don't need to get married, you don't need to sell the farm." But, my spiritual/ethical nature wouldn't allow me to do that. He asked me to marry him; we started making arrangements, and then it kept being pushed back another month, and another month. Still, we got married five months after we met, and I was still saying, "This is wrong, I'm not doing this, I have more sense than this." It was just something I couldn't stop. And right now, in spite of our obvious problems, I have absolutely no desire to leave this relationship, even though at times it is quite painful.

Anne: I understand. You know that you need to hang in there and work this thing through. When I look at the two of you at a psychic or spiritual level I see you as very much equals. I frankly doubt that there is such a thing as someone being our other half, but I have the sense that there may be the other half of an energy you need to work with to complete a sequence. So in this sense, you are two equal halves of a whole.

Judith: Leslie's energy grounds me. Otherwise I'm out there playing in the ethers. With him around I pay more attention to reality and the things I do.

Anne: Leslie, I think that to honor Judith consciously, being unafraid of who she is and what she may become, is not going to take anything away from you, in fact, it is going to elevate you to another level of consciousness. So I want to say to both of you: You need to understand that to honor each other for who they are, will take nothing away from either of you. Realize that you have much deeper work to do and that you have only scratched the surface of your capabilities. If you honor that commitment you will become equals and complete the work that you have to do together.

Leslie: I have a problem when you talk like this because I envision myself as the bag boy. That's the way I feel.

Jim: Well, I could feel that way. Several men have asked me how I stand being a "step-and-fetch-it" for my wife. Before we started working together I had been quite successful in industry. I left when I felt it was time to move on. Then circumstances pushed me into helping Anne out of a bind, and I never stopped. For years I had pushed her to live up to her potential. She is a Cancer, so she was happy living under a rock where it was nice and cool and quiet. Now look what has happened to her. And me, I'm doing what I have always wanted to do—help wake people up to their potential.

Leslie: She is very wealthy, and I'm just a country boy from Timbuktu. I am compelled to be successful, which translates—make a lot of money. I do well, but it has become a compulsion. I'm in a contest to accumulate at the physical/material level so I can feel her equal, but inside I have the emasculated feelings of a bag boy. I even changed my name from Les, which is the diminished part of me, to Leslie, which in America is a feminine name. See if you can figure that one out. I feel so masculine and so male on the inside and my name on the outside is Leslie. Johnny Cash has a song about a boy named Sue.

Judith: I'm the only one who ever calls him Leslie; everyone else calls him Les.

Leslie: If anyone else called me Leslie, I'd shut them up.

Jim: Talking about feeling like the bag boy, let me tell you a story. Anne, Chris and I came home one Sunday night after a big weekend. Anne was two or three years into her Kundalini opening so, spiritual training was pretty important in our lives. It was late, the house was cold, everyone was tired from several hours of driving, and the f-ing furnace wouldn't come on. I went to the garage, got some tools and started to try to find out what the problem was. All the time this was going on I was grumbling, swearing, cursing the furnace, the fact that I had to work on it and that I had cut my finger on the furnace cover. Suddenly I stopped. In the midst of all my profanity I recalled something I had read recently. Do you remember when Jesus washed the feet of his disciples? When reprimanded by Peter, Jesus said, in effect, that he was not above washing their feet and that they should follow his example. So don't berate your fate because you are forced to do a menial task, just ask yourself how Jesus would handle the current situation. I don't believe being a bag boy, or fixing a furnace, would be below His dignity.

Anne: It's the ego that becomes irate and pushed out of shape, not the real Self. The "Real Self" is never diminished. It is only the body/mind/personality with its feelings of inadequacy that has all this human stuff, but that is not the real you. What we are talking about is at a soul level. In one lifetime we are the stepping-stone, and in the next we have our day of light and glory. In the lifetimes that I have explored, Jim has killed me and I have killed him in some very cruel and dramatic ways. So who is to say what who has done to whom? The important thing is that we work it out now, and do not waste this particular time around. That, is what's important, not the dictates of the ego/personality. True, it takes a lot of centeredness and a lot of faith to keep going when the way gets rough.

Anne: Leslie, I experience you as very handsome, very masculine, and very capable. And I'm sure Judith experiences you in the same way. The fact that her path is different right now is really beside the point. What you are carrying inside of you is some of the strength she gave you. She gave her life at one point, she gave you her unborn child, and that still lives within you. She honored you, and now it's your turn to honor the one who gave the original gift. So, you know, there is balance and justice in life if we can go back far enough. Sex and orgasm with you means death to Judith, but not with anyone else, only you. We don't know what in Hell we are responding to when it is so deep in the subconscious.

Anne: OK, what did some of the rest of you get? If it can add clarity to these people's lives it is important, so put out what you got.

Group Member: I got the feeling of suffocation, a heart that was hot, indicating to me a lot of love and affection. There was also a half cold and a half warm heart. Then I was aware of a teepee with the flap open that reminded me of Indians and rituals. I was aware of natural triangular shapes like pine trees, and then: a sudden flash of many windows, a tiled roof on a white stucco house, and a brown shed against a fence.

Judith & Leslie: You have described the setting and the house we live in.

Anne: That is a real hit. Next.

Group Member: I didn't get very much. I got stuck immediately. I got an unbelievable pain in the pit of my stomach that radiated throughout my torso, and a great feeling of nausea. I could not get beyond that. The only thing that came up was excruciating pain around Leslie, based upon some past-life experience. That all happened immediately and I became stuck.

Anne: You will notice what I did. I had some of the same feelings but I asked for an explanation. Once the explanation comes I can then go to the next scene or phase. You have to learn to "move the film along." It comes with a lot of practice. Next report?

Group Member: I set up my stage and got Judith standing, being very pregnant. She had an apron over a very full, feminine figure. Leslie had her hand and she was pulling back. He was gentle. His figure came and went while she seemed quite clear and constant. He had her by the hand; she seemed to be resisting. He was partly coaxing and partly pulling, trying to bring her toward him. That is all I got.

Anne: Very good images, very significant.

> Note: The reports from the group continued for twenty or thirty minutes, some with significant passages and others totally off-the-wall. After all, this was the first intuition practice. So now we have arrived at the wind-up where we hope to pull most of the loose ends together so Judith and Leslie don't go to dinner feeling that their life has just gone through the kitchen meat grinder.

Group Member: I saw something happening with Judith's father at an early age, and Leslie is reminding you of your father.

Anne: Yes, I got a sense of Leslie and your father blending into one, having the same penis.

Judith: A few days ago we were fighting and I said, "You are exactly like my father. Damn it! I've done it again, I've married my father." That came up because my father is emotionally absent. He is a fantastic businessman; he has made a great success of his life—financially. He is magnificent to look at; he's built like Leslie, but emotionally there is nobody home. That is how Leslie feels to me sometimes when he gets hell-bent on his success and money making. That is when I say, "Hey, remember me, I live here, too." And that is how my father is.

Group Member: At some point you both mentioned an honesty agreement. Judith, I feel that you can read Leslie's thoughts. That doesn't make for an honest relationship. I got the power struggle issue, and one way you hold on to your power is by not having an orgasm. There were other feelings, but they were too complicated and confusing to be reported.

Anne: I could know Jim's thoughts and actions just as easily as I can know other peoples' thoughts, but it is something that I would never do. If he asked me why he had a backache, for example, he would in effect be giving me permission to seek out the cause of the problem, and it is always possible that I would see causes about which he had never dreamed. Our lives, however, have evolved to the point where we have very few secrets left.

Jim: Rather frequently, people ask me how it is living with a highly intuitive person. I tell them it is no different than living with anyone else, except if I needed some advice I wouldn't have far to go.

Anne: No, I never look. It's just not ethical. It would keep the other person on the defensive all the time. After all, one can't always be on his best behavior.

Judith: Yes, I have stopped doing that.

Leslie: The truth is I can read her mind also.

Anne: Well, do you do it? Maybe this is something you should look at.

Leslie: Well, I don't have the switch that she does.

Anne: But some part of you wants to do it or it wouldn't be happening.

Leslie: It has just manifested itself recently. I think it was part of the power struggle—if you're going to do it, I'm going to do it. However, Anne, I really appreciate you pursuing this. Hopefully, I can let it go because it could destroy our relationship.

Anne: It's all ego. That's all it is.

Group Member: I have a question for Judith. Were there any surprises? How do you feel about all this?

Judith: For me it is right on. I can see how it has manifested in our lives today, perhaps a little differently than what Anne said, but effectively it is the same thing.

Group Member: Is that true for you, Leslie?

Leslie: Where I am right now is that it is not really comforting to have those images floating around in my head.

Anne: Some of the things I have run across about myself during past lives, or during therapy concerning this life, are pretty horrific. I could beat myself over the head for the rest of my life; but you know, that "was" a way of life, it "was" the way we lived. What I saw happening during that ritual would not have been considered cruel in that culture; it "was" an accepted way of life. Our belief structures encompassed those kinds of actions. Can you imagine the Roman games—lions tearing Christians, gladiators and slaves to bits while crowds roared—coming to the Los Angeles Coliseum? That was less than two thousand years ago in a very "civilized" nation. So, Leslie, don't put yourself down. Just consciously join the human race.

> *Author's Note:* Among other things, we are not anthropologists. We have never heard of the ritual that Anne described earlier in this section. Was this just a metaphor to psychologically explain an orgasmic discrepancy of one of our workshop participants, or was this an actual ritual practiced by some obscure group in Outer Blah-Blah? If you have any knowledge of such a bizarre ritual ever having been practiced by some ancient, or current, society, please send whatever documentation you have to our e-mail address listed below. In our own way we are about as skeptical as The Amazing Randy. I tried for nearly thirty years to think like a "scientist," but I never quite made it. Still I believe

in a certain degree of logic. Thank you. — Jim
Armstrong e-mail: azoth@volcano.net

Regular Group Scan

The regular group scan has been our standard training exercise for over 30 years. We were never able to find a better one; and nearly everyone in a workshop wants to be the subject of the exercise. During a weekend workshop we would only do about five scans, and in a five-day workshop, about fifteen. So with groups between twenty and one hundred participants we needed to draw names from "The Hat"—a straw tortilla basket that has been carried all over Europe and North America for twenty years or so. This way the gods would choose the next candidate for the group scan.

In the late '70's we were leading a five-day workshop, and about the second day, after most of the group had left for the afternoon, the wind blew The Hat on the floor spilling all the names. The person helping me straighten up the room picked up the name slips and noticed the same name on two slips of paper. She called it to my attention and then looked at all the name slips. The lady had put her name into The Hat five times. My helper wanted to throw out the extra ones. I said, "No, let's just see how the gods will handle it." Not one of her name slips was ever drawn from The Hat that week. Perhaps there was a lesson in it for her.

The person whose name was drawn from The Hat would state his or her situation as succinctly as possible and the group would be given ten minutes to scan the situation intuitively and take notes. In a regular group scan, the participants report their intuitive hits and after everyone who wishes has reported, Anne gives her evaluation of the situation. The target person then gives feedback on the reports. The entire process is recorded on a cassette tape for the subject.

In addition to the intuition practice afforded by the group scans, we use many other exercises that help the participant get out of their worldly-oriented mind and into the spiritually-oriented portion of the mind. We have them begin by simply becoming aware of their feelings and emotions, and then move into exercises that help them gain control of the mind through visualization.

Feelings and Emotions

The language of intuition is built around feelings and emotions. Usually our intuition communicates to the conscious mind through our feelings and emotions, yet most of us either stifle our feelings or let them run rampant. Intelligent emotional control appears to be the optimum condition for intuitive functioning. Control of one's emotions has always been a prerequisite to serious spiritual training. It was that way at the time of Plato and before, and it is equally as necessary today. Therefore, for years we have used a series of exercises to make people aware of their feelings and emotions and then encourage them to bring these under the control of the mind, or is it the soul? Instead, most of us let our emotions control us.

Imagination and Visualization

In our "scientific" culture, imagination has received a bum rap. Recently, it may be improving, but most people have poorly developed imaginations. We use exercises that stretch and expand the imagination so that no matter what is encountered in the non-physical realms, the mind can accept it as a possibility.

Visualization is another faculty of the human mind that is poorly developed in most people. However, visualization and imagination are the driving force behind creation, and we are all Creators. Being gods in training, potentially we have the creative abilities of our Creator, so it is time to begin our practice. Creation begins with a thought and a desire in the mind of the Creator, whether it is you or God. The problem is we create more unuseful thoughts than useful ones. However, once we become conscious creators we become more discriminating. So we have exercises to train the mind to construct thought-forms that are just a shade short of being physical. To do this we suggest that the participants practice by tracing a three-dimensional figure in space and mentally moving around it so they can "see" it, and "work" on it from all angles.

Another creative imagination or visualization exercise that has worked well for thousands of people is to create an imaginal body similar to our own physical body, or perhaps an improved version. Once we have become adept at using this imaginal body we can experience being an animal, a bird, a whale, anything you fancy. In this way we begin to "feel" as they feel, as they see the world through their eyes, swim in the depths of the ocean as a whale, or fly over lofty mountains as an eagle. Or, we can perform endless, fantastic physical feats with our bodies, such as playing on the moon, flying in the imaginal body, going into the depths of the ocean, leaping a 100 feet—anything that you can imagine.

Conclusion

Throughout the past 33 years the workshop has been our basic training structure. We still meet with two, small, on-going groups in the Los Angeles area a few times a year; but basically, we have "retired" from the workshop/seminar circuit. Our hope is that someone will pick up where we have left off and continue an intuition training program that is built upon a spiritual, ethical, moral, esoteric foundation. Hopefully, there are already some out there. Teaching intuition without this foundation seems unethical and immoral.

The human race as a whole is behind in its spiritual development. It has done a great job developing the physical/mental side of its being, but the spiritual aspect has been sorely neglected. However, spiritual intuition working through a reasonably well-developed chakra system, including the Thousand-Petaled Lotus, will eventually give the individual access to all the wisdom necessary for his/her own enlightenment. And, for all the reasons that can be given for developing one's spiritual intuition, this is the best. We have more to say about this later.

CHAPTER VII:

TRANSPERSONAL COUNSELING

Introduction

Once Anne got herself healed of some, if not all, of her ailments, her therapist thought it was time for her to start helping other people. In her own therapy sessions she always knew what her major problems were, what the cause had been, and what she should or could do to improve the situation. So it was only logical that she could do the same for other people.

Anne's counseling covers a wide range of human activity, but relationships seem to be one of her specialties: marriage/family, parent/ child, and employer/employee. She possesses an uncanny ability to "become" another person, to see the world as they see it, to feel as they feel, think as they think. This is an invaluable tool when working in relationships, especially since most relationship problems are the result of misunderstandings. She is able to "know" where the person is coming from and usually why they are in that stance. She is able to put words to unspoken feelings, desires, hurts, anger and jealousy. She can "become" the hurt child or timid wife and explain to the other person why they act or react the way they do. Once you begin to think about the ability to become another person the applications are endless. Anne

153

can experience either or both partners in a relationship, "knowing" how they feel and effectively how they think. Armed with that kind of data, it is much easier to live with a difficult situation, find ways to change it or perhaps even to decide that the situation is hopeless.

Relationships

Anne was working with a man in a workshop and it became very clear to her that he was extremely unhappy in his marriage and wanted out. All she did was put words around his unexpressed desire. An hour or so after we got to our hotel that evening the phone rang and there was a very irate wife accusing Anne of breaking up her marriage. Anne explained that all she did was see the relationship from her husband's standpoint and put what she saw into words. She didn't advise anyone to do anything.

Six months later the wife called again. She said she had never been happier. She was free, had met a wonderful man and just called to thank Anne for seeing the relationship as it really was. Years later we ran into the ex-husband. He too was doing extremely well, and was delighted with the way it had worked out for everyone. As a matter of fact, we met his ex-wife again at a conference that he had organized.

Career Counseling

Ever since the beginning of her counseling work Anne has been helping people find their unique niche in our complex society. As we are growing up, our teachers and parents make suggestions as to what they think we should do with our lives, but all too many times their suggestions are based upon their own unfulfilled dreams, their own ambitions or their desire to have the child follow in their footsteps.

Such was the case with Bill who came to see Anne when he was about twenty years old. His father, a very successful automobile dealer in the Bay Area, knew that Bill didn't want to go into the auto-sales field, but since he had an interest in the healing professions, the father suggested chiropractics. Bill was in a quandary. He knew he had already disappointed his father by not going into the family business, but neither did he want to be a chiropractor. He knew that he wanted to work with people, but how he wasn't sure.

After mentally putting Bill in various professional settings, Anne was convinced that, yes, he belonged in the healing profession, but where? Thirty years ago Rolfing was becoming well established as a popular form of bodywork. In her mind, she put Bill in the Rolfing scene. He fit there better than in any other discipline. How did she know? She just "knew". Bill felt good to her when she put him in the role of a Rolfer. Now, thirty years later, he has evolved into an innovative member of the healing profession, having added other healing modalities to his original area of expertise.

Very early in her counseling career Anne had an intelligent young woman come for a session. She informed Anne that her education was as an international lawyer. As soon as Anne became quiet she could "see" that this young woman was not emotionally suited for international law. Instead, she saw a person in front of her who liked to cook. Anne told her what she was sensing, and the response was, "Oh, yes, I love to cook, bake—all that domestic stuff."

Anne suggested she bake some items and see if she could find an outlet for them and her hidden love and talents. Soon she was taking small catering jobs in the South Bay Area. Gradually, the jobs became larger; she began planning the entire affairs; invitations, flowers, decorations, as well as all the food and liquor. She truly became a culinary artist. So now, nearly thirty years later she is considering retirement from a highly successful career as one of the San Francisco Area's most innovative caterers. Within the last few years she has planned and catered two parties for us—Anne's 80th birthday and our 60th wedding anniversary.

Anne Keeps No Records

Anne has never kept a log or case notes on clients. To her, life is a fluid, dynamic process—humans are always changing, hopefully for the better. She feels that in most cases she gives her clients enough to work on for many months, and just so they don't forget what was talked about, she gives them an audio tape of the session. But she keeps no records for herself and hopefully, forgets everything about the session so that if the person comes back in a year, or so, she can start with a clean slate. Anne does her best to discourage dependency, feeling that an appointment once every year or so is sufficient, except in cases where the client is dealing with rapidly changing events.

Drug Counseling

Anne was just beginning her counseling as the drug-hippie era was getting into full swing in the mid-60's. Psychologists, psychiatrists, doctors, ministers, counselors of all kinds were beginning to work with people who were having adverse reactions to the indiscriminate, casual use of psychoactive chemicals. The professionals began referring to their textbooks for information and guidance, most of them never thinking of experiencing this fantastic state of consciousness for themselves.

So instead of getting a professional opinion, the client was getting a bunch of obsolete, rehashed opinions on psychosis, schizophrenia, and paranoia, and as usual the client's experiences were fit into some convenient box. Actually, most of the "professionals" knew nothing about the states of consciousness their clients had experienced.

Unfortunately, there were very few William James's out there who were willing to experiment with unusual states of consciousness. Instead, most of them hid in their inner sanctums and passed out textbook advice.

Fortunately, just as Anne was beginning to get seriously into her counseling work in 1964, she had an opportunity to meet and work with the directors of the International Foundation for Advanced Study in Menlo Park, California, and she had independently experienced the mind-altering capability of LSD. The Foundation had FDA authority to investigate the newly developed mind-altering chemicals until they began to be classified as illegal drugs. Anne had been experiencing altered states of consciousness for several years, and the effect from entheogenic substances was not that different. The major difference was that this one was chemically induced. So when she began to get clients, who for one reason or another needed help in clarifying a chemically-induced experience, she was in a much better position to do the counseling because of her own first-hand experience in both naturally and chemically-induced altered states of consciousness. To say, as the psychiatrists were doing, that these people were borderline psychotics or worse, was very destructive. Anne, and other professionals who had had first-hand experience with entheogenic materials were much better qualified to be advising others who had used these plants and chemicals. They were familiar with the environment these people had visited on their excursions into inner space.

In the fall of 1964 a handsome young man named John came to Anne for counseling. He was desperately seeking answers to the riddle of life, but like most of us he hadn't found them. Someone recommended that he talk to Anne.

He had a good education and had been a paratrooper stationed in Germany during the occupation. He was married with children and had a good "normal" job, but he was still looking for deep, philosophic answers to life. His "hobby" was removing large trees—ones that most other tree removal services considered too dangerous to remove from a crowded residential or industrial area. His other idiosyncrasy was ingesting psychoactive, entheogenic substances, hoping to find some of those answers he had so desperately been seeking for so long.

During their initial counseling session, he told Anne that he had taken approximately four hundred "trips" using various plant and chemical psychedelics, at times taking experimental doses that would have killed an elephant. His drug of choice was LSD. In her session with John she found him to be an intelligent, curious person with an insatiable appetite for the unknown, esoteric aspects of life. And at this point in his life it seemed to him that entheogenic substances might lead to some of the answers he was seeking.

Anne recalls that John was intense and dedicated, but there was no evidence that the wide assortment of substances, hundreds of "trips", and at times massive doses had in any way affected his mind or psyche. John's basic reason for talking to Anne over the years was to enlist her help in integrating his psychedelic experiences into his philosophy of life. It appears to have been useful because the next time she heard from him, he had established the first drug rehabilitation center in Sacramento and had assembled a huge staff, mostly volunteers. His abilities and drive came to the attention of the California Drug Commission and he was asked to join their organization. After a very up-front report on the activities of a "religious" rehabilitation organization made him a political liability to the state, he resigned.

Later when our paths crossed, John had been appointed as a juvenile judge in Nevada. After many years as a judge, he resigned and went back to his first love—removing maverick trees that no one else would even bid on. John's life certainly makes you wonder about the validity of the scare mongering by our government, the priesthood and the media.

Insights Into The Psychic/Intuitive Process

Since Anne's modus operandi is rather subtle, she is frequently asked if there are days when she is unable to make the necessary contact to do a counseling session, or if there are people with whom she just can't establish the rapport necessary for a successful session.

Even though Anne has not had a migraine headache since the early 1960's, at very infrequent intervals she has had a sinus headache or some other debilitating physical problem. I have heard her say more than once that she left her physical problem (headache) at her office door, went ahead and did a successful session, walked out, and picked up the problem at the door.

We were scheduled to do a five-day workshop at Esalen, starting Sunday evening. On Saturday Anne's doctor insisted she cancel the workshop because the doctor's initial diagnosis indicated Anne had pneumonia. Just to be sure she didn't leave town, the doctor gave her a Monday morning appointment with explicit instructions to keep it. Sunday morning Anne insisted she felt fine, and we made the five-hour drive to Esalen and started the workshop on schedule. Tuesday morning a medical doctor in our group came up to her at the morning break and said, "Lady, you don't have a cold, you have pneumonia." Anne's very quiet retort was, "Yes, but don't you dare tell anyone." He drove to Monterey during our three-hour lunch break, brought back serum, needles, pills and whatnot, and began to treat her. We finished the five-day workshop without a hitch. However, following this workshop we were invited guests at a five-day conference beginning Friday evening. During the conference Anne attended the morning and evening sessions but slept-in during the afternoons. She also asked to have her presentation delayed until the end of the conference. Again, no one knew she had a problem. My observation is that her intuitive information comes from beyond her brain/mind system and is affected only minimally by the current status of the physical body/brain/mind complex.

Energy Blocking

As to having problems working with particular clients, in 35 years and thousands of therapy sessions she can recall only two or three times being blocked by the person's energy.

In the mid-60's a mutual friend brought a young lady to see Anne; she had flown all the way from New York to Sacramento for the appointment. She'd had a disturbing drug experience and needed to talk to someone who could relate to what she encountered. However, when she sat down in Anne's office for the session, Anne drew a total blank—something that just hadn't ever happened. Anne didn't panic; she just "asked," "What is the problem and what can I do to help this person?"

The answer came to her, as do the answers to any other questions, "She is frightened, distract her."

Anne went into the living room and brought the client's friend to the room telling her to start talking to her. Apparently, when the client switched her attention to her friend, she dropped her guard and Anne was able to make contact. She said a few pertinent things and they got started. The session that followed was highly productive. Being the very responsible person that Anne is, coming all the way from New York applied a lot of pressure to do a "good job." For a moment she wondered if it was going to be possible, but the intuitive process delivers answers on all levels.

Psychic Shield

This psychic wall or shield can also be a learned, automatic response. Let me use the case of another of Anne's clients to explain. Several members of a man's family had worked with Anne and his name had frequently appeared on their tapes, so he was curious about this lady who knew so much about him without having met him.

Quite soon after his session began Anne realized that she was having a problem. She could tell him what his wife or daughters thought he was or wasn't, but she couldn't "see" what or who he really was. She tried many different tactics but they all failed. Pretty soon he realized she was having problems so he said, "You are having a problem seeing who I really am, aren't you? I think I can tell you what the problem is. For many years I was a member of the Mafia. We were taught how to shield ourselves, since most arrests are made on "hunches". But now I would like to be seen for who I am and I can't figure out how to drop that invisible shield." She never found out if he ever was able to let people really see him. Yes, black magic is still alive and well in organizations like the Mafia. It has served them well for many centuries.

Operating Rules

Anne was effectively pushed into the counseling phase of her life, so instead of looking for clients she has always discouraged as many people as possible. For one thing she has some hard and fast rules about what she will and won't do. Her first question when someone new calls for an appointment is, "Why do you want to talk to me?" If she doesn't get the answer she wants, she simply tells the person that she does not work in that area. And what are some of these areas?

To begin with, she obviously will not do medical diagnostic work since she is not a doctor. She might be able to tell the person why their soul chose this particular illness to get their attention, but someone in the medical professions will have to do the diagnosis and tell them what to do medically. She might even be able to assist in the choice of doctors—based upon their knowledge of that particular problem and their compatibility with this particular patient.

Another client with whom she won't work is one who wants to know about "past lives." If during the course of the session, however, pertinent events of a past existence present themselves, she will talk about them, but she will not go looking for them. I have often said in workshops that if you wanted a lucrative profession (and lacked scruples, of course) you would study a lot of history and historical novels and set up shop as a "past-life reader." You would have a constant stream of frivolous, curious people, and you would be perfectly safe, for who could prove you were wrong?

Another area that she does not work in is finding lost things and people. I have heard her say, "I can probably tell you why the person ran away from home or why they got themselves lost, but I don't think I can tell you where they are."

However, there are exceptions to all rules. We were eating our bag lunch beside an Olympic sized pool during our lunch break at a workshop in the San Francisco Bay area. A couple from the workshop approached us and asked Anne if she would help them find a contact lense that one of the workshop participants had lost while diving in the pool, a few minutes before. Anne just smiled and said she was no good at that sort of thing. A few minutes later she said to me, "I think I know where that lens is. Take me by the hand and lead me to the other side of the pool so I can stay in my intuitive state. About a third of the way from the deep end of the pool she suddenly stopped and pointed down to the bottom. I looked and all I could see were little moving shadows caused by the wind on the surface of the water—the bottom looked like a thousand contact lenses. No one else could see it either, so someone took three pennies from their pocket and dropped the first one where Anne was pointing. Anne indicated it was a little farther out; they dropped another, and from her directions dropped the third. Still no one could tell which of the quivering, circular shadows was the lost lens. Then someone wearing water goggles lowered himself slowly into the water so as not to wash the lens away and reached into the center of the now, triangular space defined by the three pennies and picked up the lens. Anne smiled and said, "Don't expect me to do that again."

It worked that one time because the conditions were just right. First, she had already disavowed her ability to find the item so the pressure to find it was removed, second, no one except me knew she was "looking" for the lens when we walked around the pool, and three, she had drunk a half a can of beer with her lunch so she was even more relaxed.

So it's not that this intuitive aspect of her being is incapable of consistently performing seemingly impossible tasks like finding the contact lens. It's just that the human personality is effectively incapable of giving up its desire to be right, which creates static that interferes with receiving and acting upon the very subtle, intuitive signals.

Another area that Anne shies away from is giving advice. She may have an idea about what is the best approach to take, but she tries to present the alternatives, advantages and disadvantages of each, and let the client choose. There is probably no such thing as a good or bad choice. Each way would present a different set of experiences, and who is to say which is best for that person's soul growth at that moment in time?

Unhappy Clients

Considering the nebulous basis upon which transpersonal counseling is founded one would expect a lot of dissatisfied clients. When asked, Anne says her accuracy is around 90 percent. So one should expect a certain percentage of disgruntled people, especially if most of that 10 percent inaccuracy occurred in one session. But in actuality only one or two people a year feel that their session has not been useful. Of course, just being extremely correct can also lead to a disgruntled client. The following is a good example.

Two or three of this woman's grown children had been Anne's clients, and a couple of months after their father died they arranged to have their grieving mother come for a session with Anne. After the woman had poured out her heart, weeping and crying about the recent death of her husband, Anne settled down and looked at the woman's situation intuitively. No matter how she looked at the situation she came up with the same answer—the woman's feigned grief was just a smoke screen—she was relieved to be rid of him. The problem now was how to say that in a way that it could be accepted. Apparently, in spite of Anne's skillfulness in wording it, the woman exploded, stood up and said, "Young woman, I did not come here to be insulted, my grief ridiculed, and my sincerity questioned!" and stormed out of the office. Anne felt terrible that the lady may have been honestly insulted; yet, the intuitive information was still clearly there—the woman was relieved that her husband was out of her life.

Three or four months later Anne received a phone call: "This is Annette, the lady whose husband died several months ago. I want to apologize for making such a scene when you said my grief was really a cover-up. You were absolutely right, but I couldn't face the fact that a 'good Christian woman' could feel that way. Then, to have you be aware of it was more than my ego could stand. What you did was a Godsend. I faced up to my feelings, changed my attitude, and my life is going fine. I have a new job, I have met a loving man and we plan to get married. So I want to thank you for your insight and honesty."

Becoming One With Another Person

Lisa's Daughter

Death of a loved one is always a difficult situation to handle. If the person has lived a good, full, long life, excessive grief seems inappropriate. Sure we are going to miss their company or counsel, but perhaps it was time to get on with the next phase of their life—the so-called afterlife. The death of a young person just moving into adulthood is extremely difficult to handle. It always seems such a waste to go through the growing-up process and never have an opportunity to live out a full life. However, when we stand back and look at the big picture, we realize that we don't know what the young person's script contained. Perhaps that is all the script called for, or perhaps the future looked so terrifying they felt compelled to leave before it really got untenable. A death wish can create an energy field that attracts a self-fulfilling condition. So be careful what you wish for, you just might get it.

While making our presentation at one of Stan and Christina Grof's month-long workshops at Esalen, Christina asked Anne if she could talk to a relative of hers who was at Esalen that week. The relative, Lisa, was in deep grief over the brutal murder of her 25-year-old, adopted daughter. The death occurred soon after Lisa's second marriage to her high school sweetheart, and the grieving was putting severe stress on the new marriage. Roxanne, the daughter, and her brother had been found as children buried under their dead parents after an Iranian earthquake. Lisa had been working as a nurse in the area where the children were rescued, and subsequently she obtained permission to adopt them. But the question that now haunted her was why, after being rescued and given another chance, was she murdered?

As soon as Anne became quiet she was aware that Roxanne had lived constantly with a death wish. Lisa recalled that she had drawn many pictures as she was growing up where death, misery, blackness were the central themes. When Anne merged with Roxanne so she could understand how Roxanne had felt during her short lifetime, she had the feeling that she shouldn't be alive; after all, her parents had died, perhaps while trying to save her and her brother. Anne said that as Roxanne she had the feeling that she always wanted to join the family members who had died.

Later, Lisa's brother who was more knowledgeable of the Iranian customs said that the people in the area where Roxanne was from were very family-and-clan-oriented. They felt it was unjust for some family members to be killed while others survived.

With this improved understanding of the situation, the grieving process on Lisa's part rapidly decreased. Soon she was able to again become an active participant in the new marriage. We have known them for many years, and although the awareness of the unfortunate death of this young woman is still there, it has not prevented them from getting on with their lives.

Jeannie's Ph.D.

Identifying with another person, as Anne did in working with Roxanne is not always so dramatic or life clarifying. Jeannie's case is a good example.

Jeannie was in the process of getting her third Ph.D. and the chairman of her doctoral program was giving her a real hard time, so she felt she needed to talk to Anne. Anne intuitively looked at the situation from various angles, but seeing Jeannie through the chairman's eyes was the most revealing. To begin with, he felt threatened by intelligent women, especially one working on her third Ph.D. This deep, subconscious fear was coloring the entire relationship. After due consideration of the "facts," Anne asked Jeannie how badly she wanted that third Ph.D. Yes, she really wanted it. Did she want it badly enough to play the dumb-blonde act for this chairman? Well, that answer didn't come as quickly. What was to be required of her?

Anne laid it out. Jeannie really had to play dumb. She had to make the chairman feel needed, that she couldn't do it without his help. Jeannie said that was too much for her ego to endure. However, after more discussion of the pros and cons, she decided to consider it. But just what did Anne really have in mind? Anne again "became" this professor to see what it would take to overcome his subconscious fears and prejudice. Anne's specific recommendation was to call him at home at all hours of the day and night about details of her thesis, ask his advice, make him feel like the great intellect, act and sound like the typical dumb blonde—really get into the part.

Jeannie left, still not sure her intellectual pride would allow her to humble herself in this way. In the crush of daily life Anne forgot about Jeannie's problem until about three months later when a Jag Coupe with the back seat full of flowers pulled up in front of our house. When Anne saw Jeannie get out and start carrying the flowers into the house, she knew the ploy had worked and she had her third Ph.D.

Distraught Mother

Another dramatic case of almost totally becoming another person occurred in 1964 soon after Anne began to do counseling. This very distraught woman came to Anne for counseling. Her 15-year old daughter wanted to go for a ride in a boy's, new, open-topped roadster. The mother and daughter quarreled; the teenager stormed out of the house in a huff and went anyway. The car skidded off a mountain road and her daughter and the boy were both killed. The woman briefly told her story; Anne suggested they be quiet for a minute or so, and then announced to the grieving woman that she was aware of her daughter's presence. A few moments later Anne became totally identified with the young woman who had been killed—she literally became her. Anne fell on the floor in front of the woman, put her head in her lap crying, "Mother, Mother I am so sorry for having been so impulsive." She then went on to tell her mother what happened after she stormed out of the house. She told her how much she really loved her and asked forgiveness for being so impetuous. Then she said to her mother, "Tell Anne about my poetry."

As soon as Anne finished delivering the young woman's regrets and apologies, the energy subsided and she returned to her normal self. After the mother recovered from the shock, she told Anne she would send her a book of the poetry her daughter had been writing since she was thirteen. As I write this, I have the book in front of me; as I read through it, my eyes fill with tears. Why did such a lovely, intelligent soul choose to leave so soon?

The mother left, sad but also feeling that she had one more piece of data. She knew her daughter's true feeling, and her love. Just knowing was going to make the burden lighter.

Experiencing Critters

The ability to "become" another person, animal or thing is probably Anne's most useful, spiritual/intuitive process. As discussed earlier, it was a skill she discovered very early in her development. I recall Anne and I going into the woods near Carmel, California, and sitting quietly until the animals accepted us as part of the environment and went on with their lives. Anne would put her awareness on a squirrel, for example, and will her consciousness to "become" that of the squirrel. Then she would very quietly describe to me what she was experiencing as she looked at the world from a squirrel's perspective. Next, she might "identify" with a blue jay sitting on a limb, his head cocked to one side looking at us, or perhaps "feel" like that huge hawk soaring in the clear coastal sky. Then an ant crawling on her leg would attract her attention and she could "experience" the world from his perspective or, just for fun, that of a pair of monarch butterflies mating in the warm Monterey Bay sun.

The Group Spirits

Although not as highly developed as humans, every creature has consciousness in one form or another. One of the interesting phenomenon that would happen on occasion was making contact with what appeared as the god or overlord of a particular species of critter—ants, bees, birds,etc., even worms. I don't recall her ever contacting that sort of being connected with the large domestic animals. Did you ever watch a large flock of birds flying near the ground? Thousands of birds will fly, turn, swoop and spiral as if they are a single entity, rather than thousands of apparently separate birds. They perform their intricate maneuvers as if they are being controlled by a single source of intelligence. That single source of intelligence is no doubt the group spirit.

Anne's most dramatic experience with one of these group spirits occurred many years ago, but it is still vividly etched in our memory. It was a cold, rainy morning in the winter of 1962. I was getting ready to go to work, and Anne went to the kitchen to start breakfast. I heard a loud, "Oh, no!" and ran to the kitchen to see what had happened. The sink and counter top, which I don't think had ever seen an ant before, was a black, seething mass of ant life. If we had even run the water to make coffee, we would have drowned a thousand ants. I suggested we leave the kitchen and go to the den, sit quietly and try to look at this situation from another perspective.

Within seconds after becoming quiet Anne said, "You will never believe what, or who, is standing in the middle of the room. He (it) is about 3 or 4 feet high and is the most exotic, elaborate, intricate being I have ever seen. It appears to be a composite of every beautiful, delicate, insect feature and color that one could imagine—and all on one creature. It has elaborate antennae; delicate pincer-like "hands"; gorgeous, multi-lens eyes; iridescent body plates; and in short, is the most exquisite being I have ever seen in any realm—physical or transpersonal. I sense that it is intelligent and friendly and is intimately involved with or knowledgeable of the situation in our kitchen. I have asked it why our kitchen has been invaded, something that has never happened in the 6 or 7 years we have lived here. I am being informed that the heavy rains have flooded the ant's homes under our house and they have lost their food supply."

Anne and I talked for a few moments and agreed that we would not go near the sink until 11 AM that morning. We would use the second bathroom counter as a kitchen sink, and we would put out a supply of food for the ants just outside the kitchen wall on the front porch. Anne communicated these concessions to our guest, and I returned to the process of getting dressed for work. Then she proceeded to use the other bathroom counter for a kitchen sink. She got our breakfast and set out an assortment of goodies on the front porch for our unfortunate neighbors.

A few minutes after 11 AM I called home to see if our request had been met. Anne reported that there were a half dozen stragglers wandering around the sink; the bulk of the invasion force had retreated soon after I left for work. They had found the food on the front porch and had busied themselves carrying it down through cracks in the concrete. That was the first and last time we ever had ants in the house.

We talked later that evening about the unusual happenings of the day. Anne said it was her understanding that during our meditation that morning, she had contacted the group spirit of the ants—the ant god, if you will.

The Standing Stones of Ireland

At times Anne just looks at something or touches it and instantly she begins to get pictures or information relative to the object, as the following experience illustrates.

A friend had driven us into some high, wild, uninhabited hills in Ireland to show us the Standing Stones that were scattered over the landscape. It was cold, damp, overcast and windy, but we got out and walked to some of those closest to the car. As we walked around a large Standing Stone we were aware of how much warmer it was out of the wind, especially when we put our backs up against the huge stone that earlier that day had been warmed by the sun. As soon as Anne cuddled up to this huge stone she began to get pictures of primitive people using these stones for some special purpose and she saw a huge man—at least 9 or 10 feet tall. The lady we were with laughed and said, "You have been reading our mythology." Anne looked startled, replying that she hadn't read anything but that as soon as she leaned against the stone she began "seeing" this huge fellow in some way associated with these stones. Our host said this big fellow, and she called him by name, figured prominently in the folklore of this area and these seemingly isolated, randomly placed stones.

Anne, as you can see, is an interesting travel companion. During our travels through such places as Europe, the Mid-East, and Egypt, she was frequently impressed by the history of the site we were visiting. Sometimes the information came unbidden, but usually when she or someone had asked a question. Most of the time what she said seemed logical, and at times other members of the group had information that corroborated what she had "seen" or sensed. Beyond being an interesting phenomenon it has never warranted any serious consideration.

Hands-On Therapy

For many years our daughter Christine suffered chronic back problems. She tried all the usual alternative therapies for back pains—acupuncture, massage, chiropractic, Trager, Feldenkreis, and anything else that she thought might help. Finally, in desperation she went to an MD. His prognosis was that she had a damaged disc that needed to be operated on. But before he operated she could try one more thing—an injection directly into the disc. He gave very little hope that it would do any good. It would require that she remain in bed at least 22 hours a day for two weeks.

Christine wanted to try the injection, but she needed a 24-hour a day housekeeper—perhaps her mother?

Anne agreed and told her to make arrangements for the injection as soon as possible. Up to that time Chris had never been amenable to Anne's therapy or healing approach. Anne hoped that with the threat of an operation hanging over her she would allow her to do something more than maid work.

The first morning after the injection they began before 6 AM so as not to interfere with the family's routines. They set up a massage table so Anne could conveniently work on all sides of her body. As is typical with Anne's way of working, she and Chris got into a meditative state and just waited for inner guidance. The first thing Anne did was to reach for Chris' right foot, telling her to be aware of any inner responses. Chris reported being 1-1/2 years old in the big house we had rented in Rapid City, South Dakota the first year I went back to college. An hour or more of heavy-duty therapy followed with Chris exploring feelings buried for over forty years.

The second morning they again began their therapy before 6 AM. After a short period of quiet, Anne again took hold of Chris' right foot

169

and ankle and told her to look at her life between the ages of seven and eight. Chris immediately began to get memories of friends and acquaintances of ours that she had not liked and again there followed an hour or more of intense therapy.

This same format was followed each morning for most of the two weeks. It was only after six days of intense therapy centered in various parts of Chris' body, that Anne finally touched Christine's back, the area that was giving her so much pain. Anne pushed Chris to self-discovery, only telling her enough to get the therapy/discovery process started.

After a week of this intense therapy the doctor declared his injection a success. And after two weeks Chris slowly began to return to a normal lifestyle, but this time with a much more comfortable back. Now, several years later Chris treats her back with respect, like using a back support when gardening all day, but the original problem seems to have disappeared. Was it the injection or the therapy? The doctor didn't think the injection would help, but he didn't know about the therapy. Chris is totally convinced that it was the in-depth therapy into her childhood that affected the cure. The other significant side effect is that the mother-daughter relationship reached a new high that has continued, only getting better.

Becoming One With The Machine

Intuition works at all levels of matter, so Anne can do counseling on a house, a business, or a machine. Frequently, a client will call Anne about real estate. They are considering an old house and they want Anne to "look" at the structure, plumbing and electrical wiring. She has had enough feedback to have confidence in what she senses. Sometimes there are enough positive aspects about the building that they buy it anyway. Then when they get into it they find the electrical, plumbing or equipment problems Anne had warned them about.

The Alfa Overhaul

I have had several first-hand experiences with Anne around my old Alfa Romeo. At about 100,000 miles it became obvious that the engine needed some serious work. So before I took the car to the shop I wanted to see if Anne could sense intuitively what was wrong with the engine. Anne is a typical driver. She knows that if there is fuel in the tank and you turn the key in the switch, it will start. Beyond that she has very little interest in engines.

This particular morning I asked her to sit in the front seat of the Alfa, and I gave her a crash course on internal combustion engines. I told her this particular engine had four, small, bucket-like things that went up and down inside tubes or cylinders. Above this bucket was a space that had two little things called valves that moved up and down. I further explained that the engine had two large parts: there was the block that held the cylinders and buckets and the head that contained the valves; and there was a gasket between the block and the head. Next, I explained that the up and down motion of the buckets, called pistons, was converted to circular motion through arms that connected to a weird-shaped shaft. This shaft went round and round in the lower part of the engine, and at each place where there was circular motion there was a bearing. I purposely kept it simple and vague.

I asked her to start at the front end and tell me what she sensed in that first area containing the piston, valves and gasket.

She said, "There are some circular things that go around that bucket-like object—one is broken, and one of those things above that pop up and down is rough and black around the edges. That gasket has a hole burned in it. Could there be water coming through it?"

I instructed her to go to the next compartment and "examine" the same objects and see how they "looked." Again she started with the piston and talked about the little things that went around it—they all looked good, no broken ones, and the little things that popped up and down also looked okay; the gasket between those large metal parts had a bad area but there didn't seem to be any water coming through it.

She continued describing the condition of the last two cylinder areas with the same detail, noting burned valves, broken rings, holes or no holes in the gasket. In two instances when she spoke of the ring around the piston being broken I asked her to examine the smooth, shiny surface next to the piston. Did it look OK? In both cases she said it looked fine.

Next I asked her to examine all the bearing surfaces where that weird looking shaft, the crankshaft, touched other moving or stationary parts. She said they all "looked" and "felt" fine.

I wrote down all the details, cylinder by cylinder. Then I drove the car to the shop and asked to have my favorite mechanic take the engine totally apart, carefully laying it out on a bench in the order in which it had been removed. That evening the shop foreman and I examined the parts. But before we started, I asked him to look at my notebook where I had written down Anne's diagnosis. He read it and then asked me where I got it. I said, "Oh, a friend of mine wrote it down. But now let's look at the engine parts."

We began by examining the parts from the front cylinder. There was a broken oil ring, the exhaust valve was burned, and there was a break in the gasket; the cylinder wall looked perfect. Bob said, "Where is that notebook you had? I want to look at it again."

The description of the second cylinder parts showed the same uncanny accuracy. Bob said, "I've been in this business for over twenty years and I'm pretty good at diagnosing what is wrong with an engine, but this is unbelievable. Let me keep that notebook while we look at the rest of the parts."

On cylinder three Anne had missed a broken compression ring, cylinder four had an area in the gasket that looked as if it could be leaking. The cylinder walls were as beautiful as the day they left the factory. You couldn't even feel the ridge usually caused by the top piston ring. Otherwise, the diagnosis of the top of the engine was as stated in the notebook. An examination of the bearing surfaces in the lower engine compartment indicated they were as good as new.

"Now, I want you to level with me," Bob said, "where did you get that information?"

I said, "My wife sat in the front seat; I explained in very general, layman terms how an engine works and what was inside, and then without starting the engine, I asked her to systematically examine the parts, cylinder by cylinder. I wrote down her remarks." He just knew there had to be a better answer. I knew that explaining to Bob how Anne worked was going to be more difficult than explaining to Anne how an internal combustion engine worked, but I tried. When I finished, he said, "Boy, could I use her around here!"

A year or so later the rear end of the old Mercedes began to make a lot of noise. Again I asked Anne what the problem was. She closed her eyes, got quiet for a few seconds and said, "There is a tube or rod in there and the thing around it is worn out." When I asked her why it was worn out, she answered, "That tube or rod is bent."

I drove the car into the shop and asked Bob what the problem was. He drove it, listened to it and concluded that the left axle bearing was worn out. I stood there while they pulled the axle and bearing. I asked him what had caused the bearing to wear out. He said it was very unusual and that he had no idea. I asked if it could be that the axle was bent. He said that in all his years in the Mercedes garage he had never seen a bent axle on a Mercedes. I asked if he had a lathe where we could chuck up the axle and check it for straightness. It turned out that it was at least thirty thousands of an inch out of alignment. He couldn't believe his own eyes. Again I told him I could take no credit for that diagnosis—my wife had closed her eyes, got quiet, described the problem in lay terms and told me what had caused it—a crooked axle. From then on Bob was a believer. He couldn't figure out how she did it, but he could see the results. Now he really wanted to hire her!

The Alfa Exhaust Manifold

Another time, after a $1,400 transmission job on the Alfa, Anne and I took the long way into Monterey from Carmel Valley which entailed going up a steep two-mile grade. As soon as we hit the grade I began to hear an intermittent sound as if there was a high-pressure gas leak. My first thought was a blown head gasket, but I didn't say a word. I downshifted, hoping it would go away or be drowned out by the engine noise. It continued. Finally, Anne broke the silence, "It's not the head gasket." I had hoped she hadn't heard it. Nothing more was said until we returned home. She got out to open the gate, turned and faced the front end of the Alfa and very cryptically said, "It's on a slant on the left side, the second one back from the front." She opened the gate and I drove into the yard, remembering what she had said: "...on a slant." Apparently she was referring to the exhaust manifold, but that would be a vertical surface. I waited until the engine cooled off, got a 12 mm, box wrench so I could check for a loose nut on the exhaust manifold, and what do you think—the exhaust, manifold, mounting surface on an Alfa Romeo is on a 45° slant because of the wide head to accommodate the overhead valve assembly. The second brass nut was already stripped. In my eagerness to get everything tight I stripped the far end nut. She was right, it was not a leaking head gasket, the second nut was stripped and the mounting surface was on an angle. I replaced the two brass nuts and from then on the engine sounded fine.

A Friend's Airplane

A friend/client of Anne's was preparing for a trip to Mexico in their private plane. As soon as Linda, the friend, mentioned the airplane Anne began feeling uneasy about the right brake/wheel/axle assembly. Linda told her it had been recently checked and there couldn't be a problem. But that wheel assembly kept catching Anne's attention as they continued to talk, so she mentioned it again.

When Linda got home she went out to the airstrip and found her husband. The first thing she said was that she knew what was wrong with the wheel assembly on the airplane. He countered by saying, "Yes, so do we, we just fixed it". The problem had been almost exactly as Anne had described it in lay terminology.

The Maintenance Engineer

Anne and I were doing a workshop in Boston many years ago, and during our introduction she mentioned how she did all of her counseling work on the telephone. Later on she talked about diagnosing mechanical problems on cars, airplanes and rocket engines.

A year later we returned to Boston to present another workshop. At the end of our introduction, a man held up his hand saying he had been in last year's workshop also. He went on to say that he worked for a large corporation that had complex machinery in many locations throughout the Northeast and that his job was as an expert maintenance engineer for the entire system. When something stopped functioning—day, night or weekends—his job was to get it running as soon as possible. After taking our workshop last year, he had modified his approach to maintenance. Now when a plant manager calls in with a machine down, he gets as much information as they have and tells them he will call them back in a few minutes. He instructs his secretary to hold all calls and no visitors. He then reviews the data, closes his eyes, becomes aware of his breathing, goes into a meditative state and asks for guidance. He then just sits and waits for intuitive flashes. He writes down the intuitive input and calls the plant manager back with his suggestions. About 80 to 90 percent of the time he saves himself a trip to the outlying plant, and the machine gets up and running sooner than if he had driven or flown to the site.

Anne Becomes A Rocket

As I stated earlier, my profession was rocket research and development engineering. We did just what the title says. We were presented with a need and we developed a missile that would fill that need. We researched possible approaches, materials and processes, and then designed experimental models, prototypes and finally a production unit that could be mass-produced. During this entire process we were constantly testing live units. That was expensive and time consuming, especially when there were malfunctions.

I recall the development of a small rocket engine for a top-secret mission of which I was the Program Manager. It was my baby from start to finish. This was pretty late in the defense buildup so we felt quite sophisticated. The plan was to design and develop a solid rocket engine with no money for research. Using state of the art components we effectively designed and built a production model planning to make an absolute minimum number of test firings. It sounded good in a board meeting but to an experienced engineer…well, to say the least I had my fingers crossed when we fired the first engine.

The unit was designed to run for about four seconds. When test-fired the internal pressure came up to the design pressure in approximately 100 milliseconds, then there was a loud explosion and the pressure dropped to nearly zero as the fuel in the unit continued to burn at near ambient pressure.

An examination of the malfunctioned engine and the scant test data indicated that the unit functioned as designed for 100 milliseconds until the graphite throat shattered, dropping the internal pressure to near zero. I ordered the hardware sent to our shop, the test data to my office, and I went home to think.

When I walked in Anne could tell that the day had not gone well. All the way home I mulled over the meager facts, but they didn't make sense. That nozzle design was being used in production units that had been tested hundreds of times with never a failure. Why now?

I took Anne into the den, sat her down, and this time I gave her a crash course in solid-rocket engine technology, similar to when I wanted her to look at the Alfa Romeo engine. I told her, in effect that we had a tube about 15 inches in diameter and four feet long, filled with rapidly-burning, solid fuel and a restriction at one end called a nozzle that the hot gasses passed through as they escaped from the very hot, high pressure space inside the 15-inch diameter tube. To start the fire inside there was a big match called an igniter. At the zero point on the countdown this igniter would inject a white-hot flame the length of the tube to light the entire surface of the propellant and bring the unit up to operating pressure for the next four seconds. At that point the fuel is totally consumed. Then I suggested that she "become" that rocket engine for the first 100-150 milliseconds, and tell me what she observed.

She became quiet for a few seconds, took three or four deep breaths and allowed her consciousness to "become one" with the rocket engine we had test-fired a couple of hours earlier. She said, "I am inside the rocket engine, I'm aware of the hot flame igniting the propellant...isn't that what you call it? Then I am aware of something rushing down the inside of the tube, striking the back end, returning very rapidly to the front end and then very rapidly repeating this cycle from end to end."

My mouth flew open in amazement. My wife, who had never seen an operating rocket engine, was describing the high frequency, burning syndrome in perfect lay terminology. We had high frequency burning and the powerful shock waves that it creates had shattered the hard, brittle graphite nozzle. Now all I had to do was to "back into the data," to prove Anne's discovery.

The next morning I sent a rocket-engine assembly and a set of chamber, core and nozzle drawings to the high-frequency laboratory asking them to analyze the unit for possible high-frequency burning characteristics. Late that afternoon a call came from the lab, "If you had designed the length over diameter ratio of the initial free space in the unit to create high-frequency burning, you couldn't have done a better job." We replaced the brittle, solid, graphite nozzle with a laminated, carbon, fiber nozzle, and except for a slight slope in the burning curve caused by nozzle erosion, there was little change in the performance. The analysis of the problem had been correct: the change of nozzle material had corrected the problem.

Before the unit became operational, the program was scrapped because of a biological warfare treaty with Russia. I hope they did the same with their delivery system.

A Bit Of Humor

I think a chapter as serious as this one should have a bit of humor to bring it to a close. In the late 70's we had sold our house and bought a large two-story condominium. Anne's office was just down the hall past the formal dining room. Most of the time, as we did that day, we ate in the end of the large living room next to the kitchen. It happened that we had a guest for lunch and were not quite finished when the doorbell rang. It was Anne's 1:30 PM appointment. Anne put the client in the office, telling her we were a bit late with lunch. She had seen us eating when she came in and could still hear us from Anne's office down the hall.

After our luncheon guest left, Anne joined her client in the office. As they were sitting down to begin the counseling session Anne could feel the tension in the room. The client was someone she had seen a few times before, so it wasn't that she didn't know what to expect. Anne assumed that the tension she felt was the person's reason for making the appointment, so she didn't say anything.

She settled back, closed her eyes and relaxed after a very pleasant, lively lunch, and was just getting ready to speak when the client erupted. "I just don't know if I want to talk to you—I never thought of you eating!" She got up, picked up her purse and said, "I don't want to talk to you," and stormed out the door, never to be heard from again.

PART TWO:

Kundalini Process

CHAPTER VIII:

KUNDALINI
BACKGROUND

"I do not wish to cause you pain. You are part of me, and I am part of you, but I have a job to complete, and I need your cooperation to facilitate my energy in your body. My desire is to connect your physical being with a whole other part of yourself, so that at some point in time you will become complete. And, unfortunately, the process is painful, at times. My preference is to do this through understanding. The distractions of the world have enticed you away from the major theme of your life, so if pain and discomfort are the only ways of getting your attention . . .well, then that is the way it must be. I will keep trying until your soul and I find the best approach. Perhaps the best way is to re-write the script so you understand at the deepest level that you are a Divine Being making temporary appearances in a physical vehicle. To help you remember who and what you are; let me say that your true Home is a realm beyond your wildest dreams; and that you are an inseparable part of this energy that you call God. But right now look upon me, Kundalini, as your closest and dearest friend—so close that I can't tell where I leave off and you begin."

Kundalini's Playground

Kundalini—an enchanting Goddess who plays by her own rules. Everyone who has experienced her caress has a different story to tell. Perhaps it is because we humans have free will; we are all different; hence, her program is different for each one of us; or perhaps it is because our sample size is so small that the pattern hasn't yet emerged; or maybe it's because fourth, fifth or sixth-dimension rules are incomprehensible in a three-dimensional world. Whatever the reason, when Goddess Kundalini begins to "shower her blessings," you feel that somebody is making up the rules as the game is in play; or it might be that there are no rules, as we understand them, and that part of the process is learning to function in a realm where three-dimensional rules do not apply.

Since this is an unscientific document, as I'm sure you have discovered by now, I intend to review the only set of data I can vouch for, and let you, if you are so bold, draw your own conclusions. However, before we begin to consider the data, let us briefly discuss Goddess Kundalini's playground, the chakra system as viewed by Kundalini Yoga.

When one looks at the major religions of the world from an esoteric viewpoint, it becomes clear that they all evolved from a common source. The original prophet or teacher, of course, had some cultural biases, and the succeeding followers and organizers also built in theirs. Within a few generations that group had developed a typical exoteric philosophy. Fortunately, these cultural biases differed, so humanity has had many religions and philosophic approaches from which to choose.

The cultures of India and Tibet, especially the esoteric sects of Hinduism and Buddhism, developed philosophic systems that stressed individual spiritual growth. These esoteric branches constantly improved their spiritual practices by incorporating insights from non-ordinary reality. Although many ancient cultures were aware of the chakra/Kundalini energy system, the cultures of India and Tibet currently possess the greatest storehouse of wisdom concerning this system. So in this very brief discussion on the chakras and Kundalini (both of which are Hindu and Buddhist terms), we will draw heavily upon the writings of the East for theory, nomenclature, practical knowledge, and techniques. If you are not already aware of the Goddess, this very brief discussion on the chakras and Kundalini energy, hopefully, will be enough to whet your interest into further study of the subject. Please refer to the bibliography for a few basic texts in English.

The term chakra is a Hindu word that literally means wheel. Clairvoyants of all cultures, when viewing the subtle bodies of a human being, are frequently aware of spinning vortices of colored energy. The Hindu yogis and Buddhist "holy men," apparently through clairvoyant research or soma-induced states of consciousness, determined that there were seven major vortices of energy positioned along the central axis of the body, beginning at the perineum, or the base of the spine (depending upon the authority being quoted), up to slightly above the head. The classic drawing of a yogi sitting in meditation, Fig. 1., shows the relative positions of the seven chakras. At times the Tibetan Buddhists refer to the two chakras in the head, the Ajna and Sahasrara, as one center, and the Muladhara and Svadhishthana as one center. In this brief discussion, we will describe the system most often used in India, China, Japan and the West.

Let's start at the bottom of the chain of centers and move upward. In most of us the chakras would be perceived as wheels of light or local auras of various colors, probably quite different from a yogi who has spent years meditating and living a "holy life." Our discussion will include the colors traditionally associated with the various chakras. Frankly, in my reading over the years, I have found a considerable variation in the colors that the experts assign to the various chakras. Any particular set of data, no doubt, is strongly influenced by the spiritual development of the observer and the observed, so I wouldn't take the color data very seriously.

The relative positions of the seven spiritual centers, according to the Kundalini Yoga tradition, are illustrated below.

Muladhara Chakra:

This is *the* first spiritual center, located in the area of the coccyx or perineum. In classic Tibetan Buddhist and Hindu drawings, the latent primordial force, the serpent, represents Kundalini, with three-and-a-half coils around the Lingam in the center of a triangular Yoni. The reported colors associated with this chakra vary from yellow to red. Physiologically, this center is linked with the sacral plexus that controls the organs of generation.

Svadhishthana Chakra:

This is the second spiritual center located three or four finger widths below the navel, sometimes referred to as the abdominal center. The color varies from white to vermilion, probably depending upon the development of the person observed. This chakra is physiologically associated with the plexus hypogastricus and the inner organs of secretion **and reproduction.**

Manipura Chakra:

The third chakra is located in the vicinity of the navel, frequently referred to as the Solar Plexus Center. The colors observed from this chakra vary from red to blue to green. Its physiological counterparts are the plexus epigastricus and the nutritional system.

Anahata Chakra:

This fourth spiritual center is located near the intersection of the median line of the body and a line connecting the nipples. It is also called the Heart Chakra. The colors attributed to it vary greatly from gray-blue to red or golden. The physiological counterparts are the plexus cardiacus, the heart and circulatory system.

Vishuddhi Chakra:

The fifth spiritual center is located in the throat and is frequently referred to as the throat chakra. Again the colors associated with this chakra vary from white to violet. The physiological counterparts are the plexus cervicus and the respiratory system.

Ajna Chakra:

This is the sixth spiritual center, usually considered to be located between the eyebrows. Actually this is the outer manifestation of the activation of the pineal and pituitary glands by the rising Kundalini. It is commonly known as the third eye or the head chakra. When fully activated it is said to appear to a clairvoyant as a white light of great intensity. Physiologically this chakra is associated with the medulla oblongata and the non-volitional nervous system.

Sahasrara Chakra:

This is the seventh spiritual center and it is located at the top of the head, or perhaps slightly above. It is frequently referred to as the Crown chakra or the Thousand-Petaled Lotus. Tradition has it that when the Gate of Brahman in this chakra is opened, one can leave the physical body at will and enter the transpersonal realm. The physiological counterparts are the brain, including the pituitary and pineal glands, and the volitional nervous system. This chakra is perceived as a sphere of golden or rosy light, extending a considerable distance from the head of a highly developed person.

The Nadis:

The Kundalini energy is said to flow through the chakra system in conduits called nadis. There are said to be many thousand nadis, but only three are of primary importance to the chakra system: the Sushumna, the Ida and the Pingala. (Refer to Figure 1.) The Sushumna is said to be in the central channel of the spinal cord, extending from the coccyx to the Gate of Brahman in the Thousand-Petaled Lotus.

(It is represented by a vertical line through the center of the body.) The Ida and Pingala, according to ancient writings, start at the left and right sides of the Muladhara, proceed through the chakras and terminate at either nostril. Efforts to closely link the chakras and nadis with anatomical components of the physical body have not been very successful. A study of ancient texts has always indicated that the chakra and nadi systems are associated with the subtle bodies, and that their function is to act as transformers and conduits of energy. There is, however, a significant correlation between the nadis, the meridians, and points in the acupuncture system, but that is a whole other subject not pertinent to our current discussion.

The above brief description of the chakra system will serve as a basis for the discussions that follow. However, if this subject is new to you I would suggest you read Energies of Transformation, a Guide to the Kundalini Process by Greenwell, (see Bibliography). It is a great book for the person who needs an introduction to the Kundalini Process. All the material that follows presupposes a working knowledge of the Hindu and Buddhist theories related to the chakra system.

Introducing Miss Kundalini

Kundalini, even more so than other phases of spirituality, is difficult to discuss. I have recorded many discussions about Kundalini that Anne has intuitively obtained. However, I find them difficult to paraphrase in terms that satisfy the human thirst for factual information.

Kundalini, like most aspects of spirit, can only be discussed in metaphors—it does not lend itself to physical description because it is not a physical "thing." And I frankly believe that attempts to treat Kundalini as a biological, physiological thing is always going to fall short.

Anne, as well as many other investigators who have firsthand experience with Kundalini, has spoken of it as an "entity", just as we are a spiritual entity that also has an evolutionary path to follow, and a function to perform in the universal plan. The other aspect that investigators, including Anne, have observed about Kundalini is that it is a female entity, or energy. Many times Anne has had the discourse presented by this beautiful-beyond-words female figure that calls herself

Kundalini. In India she is spoken of as Krishna's Shakti, the female aspect of Creation.

This energy, also frequently referred to as a "flame", is composed of a particular type of energy different from any other in the body. Most of us accept that everything that exists is a part of The One, and yet that Oneness in this case has chosen to separate itself into many segments so it can occupy a place within each living thing—plant, animal and human. However, the highest expression is found in humanity. In this way there is a simultaneous, ongoing development in the many lifewaves.

Our responsibility, our duty, is to clear ourselves to the best of our ability so this flame within will encounter the least resistance or fewer obstacles as it moves up the spine. Humanity's major task is to become aware of this energy and clear the path, as one would clear the banks of a river to allow for the free flow of the stream, so it can rise smoothly from the base of the spine to the top of the head.

The spiritual centers or chakras have existed as long as Man has had a physical body, and the work of developing the system is a continuous process whether in or out of the body. Although the work during the "death" phase may be of a different nature, it is still a continuation of the same process.

Originally, Man had spiritual centers below the root chakra that no longer exist. Apparently, they were associated with a very early development reminiscent of the crudest of energy, and states of consciousness we have long since outgrown. One such chakra existed between the knees and another between the feet or ankles. I have seen reference to seven lower chakras, the Muladhara being the uppermost one. However, at our stage of development these obsolete chakras are only of academic interest. Clairvoyants who have experienced mankind at that stage of development have reported a grossness that defies description. They say it makes our vilest thoughts and deeds at this stage of development seem near divine in comparison. Andrija Puharich talked about experiments he did with a very capable clairvoyant.

Now let us examine the energy of the root chakra. This center contains both the negative and positive aspects of the creative energy from which our bodies have been constructed, and will continue to be constructed. Currently, we are interested in perfecting the physical form, and the root chakra can be looked upon as the foundation and the source of the basic building materials for this project. Apparently, a specific type of energy, containing both the positive and negative aspects, was developed for our particular lifewave so we could operate in a world of polarities.

As we postulated earlier, this Kundalini energy is really an entity that has undergone an evolutionary process to arrive at its present state, where it can assist in the development of our particular lifewave. Much of the development I'm speaking about occurred in the very early stages of our evolution, some even before we had a physical form. It seems to be a symbiotic relationship. We give it an environment in which it can develop, and in turn it assists us in our development. So it is a composite of everything we have ever been, and through it we have a memory of everything we have ever experienced. This "energy" is a vital, living entity, not significantly different from our own lifewave and eventually through it we will become aware of all other existing states of consciousness—those that have existed in the past, and will exist in the future—for this is a growing, evolving essence or energy.

Mankind's role in this symbiotic relationship is creating the conditions whereby the energy can readily rise from the root chakra to the head chakra. This is our contribution to the evolutionary path of this energy/entity. Then at some distant point in time, this same energy will go into a different state of consciousness, perhaps into another lifewave and continue its individualized path of development. The spiritual centers themselves are storehouses of energy that help lift the root chakra energy from center to center until it reaches the head centers—its goal.

Everything we do touches these spiritual centers. We are the guardians. In effect, it's like being in control of a tremendous source of electricity. And by our attitudes, our acts, our words, our thoughts and feelings we either close the gate on this energy, or open it so it can be utilized. The energy is already there, but through our free will we will learn to activate these centers and release their energy. If these centers are not activated, the spiritual energy will lie dormant at the base of the spine, having no way to express itself.

Perhaps this energy at the base of the spine is similar to "Universal Mind", from which we all came. To seek individualized expression and find its own evolutionary path, it fragmented and became a part of our lifewave so it could experience, grow, and evolve through our spiritual growth. So this is truly a symbiotic relationship, and in the process everyone wins.

It is frequently asked if there are specific formulas, programs, or rituals to follow that will bring about the activation of the chakras and the lifting of this root chakra energy. No, none of these are necessary. However, by becoming aware of the responsibility we collectively and individually have taken onto ourselves, we begin to live our lives in a manner that stimulates the spiritual centers, which in turn generates a field of energy that begins to activate the spiritual fluid at the base of the spine. Then very rhythmically it writhes its way up through the spiritualized body until finally it reaches its goal in the head center.

There was a time, even before Atlantis, when simply by thinking we were able to lift this energy to the head center. But as we became more and more steeped in materiality, the spiritual centers became heavier and denser, until the impulse was lost, and effectively the centers became dormant. The energy drained back into the receptacle at the base of the spine, where it remained for a very long time.

Mankind in general during this period was literally separated from this entire state of consciousness, so in recent millennia our project has been the redemption of this energy. The spiritual centers can be looked upon as a road map back to the Godhead; and as we begin to take this work seriously we realize that every thought and every deed becomes a part of the process.

As we have progressed, the spiritual centers have become more refined and have begun to rotate smoothly in a clockwise direction. This action has begun to pull the spinal energy up through the various centers, but not necessarily in sequence.

Since the spiritual centers were active in the development of the various subtle bodies that we operate through, some chakras developed ahead of others. The "root chakra", furnished the foundation and building material for the physical body; the solar plexus center was active in the formation of the desire or emotional body; and the head center was involved in the development of the mind body. Right now most of humanity is working its way through the throat chakra—the center of the will—so the heart energy can move into the head center, thus integrating the love force with the intellect, something that is long overdue.

I believe our goal at this stage in our spiritual development should be to develop all the centers more or less equally, creating a balanced system whereby this Kundalini energy can move freely through the entire system.

Meditation and certain visualization exercises are particularly valuable in activating and developing the various chakras, and encouraging this highly specialized energy to freely circulate through the centers. Meditation teaches us to control and quiet the mind, and the visualization of this energy moving up the spine convinces the mind that it is really happening.

Mankind's spiritual development moves slowly forward age after age. The Egyptians worked with this spinal energy for thousands of years after the fall of Atlantis. Then during the last couple of millennium the esoteric branches (the "secret societies") of the major religions have maintained an awareness of the importance of the development of the spiritual centers and the Kundalini energy. The Tantric traditions of India and Tibet, Taoism of China, the Hebrew Kabbalists, the Sufis of Islam, the Rosicrucians, the Alchemists, Freemasons, and other "secret societies" of Christianity, are a few of the esoteric groups that have kept mankind aware of the Kundalini energy. Even the Mayan culture of Central America had Quetzalcoatl, the feathered serpent, obviously associated with the serpent energy in the spine. References in shamanic cultures may not always be that obvious, but there is no doubt that the entheogenic drugs, drumming and other rituals made Kundalini known to them in various ways. And now again at the end of the 20th Century and the beginning of the 21st Century there is a resurgence of interest, especially in the West, in the continued development of Kundalini. Therefore, it is to be expected that the transpersonal realm is inspiring certain individuals to bring forth wisdom relating to the activation of the Kundalini energy and the conscious awakening of the spiritual centers.

Kundalini Speaks

In this esoteric field, the Kundalini energy has always been surrounded by a great amount of mystery. Whole books have been written warning of the dangers of prematurely awakening this energy, especially without a guru or spiritual master. It was the activation of Anne's Kundalini in 1959-60 that brought about her dramatic physical healing and spiritual awakening. In Anne's case the activation of this energy seemed to be under the guidance of some inner or transpersonal teacher. Apparently it was the resistance to the natural opening process in 1943 that caused Anne's discomfort for many years prior to 1960. However, since 1960 we have been very respectful of the Kundalini energy, and have consistently advised our workshop participants that they do likewise, and the same goes for the readers of this book.

In the late 1970's Anne and I developed, with transpersonal assistance, a series of chakra exercises to use with groups. During the recording of some of the basic material associated with the root chakra, Anne gave voice to the energy (or entity) that presented itself as Kundalini. Since Kundalini has been consistently referred to as feminine energy in occult or esoteric literature, we have always jokingly called this "Miss Kundalini's Soliloquy!"

> "If I appear reluctant, when you begin to re-direct me to the higher centers, it is because I wish to experience the most powerful expression of which I am capable. So I ask, how am I to be used? If I am to move up the spine, will I be given the proper encouragement and dedication that is necessary for me, Kundalini, to achieve my purpose? If this is not a serious intent there will be reluctance on my part to even listen. For I want to express myself in the most powerful way. At a personality level I really have no preference as to how I express myself—at the sexual level or as illumination. I am energy and I want my potency to be used in its entirely.
>
> "However, at a deeper level I realize that I too have a purpose. My purpose is to energize the chakras and create a course from the base of the spine to the

top of the head through which I can travel easily and harmoniously. To be allowed to do this will bring me the greatest pleasure, for I would feel that my potential had been acknowledged. But it takes a lot of courage to court me and interest me in moving up the spine. If the effort on your part is going to be feeble I am not interested. I want to experience my full potency. I know that if I remain solely as a physical or sexual expression I will not grow. So, I want to be recognized and acknowledged for what I represent, for I too wish to blossom and to fulfill my purpose, as well as the purpose of those who are willing to focus their attention on me and their spiritual centers.

"There is always a calling from the higher centers for my energy, so I know I am very important. But regardless of the intensity of the call, I cannot fulfill the request unless the path through the intervening centers is clear. To jump from the root center to the head center can be a powerful experience—possibly a very negative experience—for if the vehicle is not prepared, the nervous system can literally be shattered. I represent power in many different forms so I need to be awakened gently, but firmly. To be awakened I need to be acknowledged for who and what I am, and for what my ultimate purpose is. And then I need to be wooed gently.

"Now, I would like to have you visualize me as a seething mass of very powerful energy. Be aware that this energy can manifest in many ways: The power to fight for survival; a powerful sexual potency; or as a ribbon of light that has the power to move up through the centers to the head and to create a state of illumination. Visualize me in my most aesthetic sense—a white lotus blossom that is gently opening, petal by petal, to reveal the center and the dormant energy contained therein. I have been pictured as the sleeping serpent, but I prefer the lotus blossom. Visualize this lotus blossom at your root chakra slowly opening, petal-by-petal. Once it is open, "see", a stream of energy being emitted from the center of the blossom. "Feel", this energy welling up at the base of the spine. Now follow the stem of the lotus blossom down into the earth. Realize that the root chakra is a center where earth energy is transmuted; that the energy of this center is a combination of your own energy, and the energy of the earth.

"Picture this energy any color you like. Now allow this stream of energy to very gently move up the right side of the spine like a ribbon of light. Be aware of your breath. Imagine that the breath is gently drawing this energy up the spine through the various chakras. Just "sense" this ribbon of light slowly moving up the spine, and realize that it is not to be rushed.

"When this ribbon of light has reached the head center, let it rest there for several breaths. Just be aware of its presence as it encourages the mating dance between the pituitary and the pineal glands—the head center. Now allow the momentum of this ribbon of light to carry it back down the left side of the spine to the root chakra, making a complete cycle. Each time you visualize this ribbon of light completing this course you reinforce the resonance between the root chakra and the head chakra, so they can begin to work in unison.

"Remember, I'm your closest companion—as close as your breath—I'm Kundalini."

If you wish to become better acquainted with "Miss Kundalini," practice this simple little exercise several times a day—it only takes a few minutes. It is a good way to develop an awareness of the energy at the base of the spine.

Spiritual Centers

From 1960 to 1967 Anne and I regularly sat together during our daily meditation. Once or twice a week there would be a bit of personal information for us that we usually recorded. This recorded wisdom has become our way of life for the past forty-five years and the basis of the teachings in thousands of workshops and seminars that we have presented since 1964.

In previous discussions about the spiritual centers, or chakras, we talked about them developing a color and a tone, as one gets deeper into the chakra work. I'm sure the mere fact that we are privy to this discussion indicates we have done sufficient work on ourselves to activate the sound and color connected with each center. So let's discuss the path that this energy follows in the subtle vehicles associated with the human body, and how this movement is brought about.

A spiritual practice is not complicated. In fact it is quite simple. It begins with the sound vibrations we create when we speak, which includes the thoughts and feelings we have every moment of the day. On a very subtle level, each word, thought, and feeling carries its own color and sound vibration. So a spiritual practice begins by being aware of every feeling we have; by being aware of every thought we have; being aware of every word we speak (and the way it is spoken); and every action we perform with our body. That is where a spiritual practice begins. It doesn't begin with a bunch of spiritual or religious rituals. Awareness on the level just outlined is simple, though probably the most difficult thing we will ever attempt. But we have no choice; there is no other place to begin. We must start with an awareness of what we are doing with our lives. We must become acquainted with every detail of our lives to date, and every attitude, thought and feeling, and how they are affecting everyone in our environment. We do that by becoming aware of the significance of the different energies connected with our emotional patterns. Then through an act of will we begin to bring our lives into the balance that we now know is necessary—a balance of purity, clarity, and truth. So this is where the work begins.

My editor has again reminded me that I have written the same thing before—probably more than once—yes I know! And, if appropriate I may write it again. If you get no other wisdom from this book except the essence of this last paragraph, your time will have been well spent. On a conscious level we begin to align ourselves with all aspects of the truth. By discrimination we learn to set aside that which is not truth, to the best of our ability. As we work with this process we find we are moving closer and closer to a pattern of alignment, which of course is the purpose for following this path.

I would like you to visualize or imagine a human body with the spiritual centers glittering like jewels, each one with its own degree of brilliance and color. Don't worry about what shape or color someone else says they should be. Just imagine the different centers, and allow them to be whatever shape and color they choose to be. Now be aware of a thought pattern entering the environment of this human form. The emotional pattern registers upon the mind, the mind breaks the pattern down into stimuli, and the spiritual centers begin to respond to these stimuli. It is similar to what happens in a piano when a note is struck, (and the damper is released) the note being symbolic of a thought pattern. The vibrations of the note travel across the strings, resonating with strings tuned to certain other frequencies that are harmonics of the original tone. So not only the original string is affected, but all those strings whose frequencies are harmonics of the original tone. And so it is with our own thought process. The reverberations of a single emotion are nearly endless. So here is where the will intercepts the spiritual path—we begin to control the thoughts and emotions that we allow to enter our mind/body complex. Normally, the untrained mind allows the entirety of any thought or emotion to enter, causing the whole being to respond, and as a result each center becomes activated. But when through practice and awareness we learn to control the way a thought is received, we allow only the essence of the thought to enter the system. In this way only the centers involved with this thought pattern or process respond, and the other chakras in the system are unaffected. Thus we become selective of the emotional material or impressions we take into our systems. This is a primary lesson for each of us to learn, and to practice every moment of the day. Because if we allow random impressions to enter the mind/body complex, and affect the entire emotional system, involving all the spiritual centers, we collect unuseful energy patterns and store them in all the spiritual centers.

There comes a time when we must clear each center of these random stimuli, until they register only that which is truth. Most of us, when we start upon the spiritual path, find these chakras overloaded because they have been collecting data or stimuli that is not pertinent to their function, all because the mind process was not organized and controlled.

Through the practice of meditation, organized thinking, and greater awareness we begin to methodically stabilize, and therefore cleanse, each one of the spiritual centers.

We have always been told that the spiritual essence rests at the base of the spine, and when the spiritual interest is awakened, and we consciously set about the task of lifting that essence from the base of the spine to the head center, the spiritual journey begins. But before this spiritual essence can reach its goal in the head center, the channel must be cleared. Therefore, most of the "weeds," in the form of emotional patterns, discord and imbalance must be removed before this spiritual essence can make its way into the head center.

This clearing process begins with "knowing", not just being intellectually aware, or believing, but "knowing", beyond a shadow of a doubt that the spiritual counterpart of ourselves, the Monad, is already perfect. No matter what fate befalls us during this physical life, we must never lose this realization. It must be indelibly etched into our consciousness that "spiritual attainment" is already ours. It is only the realization of this status that we need to accept within ourselves.

Now be aware of the cell structure of the physical body. And remembering the pictures in an anatomy or physiology book, imagine or visualize this cell structure.

This is where the conflict with the concept of "already being perfect" begins. The cells of our body seem to have been etched with the concept that we must really struggle to attain spiritual perfection or illumination. The cells keep chanting this message, playing it over and over again until our minds become so conditioned that we believe all these steps in the spiritual process are necessary to attain perfection. However, in this moment in time, these steps are necessary, because we do not seem to be able to make the transition from this mental set to the state where we are already perfect. It is, therefore, hoped that some place along the path we will accept this realization, and eliminate some of the steps. But since we are so conditioned we devise game plans by which we go step by step to attain illumination. So our job is to design a game that will satisfy the cells (the mind) while making giant strides to close the gap as quickly as possible, but at the same time, realizing it is only the limitations of the mind that are keeping us from accepting this premise.

Meditation is probably the best game plan yet devised to take these giant strides toward that ultimate goal. The problem is, that most of us don't know how to enter into meditation, or what to do after we get into that relaxed, quiet state. To begin with, meditation is not to be looked upon as "work" toward enlightenment. Meditation is something that one does just because it is there to be done. It's like the question to the mountain climber, "Why do you want to climb the mountain?" "Because it's there." Meditation is the same—it's there. Meditation is not something you do for thirty to forty five minutes a day; it is a state of awareness that one carries with them every waking moment of the day. And how does one maintain this awareness all day? By being constantly aware of one's thoughts, attitudes, feelings, words and deeds. Another thought in passing, is that after becoming relaxed and quiet in an attitude of meditation, realize that you are already perfect. Then keep that thought with you throughout the day. So now let's return to the spiritual energy at the base of the spine.

Since we live in a realm of duality, energy seems to be divided into the positive and negative, the two making the whole. This seems also to be true for spiritual energy. Hinduism speaks of positive and negative energy in the spine. We also know that the spiritual energy and the sexual energy are the same—both creative energies.

As you are reading the next few paragraphs, I suggest you visualize, experience and sense what is being discussed. Let's begin by being aware of the spiritual essence at the base of the spine. Actually, begin to "feel" its warmth, because it is a "flame". "Feel", "sense", or "imagine", that this energy is divided into positive and negative aspects. Then "see", or sense this energy being lifted from the base of the spine, dividing into its two aspects at the pelvic area, each tracing a pattern of light like a butterfly wing and coming back together at the spine. "Feel" its warmth for a moment, realizing it is a flame, and that both aspects are again one. "Sense" it, continuing up through the spine until it divides again in the area of the solar plexus. Here the two aspects encircle this spiritual center—one energy going clockwise, the other counter-clockwise, and again joining at the spine. The returning energy again moves up the spine to a point between the shoulder blades. This is an area where many ganglia and their spiritual counterparts are concentrated. Here the spinal energy again separates and the two energies encircle the heart chakra, one clockwise, and the other counter-clockwise. The returning energy enters the spine, combines and moves upward to the throat chakra—the seat of the will. Pause here and again realize that you are perfect and that you have always been perfect. Realize, also, that through the effort of the will you have lifted the spiritual essence in the spine and traced the butterfly wing patterns just described.

This is as far as it is advisable to move this energy at this time. But by repeating this exercise during meditation we mentally burn away confusion, and much of the residue stored in the spiritual centers by the thought stimuli we have allowed to invade our emotional body. It is through the mental process just described that one can burn away the misused energy stored in the spiritual centers. However, the only way these centers can remain cleansed is by being so completely aware that one does not repeat the same mistake again. For if we perform these exercises during meditation but continue to allow the mind to receive and store useless impulses of energy, the unuseful emotional patterns and residue will return. The positive energy we have generated by the exercises will be erased by the negative energy we allow to return through our emotional binges. So it is very important to become aware of our attitudes and emotional patterns.

As we continue to refine our thoughts, emotions and attitudes, and to maintain this kind of balance in our lives, another very interesting and beautiful phenomenon begins to occur. Within one of the etheric bodies (I believe it is the vital or astral body) a vine-like structure begins to appear. At first it is very faint, but more and more substance is added as one becomes increasingly aware. In time the spiritual centers become beautiful, open flowers on this vine-like structure. A suitable climate for the growth and final blooming of this "vine" is created when we begin to rid ourselves of destructive emotional patterns. It would definitely help if we would begin to "see" ourselves as gardeners tending this very beautiful, exotic plant, "knowing", that our feelings, thoughts, words, deeds, and attitudes will give this plant life, or destroy it.

Now be aware of the circulatory system, the blood in particular. An involvement in a spiritual program of this magnitude actually begins to change the chemistry of the body, especially the blood. The cleansing process begins when the negative attitudes and thoughts are removed or radically changed for the better. Even the color of the blood begins to change as debris is removed from the subtle bodies. Spiritual development is a hybridization process. We are starting with something that is very earthy; then we begin to refine it by introducing these higher principles, thus changing the structure of the system. It's not a tangible process, something we can measure with a pair of calipers, but a very subjective procedure producing quite obscure results.

If the reader is serious about walking the spiritual path, it is recommended that they follow the procedure outlined above for the next few weeks, morning and evening. Remember to be especially aware of your attitudes and thoughts throughout your entire waking day. It is not something one does just during meditation, but it is an awareness that one attempts to maintain throughout the day. And above all, remember each moment of the day that perfection is already yours. Basically, what a spiritual practice does is open the door to the realization of that perfection.

Highlights of Anne's Kundalini Opening

For these discussions on Kundalini I am going to use Anne's personal experience since that is the only one we are intimately familiar with. I would like to say that her experience was typical, but there is no typical Kundalini experience. Anne's misery, over thirty years of it, came before the last opening. But since this opening, her health has only become better. Perhaps she was lucky that the thirty years of ill health left no permanent scars in her body. We have all the issues of "Shared Transformation", a newsletter or journal that, among other things, is a mouthpiece for current day Kundalini recipients. Nothing that I could write would do justice to the misery that people have had and are experiencing as a result of Goddess Kundalini's "caress." Sometimes when I finish reading a new issue I lay it down, with my heart and stomach in a spasm, and thank God that Anne emerged unscathed from thirty years of suffering. Migraine headache victims have remarkably strong, healthy, young-appearing bodies—a medical verity—and once the headaches went away, so did the other maladies, except for almost perpetual tiredness, she is still in excellent health. Anne's transition, once it began to unfold was so smooth that I don't think she was really convinced that she'd had a classic Kundalini opening until she read

Swami Muktananda's book, *Kundalini, the Secret of Life*, about twenty years ago. In the earlier chapters of this book we made several references to Anne's spiritual or Kundalini opening. However, since the references are scattered over many pages it will probably be advantageous at this point to sequentially relate her entire Kundalini process, even at the expense of some repetition.

Up to 1959, the term Kundalini had no particular meaning to us. We had seen it in classic books on Hinduism but we had nothing to relate it to (we thought), so it made no impression. In early 1960 we began to study books on Yoga so we could identify the asanas and intricate breathing patterns that Anne was performing spontaneously. However, to fully understand Anne's Kundalini opening it is necessary to start our story in 1942, a few months after we bought a home in Farmington, Utah, 17 miles north of Salt Lake City.

My Aunt Geraldine, whose books got me interested in Eastern philosophy when I was a teenager, moved to Salt Lake City in 1941, and it was through her that we started attending lectures on Rosicrucianism (The Rosicrucian Fellowship in Oceanside, California). We became interested in the philosophy, which is an aspect of esoteric Christianity, and purchased Max Heindel's book, The *Rosicrucian Cosmo-Conception, or Mystic Christianity*. Along with the book we subscribed to a series of lessons-by-mail based upon the material in the book. It might be useful to note here that this current organization is based upon a lifetime of clairvoyant research by Max Heindel, and is following in the tradition of the Rosicrucians of the Middle Ages, an attempt to preserve esoteric Christianity. Before their members went underground during the inquisitions, many were persecuted, tortured and killed as heretics by orthodox, organized Christianity. The alchemists were also dedicated to preserving esoteric Christianity. They hid their philosophy behind or within their alchemical experiments. The transmutation of lead to gold was symbolic of the transmutation of the common man to a god through the refinement of the mind, body and spirit. We found the study of modern Rosicrucianism to be quite fascinating, as well as enlightening.

Anne and I studied The Rosicrucian Cosmo-Conception, and completed and mailed in the lessons for many months. Meditation and visualization were standard practices that went along with the reading and studying. As I mentioned earlier, Anne had more free time than I did to practice meditation and spiritual exercises. Within a few weeks she began to feel lightheaded and dizzy after the meditations, but wasn't concerned. Then one day while meditating she realized she could "see" herself—her body—from a position near the ceiling. She felt totally present in that awareness near the ceiling, and completely detached from her body, which was still seated below, meditating in the chair.

It suddenly occurred to her that she might not be able to get back into her body, or worse yet, that she might already be dead. Needless to say she panicked, and in an instant was back in her body, her heart racing and unable to catch her breath. From then on every time she got into a meditative state she began to feel a spinning sensation, then a loud roar, and a moment later there was dead silence, and she realized that some aware part of her had again separated from the physical body. Again there was the panic, and rapid re-entry into the body. Something similar happened any time her mind became fixed on a movie or a lecture. However, in those cases the split was horizontal, and I would see her looking first to one side and then the other, trying to determine which was the real body and which the double. Any time she lay down to go to sleep the separation would begin. If I were there she would cuddle up very close and go to sleep. If I were working the night shift at the airbase, however, she stayed awake until I came home, even if I didn't get home until 8 AM the next morning.

The sense of having two equally real bodies, one physical and the other ethereal became an on-going condition in addition to the sensation of floating a few inches above the ground, creating more instability. Anne consulted a Salt Lake City doctor. He told her she was neurotic, and gave her pills and shots to clear up her condition. If anything, it made conditions worse. Finally, one day in desperation she said, "Before I started all this esoteric study and all these visualizations and meditations, I had my regular illnesses—migraine headaches, asthma, hay fever and back problems, but at least I was functional. I'm going to stop all this spiritual nonsense and go work in my garden." And that she did. Gradually, over a period of months the dizzy, unstable, floating sensations went away. However, her previous illnesses became intensified and new conditions began to appear. A year or so later, I quit my job with the Air Force. We sold our house, moved to San Francisco, and I joined the Navy. I was promptly placed on inactive duty and assigned to Pan American Airways. Pan Am had a contract with the Navy to do repair and maintenance on their pacific air transport fleet.

Within six months we moved into a two-bedroom house just south of San Francisco near the airport and rented the second bedroom to Carl, another Navy man. He had been part of the Rosicrucian group in Salt Lake City so he shared many of our interests. One of our common interests was the human aura. Carl's immediate goal was to build an electronic instrument that would detect the aura, record its location, and hopefully its intensity. Anne had been aware of her ability to see auras ever since her abortive meditation experience in Utah. Carl had proven to his satisfaction that Anne could see auras, so now if he could design and build an electronic instrument that would do the same, they could be used to substantiate each other. As mentioned in a previous chapter, Anne was able to detect changes in my thought pattern by observing my aura against a color-neutral background. The data was very reproducible and we felt it would make a good check against an electronic instrument. But one night we put our experimental instrument in our car so we could take it to the instrument shop the next day, and during the night someone stole our car. That was the end of the aura research. Since that time Anne has lost her ability to physically see auras, however, infrequently she reports sensing a person's aura intuitively rather than seeing it.

From 1943 until the fall of 1959 we lived in a purely physical mode—going back to college, becoming established in a profession, raising a daughter, owning two more homes and all the attendant householder duties that one has in our busy society. During all this time Anne's health was deteriorating. She had migraine headaches three to five days a week, as well as bouts of hay fever, asthma, back problems, a goiter, endometriosis and I'm sure, others. In spite of these problems she kept up her household duties as well as becoming deeply involved with the Brownies, Girl Scouts and Summer Camp.

Then in the summer of 1959 a family moved in next-door and the wives found they shared a common problem—migraine headaches. A month or two later the next-door neighbor gleefully reported that she had been cured of her headaches, and strongly recommended that Anne get an appointment with her doctor. When Anne found that Phyllis's psychiatrist had used hypnosis to uncover the problem, she simply refused. All the esoteric literature we had read warned against hypnosis. However, her fears were allayed and she soon found herself back in the meditative state that she'd been avoiding for nearly 16 years. True, brainwave studies show hypnosis and meditation to be different. But there are enough similarities that Anne picked right up from where she'd left off many years before. Only this time she had a therapist who knew what was happening, and I was not only sympathetic and informed but I was willing to work with her in any way she needed me.

The apparent past-life therapy that Dr. Irene Hickman and I did with Anne seems not only to have furnished a key to the cause of Anne's headaches, but it held her attention long enough for the real Kundalini opening to begin. For the first 6 or 7 weeks Irene and I always used a hypnosis routine to prepare Anne for a therapy session. Very rapidly Anne began to add accomplishments to her already remarkable ability to recall past lives. She found that she could do psychometry, controlling her consciousness in various ways such as projecting it into objects, people and animals, and was beginning to sense other realms of consciousness. Then one day about six weeks into the hypnotherapy I was sitting with Anne discussing the interesting things she was able to do in the hypnotic state. She looked at me and said, "I'm doing those things right now without being hypnotized." From then on, when she wanted to enter that state of awareness for therapy or to perform one of her other psychic/intuitive functions, she would simply relax, close her eyes, take a few slow, deep breaths and quickly settle into an aware, conscious, yet altered state of awareness. She was always totally conscious when she did therapy or other intuitive tasks.

During those first 6 to 8 weeks of therapy, there were no outward signs of a Kundalini opening. Her health was improving, her spirits were high, and she was excited about all the new things that were happening to her, so when during meditation one day a very clear "voice" directed her to set aside one to three hours a day for training, she complied though she had no idea what she was training for. Up to then, everything she had done had been a positive experience so what could it hurt to see what this "training" was?

In hindsight we realize that the real Kundalini opening began with directed training. As stated in an earlier chapter the work began with conscious, aware breathing, rapidly becoming more and more complex. I recall Anne showing no signs of breathing for several minutes, while at other times her breath was extremely active. Soon she began to spontaneously perform yoga asanas, asanas not discussed in locally available yoga books. One in particular that I recall was called "Moving in the Void". An advanced yoga book described it as a technique used by Kundalini practitioners to stimulate the flow of an etheric elixir from the head chakra to the heart chakra.

At about this point in the process Anne became aware of the director of this training program. A beautiful Hindu, white turban and all, appeared about 18 inches above her head, and a little to the right. All she had to do to make contact was put out her hands, palms up in a mode of supplication, look up to her right and there would be the face of this beautiful guru smiling at her. Mr. M, as she called him for lack of a better way of addressing him, was there for any request she had—her own Genie, only he wasn't in a bottle.

The training continued week after week, becoming ever more rigorous and complex, the asanas and breathing patterns continually changing. I was amazed at her agility in spite of her forty years. And all the while her intuitive skills were constantly increasing in number and accuracy. It was during this period that Anne, Al and I conducted the consciousness-shrinking experiments where she did molecular-structure and inner-atomic investigations, just for practice.

Al was a fellow research engineer from work. He had previously been an engineer on the Manhattan Project—the development of the atomic bomb. I don't recall how he found out about Anne's unique abilities.

Irene and I continued our therapy with Anne, unearthing more past life material and working with the imprints that her childhood experiences had made on her psyche. Anne was rapidly gaining control over her new found skills of clairvoyance, and that sense of just "knowing". Although she was able, at will, to visit other realms of consciousness, it was only on rare occasions that she would have what might be called a transcendental experience, with the feeling (knowing) that everything is One; the system is perfect; and with the elaborate visions of celestial landscapes, and the vivid colors and cosmic sounds. But when these experiences did happen the joyous yet wistful longing for those realms lingered for days and made our world look like a Tinker Toy exhibit.

Along with the intricate breathwork and complicated asanas, came endless discussions on right living, eating, sleeping, thinking, emotional attitudes and control, morals and ethics, much of which was just plain good common sense, but it sure bore repeating. What now seems interesting is that I don't recall ever hearing the word "Kundalini" in any of the instruction material that Anne received that first year for her own training. That indicates to me a lot of moral, ethical, emotional, mental, physiological, and psychological work needs to be done before one even thinks about so-called "spiritual work." That may be why so many people have problems with abortive Kundalini openings. They get the cart ahead of the horse. Anne was without a doubt in a self-improvement course for the soul. But along with all these extremely interesting happenings, she was carrying on her normal everyday activities as Girl Scout Leader, Camp Director and mother to a ten year-old daughter.

Speaking of a ten year-old daughter, there is one bit of advice we would like to pass along to other parents:

Handle a spiritual awakening in the family the same way you talk about the subject of sex with your children. Tell them as much as they can deal with. Keep them informed and don't try to keep it a secret or avoid it. We made the mistake of not talking about what was happening, and the lack of communication led Christine to speculation and erroneous conclusions that stayed with her into adulthood, even coming up in her own therapy. In spite of it, however, she is now a fine psychotherapist in private practice.

In about six or eight months, the intense training, apparently under Mister M's direction, diminished and one day he just waved goodbye, as much as to say, "You are on your own."

One of the intuitive areas Anne moved into very early in her development was delivering profound spontaneous esoteric lectures. Many of the lectures that she delivered less than three years after her first therapy session, are as fine as anything she has ever done. Many have been published in The Azoth Journal of Esoteric Wisdom. This high level, esoteric lecture work continued through 1967. By that time the Friday Night Group (FNG) had disbanded, Anne was starting to do more workshops at Esalen and other growth centers and her private counseling was taking a lot of her energy. We considered the lecture material recorded during the FNG sessions to be for the group and ourselves (as well as a few special friends with whom we had worked over the years).

So up until we began to publish The Azoth Journal of Esoteric Wisdom in 1995, we simply used the material for reference, drawing upon it for meditations, exercises and background for our workshops, as well as our primary source of spiritual guidance. The exceptions were the dozen or so unedited lectures that were reproduced on tape for workshop attendees.

As time went on we began to fully appreciate the wisdom in those spontaneous lectures, frequently finding material in them that is found in no other reference I am familiar with or the references, if available elsewhere, are so veiled or vague that they are effectively useless. So what follows is a composite of wisdom garnered from Anne's spontaneous lectures recorded for our own use between 1962 and 1967 and from another series recorded between 1993 to 2002.

Ancient Hindu and Tibetan Buddhist texts refer to the Kundalini energy in the spine, but much of it is written in metaphors that seem to hide rather than reveal the truth of this illusive energy or force associated with spiritual development. Even recent books by Gopi Krishna and others seem to generate more questions than answers. The material we have compiled over the past forty-four years also leaves a lot of unanswered questions, so if anyone has any answers please send us your references and we'll see if we can fill in some of the missing pieces in this Kundalini puzzle.

CHAPTER IX:

KUNDALINI PHILOSOPHY

The Basics

At least once a week for years Anne has received a call from someone having very bizarre physical and emotional experiences that their doctors and psychiatrists can't diagnose or cure. All the client knows is that they want it to go away—can Anne rid them of their problem?

After several minutes of discussion it frequently becomes obvious that they are being nudged by Miss Kundalini to begin to take note of their own spiritual development, and the last thing Anne is interested in is "taking it away." She wants these people to realize what is happening to them, hoping that understanding and acceptance will start to relieve the symptoms. This person's resistance to creating a balance in his or her life has caused the problem in the first place, and since this may be a several-lifetimes condition, it will probably take more than a few weeks to turn the situation around. God only knows how many centuries they have insisted upon a purely physical existence with little or no thought about truly spiritual matters. While they may have gone to church on Sunday, Monday morning it's business as usual—nothing morally, ethically or spiritually has changed. They are the same physically oriented person they were on Friday or Saturday evening. So it is time, actually past time, to start thinking about the spiritual aspects of life.

A few years ago, after talking to Anne about the rash of Kundalini cases that she had been getting, she suggested we "sit" together and see if Consciousness had any wisdom that could be passed along to these new, Kundalini recruits.

Kundalini's Dilemma

After being quiet for a minute or so, Anne began to talk and here is what she said:

> "I have asked that I be given specific information that I can pass along to people who are interested in the Kundalini process or are having preliminary Kundalini experiences. The first impression I get is a "timeline" that relates to this on-going saga that we refer to as "life," as we move toward greater awareness. There seem to be markers on this timeline referring to steps of self-development. First, mankind had to master the physical realm. The experiences we have gone through appear to me as building blocks necessary to construct a proper foundation, one that was psychological as well as physical, upon which our quest for higher knowledge could rest. And looking at the timeline, it has taken a very, very long time. But as a whole, this lifewave has finished laying the physical, psychological, and emotional foundation, and is now ready to awaken to the next level of consciousness—one that has lain dormant in many of us for eons. And this awakening is being spearheaded by Kundalini in the spines of an increasing number of members of this lifewave.
>
> "Most of us have done a masterful job of placing these foundation blocks so we could live successfully in the physical world, but we appear not to have had the intelligence or inner wisdom to see that the physical phase was only one step in a long on-going process. The intellect has, however, become very creative

materially, and instead of moving upward, it has spread laterally until the foundation is immense. I see how our mind has become involved in peripheral situations that are far beyond what was appropriate. It has been a battle between what was a natural progression and the inventiveness of the physical mind. So instead of seeing that shifting to the spiritual journey was the natural progression, we have gotten sidetracked using all this creative energy for purely physical purposes. It would have been much better if some of that creativity had been used for refining the Kundalini energy and lifting it smoothly up the spine. True, the mind has created some very wonderful things, but at the expense of not staying focused on our true nature, of not staying focused on who and what we are, and the path we are to follow. I have the feeling that this energy has been so dispersed that, as a lifewave, we are hardly aware that there is a specific direction to be taken, namely, to clear the path that allows the Kundalini to begin to freely move up the spine. But there have been so many other fascinating things in the world that catch our attention! So we continue physically building a better world, but because we've been distracted, we forget to include our own inner spiritual development. I feel that we were meant to use some of that constructive energy to build a channel for Kundalini. Instead, we have become sidetracked on all these wonderful "things." So in a sense, we have lost the map and forgotten that we have the responsibility to move forward and use our spiritual energy—Kundalini—as well as our intellectual/physical creativity. This physical playground has been great fun, but we have forgotten that its main purpose was to help us find our way back to the Source, back to God.

"Along with the various energies, mankind was given freewill to do whatever it felt needed to be done. However, the hope of the gods was that our spirit's or soul's purpose would always parallel what was happening in the world, and that somehow we would listen to the more subtle energies. But instead, we have been attracted to that which was the most fascinating, and which served us in the most practical way. It would seem that the 'committee' underestimated the willfulness of a lifewave with freewill! We appear to have lost our sense of balance and been trapped by our own creativity, not realizing that as we developed the outer we needed to develop the inner. And that does not appear to be happening.

"This lack of balance is reflected in the excessive violence and crime we are experiencing in our "civilized" societies; the spiritual has not kept pace with the material. We have tapped into great power, but the spiritual balance has not been maintained. We misguided ourselves by believing that this material development was the solid, scientific, and logical path to pursue. So it would seem that the original intent of our creativity has been over-shot, and we have lost our way. It's as if we had two paths to choose from, and we have chosen the most glamorous way to build a 'better world.' This energy that is Kundalini has been pushed aside, and to make its presence felt it has had to do some pretty dramatic things in the hope that we would become aware of its potency. It doesn't mean that we shouldn't use our creativity to build a more pleasant, comfortable place to live; it only means that there is a parallel path, that if included, will, at the same time, maintain our connection with God. It was intended that in spite of free will we would have the wisdom to recognize the other path and continue to build the inner strength by raising this other energy up the spine to the top of the head. Then eventually, we would not only have a better physical world, but we would have developed the most precious energy in our mind/body/spirit complex—this energy that is truly our 'gateway to freedom.' For it is only through the spiritual use of

Kundalini that we can finish our work on the earth plane and eventually return to the Godhead.

"The image I am aware of is a fearsome energy mass, almost like a thought-form, representing our mental/intellectual state, completely out of proportion to the energy that has been allocated to the lifting of Kundalini. We seem to have lost sight of the fact that we are spiritual beings having a physical experience. It is important to enjoy this physical life, but we shouldn't forget that the basic purpose for being here is to achieve some degree of illumination, not forgetting the Source that we came from, or our responsibility to our Divine Self. It was not intended that we would get so involved in this fascinating physical world that we would forget our true heritage.

"We are just not using this energy in the proper way. We sense this power within, but we have lost sight of its liberating force. So I believe we will experience much more physical, mental, and psychological pain until we recognize that there are other ways to advance than through the intellect. Most of us are just lost, wandering around, using our creativity and energy to build wonderful new "things," but leaving behind our most precious possession—the map of the route the Kundalini energy will follow in the spine. However, when the intellect that we have exhibited in the physical world merges with the creativity of Kundalini, we will have an unbeatable combination. It is as if the energies inside us have become confused. Creativity is alive and well in the lifewave, but for thousands of years we have equated creativity with developing more and more 'things' in the world of form, because that is where the recognition has been. In the meantime, Kundalini has been ignored.

"We have forgotten that there was a dual path we were to take—to glorify the earth and to find our way back to the Godhead. We have put so much energy into the physical that we have completely ignored the Kundalini energy that was also to have been incorporated into our sojourn upon the earth. Kundalini is the epitome of creativity. And since nearly all of us have ignored Kundalini's energy, she has devised an endless number of ingenious ways for getting our attention—all sorts of common and exotic illnesses, many for which our medical establishment can find no cause or cure. No, she isn't being sadistic—just trying to get our attention. It appears that the soul is willing to use any means to awaken the personality to its parallel path of creativity.

"Unfortunately, pain is the most effective means of communication yet devised to get a human being's attention. (It took 33 years of migraine headaches and a number of other illnesses to get my attention.) Unfortunately, the majority of people have never heard of Kundalini; and if they have, they have no idea how they are blocking its flow. Our constant attention to creation in the physical realm has effectively shielded us from the energy that is ultimately 'our gateway to freedom.' Until we recognize and honor the presence of Kundalini as a component of our physical and energetic bodies, it will continue to push its way up the spine in a desperate attempt to raise our level of consciousness. Unfortunately, Kundalini uses up much of its energy confronting our psychological and emotional situations and in attempting to get our attention so we will wake up. One of the results is a great deal of confusion and a feeling of having lost the meaning of life.

"It is being made very clear that if it is deemed necessary to eliminate disturbing elements in our environment that can no longer be tolerated by consciousness, it can and will do that also. So this refining process can become difficult and harsh if we don't learn to lift that energy up the spine to its rightful place in the head.

"I am now aware of "seeing" this energy pouring like rain from the transpersonal realms, but since we do have free will we can use it any way we choose. It can be used as sexual potency and personal power (as many of our leaders have done, and are still doing) or for varying degrees of illumination, with hints of sexual and personal power (as has been the modus operandi of a wide range of current gurus), or for full illumination and transcendence.

"With the current increased flow from the transpersonal realms, the opportunities to misuse this powerful energy are greater than ever. This energy has always been confused with personal power because Kundalini energy at the root chakra level is a powerful sexual and survival force. The same energy can be used to create unbelievable havoc or the illumination of a Buddha or a Christ. It is up to us individually to use this potent energy wisely, for en masse, humanity has created spiritual chaos with its misuse. In spite of this, Kundalini, like God, will never abandon us. It is there to serve us, and to guide us back to the Godhead. But to use this energy fully we must become aware of its presence, its unlimited creativity, and the basic purpose for its presence in our spine.

"Simply stated, Kundalini's purpose seems to be: to glorify the earth, to glorify God, and ultamately to return humanity to its "Source". Unfortunately, it seems that it is only through pain that many of us, in time, become aware of the blessings of Kundalini. Hopefully, in time, the masses can be taught the truth of Kundalini and spiritual development, thus sparing humanity untold suffering. The question still remains: Do we have the intelligence to wake up?

"Kundalini has charted its course in every member of the human race, but lamentably the path has become twisted and blocked. Our souls keep crying out, "Wake up! You have a job to do". And really all we have to do, when the time is right, is to create the proper environment inside ourselves so Kundalini can move rhythmically up the spine. Until we awaken, however, to the responsibility with which God has entrusted us, we won't have the means to end the pain caused by believing that we are lost and disconnected from God. We have never been disconnected from God and we never will be, but it is a common belief when things get very rough. We may have lost the map, but all that is needed to correct our course is for us to awaken to the realization that we have the guidance within to return to the Godhead—the Source from which we came. We are like lost children, crying out for help, not realizing that the answers are within us. Actually, the map has never really been lost, but it takes a certain degree of awareness just to recognize that. Just as it is in everyday life—we may go for therapy for twenty years, but sooner or later, we have to do the work ourselves. There is no other way. The answers are within ourselves; all we need do is learn to listen. So just remember: We have never been lost, for we are still searching; we just need to continue the search in the proper quadrant, for we haven't, and never will be, abandoned; we have only become distracted.

"As human beings we contain two levels of energy— the physical and the spiritual. And it seems to be our responsibility, or at least one of our tasks, to blend these two energies so the human race can continue to evolve. It must be done on an individual basis, for that is the way we grow spiritually. As a group, mankind has placed more emphasis on the physical because that is what is more readily available, and that is the realm in which we function more easily.

"The best way to bring about the blending of these two energies is to become well established on the physical plane, and then begin to obtain information about, or from, the other levels of consciousness (which incidentally are also a part of us).

"Information from these other levels of consciousness is similar to spotlights that illuminate certain areas of our lives making them available for use at the physical level. However, we must maintain a balance, neither too involved in the physical or the spiritual. In most of us there is a whole other part of the self that needs to be brought down and incorporated into the physical level. Only in this way does the physical body become capable of greater things. And I want to say it again— potentially, all these other so-called spiritual levels are within us, but it seems that we must have an awareness that they are there before we can incorporate them into our physical/mental/emotional-structure.

"Now I see Kundalini waltzing toward me as a ribbon of beautiful light. She is saying, "I am the link that brings the physical and spiritual realms together. It is my responsibility; and I have chosen as my abode the base of your spine, because my initial assignment is to make you fully aware of the physical realm, to activate the root chakra, and to devise ways of dealing with and surviving in the material world. It is just like building a house. First, you must construct a firm foundation for your structure. However, it is very easy to become stymied at this level and just keep extending and improving the foundation for lifetimes.

"We see this everywhere in our physical world today. We have spent entirely too much time expanding the physical base so we can feel safe and secure on this earth plane. Survival is important but perhaps we have overdone it. Shortly after we are born, we are impressed with the importance of creating a physical foundation—a healthy physical body, an education and learning coping skills for survival. Then after 12 or 14 years, the sex hormones kick in and a whole other level of physical enticement and survival instincts become manifest, and we begin making more adjustments so we can live comfortably in the physical world. All of this leads us more and more to forget that place we just recently came from and the reason for this sojourn on the earth plane.

"Slowly we work our way through the survival stage (the root chakra); then we move up to the social/sexual phase (the second chakra); and then up to the emotional phase of life (the third or solar plexus center). It is not until we reach the heart chakra that the inspiration to seek higher states of consciousness re-enters our beings. In spite of all this logical progression there are some big gaps between the root chakra and the heart chakra. This seems to be where all the psychological garbage and just "stuff" are stored or filed as we make our way through life. And literally no degree of illumination can be experienced until we push our way through these psychological barriers, we, ourselves, have created by the way we have related to our parents, teachers, and the world around us. This is where we have stored all the things we have learned: the methodology we have developed to relate to the world, how we behave in our environment, and how we have learned to acquire and handle power. This is the large gap sensed between the root chakra and the heart, the no-man's-land we get lost in during the early phases of our lives. Some people never escape from it. This is where we develop our psychological format. This is where we try out ways of surviving, coping with our environment, getting ahead in the world, finding our power, and unfortunately for most of us, this is where we have become so psychologically 'screwed up'. And it is during this time that we make decisions about how we are going to apply our power, and how to respond to other people's power.

"This is about the time that the mental level begins to wake up and wants to participate. The mind force is very powerful compared to the instinctive nature that has been operating through the body for the first two decades. At about twenty, the mind suddenly decides to take charge. Now the mind, or at least a part of it, is very connected to the earth plane, so is strongly survival oriented. And because of the similarity of goals, the mind and the body become allies—the mind becomes the director and the body the response vehicle, the doer. At this point, the mind begins to challenge the Kundalini that has begun to rise from the base of the spine. Symbolically, they are like boxers in a ring with the soul as referee, saying to Kundalini, 'Don't abandon me because I am the part of us that can guide us through this life so we will stay balanced and grounded, very necessary attributes on the earth plane. Survival is important but at the same time we need to have access to the transpersonal realm, a part of our heritage.

"There are these two opposing forces, the mind with the power of the physical realm behind it, and the Kundalini energy that is subtle and fragile—the logical directive energy of the mind in opposition to the feeling, more knowing energy of Kundalini. At about this point in the struggle for control of the body/personality, the intuitive aspect of the mind says, 'Don't forget that I am available and that I am an ally of the Kundalini energy. I am the part of the mind that encourages humans to open to the subtle spiritual realms of non-ordinary consciousness, the role I will continue to play during this physical existence.

"The intuitive aspect of the mind wants to join forces with the Kundalini energy. Again we are dealing with a subtle force, one that is not as aggressive as Kundalini, yet is capable of taking a stand. So depending upon our awareness, our body can become a battleground for these opposing forces.

"Not too many years ago this internal conflict would have been looked upon as a left brain/right brain battle, but life and our physiology are just not that simplistic. Instead it seems to be a conflict between the highly polarized aspects of the mind: The purely physical, logical, linear aspects at one end of the spectrum concerned primarily with survival of the species, and the other extreme that "knows" it is an aspect of Creation; therefore, is eternal, all powerful and all knowing, truly an attribute of God. Naturally, what we are dealing with in this lifetime is a watered down version of these two extremes.

"It appears that the linear, logical aspect of the mind and the energy in the lower three chakras are basically interested in the survival of the physical vehicle and the development of the material aspects of life while the intuitive aspect of the mind and the energy of the upper chakras, the heart chakra and above, are interested in the development of the spiritual nature of man. And so the battle continues. The worldly people around us say that the most important aspect is survival, and to assure it one must be streetwise, powerful, and cunning. But if we were to look at it from the heart chakra's viewpoint, we would see that with greater awareness we would not be influenced by the power of the lower chakras and the survival forces of the mind. Literally, this is a battle in which we can truly lose ourselves. It's as if we are being forced to make a choice without being aware of it—do we go with survival and power or do we choose the more subtle feelings and knowings? At this point in our evolution, we may not be aware that to be truly balanced we must operate at both levels at the same time. It is not an either/or choice, but realizing that they are both equally important.

"In this discussion on survival and power there is one factor that we did not consider—love. Love also contains a huge amount of power. It is through love that we discover that we can be very powerful and not be destructive. We don't deny that survival is important, that maintaining a healthy body and a sharp mind—so we can become more aware, gain knowledge, and logic—are proper goals. All these are necessary so that we can take care of ourselves in the world, but we also need to awaken to the spiritual level of our being and fully realize what it represents. In early adulthood the survival and the spiritual components of consciousness should begin to blend, for only in this way can humanity make the best possible choices. But it appears that the survival instinct in mankind continues to grow larger and larger—like a gigantic, seductive thought form, while the spiritual aspect shrinks, unable to compete.

"It is at this stage of development that the individual needs a mentor, someone to explain the existence of these two levels and how they can be brought together. ***The heart can be that mentor!*** The awareness and power that lies within the heart, which is closer to our Source, closer to who and what we are, can be the illuminating energy that will help us move through the physical world with facility. We will miss nothing; instead, we will handle each and every opportunity more deftly, and our survival skills will continue to strengthen. We will come to know that there is a wealth of information at our disposal—spiritual aspects that can be incorporated into all areas of life, meeting every new situation with equal clarity and power. This is the way it was intended to be.

"The preachers, priests and rabbis of all faiths and denominations are forever taking to their pulpits trying to awaken humanity. Their message may not be too clearly presented, but at a deep level the motive behind it is sincere. However, they seem to be unaware that there are two factors in the equation the spiritual component and the survival aspect. For, running through the foundations of humanity is the Kundalini energy, an energy that not only contains the very necessary survival energy but also a beautiful light energy that is working its way up the spine to the head centers to eventually bring about an awareness of who and what we really are. The priesthood in general would have us believe that spirituality is the 'best', seemingly not realizing that a balance of the two is far healthier. Our job on the earth plane is to bring the physical and spiritual into balance. Truly, we are infinitely more than a physical container, so we need to balance it with the spiritual component.

"The balance between the spiritual and the physical can be represented by the caduceus, the winged staff, carried by Mercury. Instead of snakes, however, I prefer to see it as two intertwined ribbons of light, with a flame at the top. There are six places where the snakes (ribbons of light) cross, representing the six chakras in the body and the wings (flame) at the top representing the Thousand-Petaled Lotus (seventh chakra) above the head. This is a true representation of the balance we are all seeking, consciously or unconsciously. At this juncture of balance in our development, the Kundalini energy fills and eventually overflows the heart chakra.

"When that happens, we truly begin to awaken, often brought to a crescendo by falling in love. At that point the energy is often misused, and the final heart opening is completed when the romance fails and the "heart is broken." (Sometimes it takes a failure of the romance to complete the opening of the heart chakra.) If the process is recognized as an opportunity to move further toward a physical/spiritual balance, the overall experience can be very positive. Unfortunately, it takes a certain degree of spiritual sophistication to profit from this unpleasant experience, and hopefully, to begin to reconnect with the God within. Falling in love can awaken these energies, and it is then that the two energies begin to entwine with each other. If we handle it in a positive way, it's a win; but if we don't, the survival instinct becomes stronger and we become warriors. If we are wise enough, and have enough teaching, we begin to awaken to the spiritual realms and find that there is a whole different kind of power and wisdom available. Then literally, the gate opens so these two energies can move up the spine toward the head. So it isn't denial of one or the other of these energies, but rather, a union of the two forces that is the beginning of true wisdom.

"Unfortunately, the survival aspect of the mind believes that in joining forces with the spiritual energy it will lose part of its power. It is true that by this time in our personal development, the mind has become very powerful; for the stronger we become in the world the stronger that aspect of the mind becomes. The mind has begun to develop its own set of rules by which it wants to live, applying the principles that have brought about success in the physical realm.

"But what about the intuitive/spiritual aspects of the mind? During the survival phase of our development it has very little power to assert itself—it is just not up to conducting a successful campaign against the survival aspects of the mind. So at some point the soul, who has been watching this battle says, 'Let's call it a draw and collaborate with one another.' However, this doesn't always work because the soul is asking for the use of logic that may have been lost at this point in the development of the individual.

"There is great confusion in the individual when the Kundalini energy begins to activate the heart chakra, for we literally don't know which path to take—continue in the survival mode or start incorporating more and more of the spiritual teachings. The survival/physical aspect of the mind knows that its rules have led to success in the physical realm so it can see no reason to change. It effectively says, 'I can win by continuing to work the way that has proven successful. Why should I change?'

"However, the more the mind continues with this line of logic the more our connection to the spiritual is weakened, and the connection between the two extremes of the mind/brain becomes more tenuous. Yet, this is where the bulk of humanity now stands—on a great battleground filled with terrible confusion, with the light of its soul becoming dimmer and dimmer—almost as if it is being threatened with extinction. Unfortunately, humanity's confusion is being reflected into the world, and it is also becoming a giant battlefield. We seem to have completely lost sight of the fact that we do have a goal and that goal is returning to our Source—to the Godhead. Seen from a psychic level, the earth is a ball of confusion, and the people who are still very much on the path are trying to find a way to straighten it out.

"The positive energy involved here is almost like an entity trying to protect itself. The danger here is that this very high frequency, Godlike energy could be destroyed to some degree by this very confused, unuseful energy, so it must back away. Furthermore, everyone has free will to choose the individual path they will follow. If we wish to follow these unsavory ways, (and the individuals who are leading), it is our choice. The question is where and when will it end? The word 'salvation'—you know, the one ministers are always using—comes into my mind. Only in this case it means when the Kundalini energy can move freely from the three lower centers to the head centers with no restrictions—that is salvation from our soul's standpoint.

"To reiterate, this must be our choice. We have free will and it cannot, and will not, be taken away or encroached upon, even by the Creator Itself. So we have literally reached that level where the 'good' and the 'evil' (both inside of us) are taking stands. Kundalini is really struggling to make us aware of her presence. Unfortunately, as stated before, the most successful method of getting a human being's attention is pain.

The soul has every level of illness and disease to choose from to help us become aware of Miss Kundalini's presence. Very few of us turn inward without some degree of pain, and the best way to stop the pain is to start becoming aware. Only your soul knows how aware you must become to stop the pain.

"Whether they know it or not, that is why the churches are working so hard to wake up humanity. It matters little what methods are used as long as people begin to awaken to the God within and begin to balance the physical with the spiritual. What is needed now is for us to choose God's Will above our free will. Toward that end, Kundalini is manifesting herself in many weird and painful ways. No one likes the purifying or awakening methods sometimes used by Kundalini, but when it's necessary it happens. Hopefully, it will cause the "victim" to begin to ask questions.

"In most people, the Kundalini energy is stuck in the solar plexus chakra. And since it is restricted, the energy spreads out and disrupts all parts of the body—including the weak areas where illness can begin. As has been said before, Kundalini is not sadistic, she is simply performing the assignment she has been given—to move that energy from the base of the spine to the head chakra and bring about enlightenment. And, yes, Kundalini's campaign to bring about enlightenment of the human race seems to be speeding up. We are being given a choice—decide to start balancing our lives by allowing this spiritual energy to move freely through our spines, or resist and suffer the consequences of a very persistent energy that has infinite ways to get our attention. Without doubt, our 'karma' over hundreds of lifetimes furnishes ample opportunity for unresolved pain that the soul can call forth at this time.

"In her efforts to speed up the enlightenment process, Kundalini is meeting a great amount of resistance from humanity. The general public has no understanding of the Kundalini process. The professionals—priests, doctors, psychologists, and scientists—have little or no real knowledge about the enlightenment process in general and Kundalini in particular. When, therefore, a person begins to sense a reality different from the familiar physical realms; 'know' things that there is no logical way for them to know; 'see' things or beings that 'normal' people don't; or experience any number of conditions that the professionals have labeled psychotic, schizophrenic or just plain weird behavior—they become a menace and a threat to society and are given drugs and shock treatment so they will conform to 'normal' behavioral standards. In other cases, when some of these signs of heart chakra activity begin to occur and the person seeks ways to stop the process, Kundalini may use other more unpleasant ways of convincing them that it is time to begin to balance out the physical/survival syndrome with some awareness of the transpersonal realms. This may take the form of 'weird illnesses' that the medical profession can neither diagnose nor cure, or it could be one of the many known 'incurable diseases.' Kundalini and our souls have quite a list to choose from, depending upon the resistance of the subject. But from the apparent increase in the number of people experiencing some form of Kundalini activity in their lives, it appears that she is gathering the strength to accomplish the task in spite of the lack of awareness and general resistance. So you decide—do you wish to welcome Miss Kundalini with intelligence, awareness, and understanding, or do you wish to choose one of the more unpleasant routes before allowing the balancing to begin?"

The Prototype Human And Rebirth

Perhaps another way to gain an insight into Kundalini's philosophy is to follow a prototype soul (or entity) that has completed the necessary "between-incarnation work" in the state referred to as the "afterlife," and is again ready to plunge into another earthly existence. From this point on I am going to assume the position of this entity and describe what is happening to me. I find myself looking back and saying:

> "Am I going to leave this lovely place where I have been for so long—an existence that I have come to love and understand—and again go through that veil and plunge into the earth plane?" During my stay between lives, little by little my memory of the previous earthly existence has faded away, and suddenly I realize that I am to be reborn in a strange place with different rules to live by. I find myself standing on the other side of that curtain that I know I have gone through, back and forth, throughout the ages.
>
> "Again I am back on the earth plane realizing that this is my next experience. I feel my heart beating rapidly wondering if I am prepared for this. I feel that I have just come from a place where I was cleansed. Symbolically, I'm shiny and sparkly, feeling that all that old stuff from previous incarnations has been placed in the proper perspective—whatever that might mean. Now here I am again parting those curtains, knowing that I am about to make another appearance on the earth plane.
>
> "I'm aware of the pregnancy and that feeling of comfort and security, hoping someone is taking care of me for a little while at least. I feel that I am being prepared for the next segment of this path. There is a sense of ambivalence about coming from a place of peace and beauty to this unknown; yet tucked back in the corner of my mind I know that this is not a strange place. I'm simply returning to a place that has been very familiar to me—perhaps hundreds of times. Still, there is that wonderment, 'Am I prepared to take on this project again?' The feeling is like when we are getting ready to die. Are we prepared for this next step? There is the same feeling of fear and ambivalence about

it; yet someplace inside is that voice that says, 'You can do it because you have done it many times in the past. This is simply another segment of an ongoing process that you have gone through many times before.' However, I am very aware of the trauma that can be created both by being carried around in the mother's womb and again breaking that barrier and coming back into physical existence. As I stand here and deliberate I know that I belong to both realms, the place I have just come from and this earth and the process that we call life. I know that the place I have just come from is my true home, and of course I am reluctant to leave it, but I also know that there is that other half of myself—the physical—involved in this thing we call "our life," that also has to be cared for. Incidentally, we should not overlook the fact that we did choose this new existence. It may not have been the best choice because once the energy is mobilized, and we are all fired up to make another appearance on earth, situations become scrambled; and frequently we have to make choices that are not the most advantageous. Coming from that place of perfection, where we experience ourselves as being whole, perfect, and close to our Godself, we have the feeling that armed with that kind of energy we can literally take on any job. Of course we have forgotten that when that curtain is pulled down we're faced with a totally new way of experiencing ourselves. There is always the hope that we will remember portions of the training that we have had on the other side so we can apply it here. But the memory of the existence that we just came from gradually fades away. I'm aware of the gradual transformation from a well-anchored, safe, perfect existence to the turmoil that we know as life. Deep inside is the feeling that each time I have come back into incarnation I have moved along a bit farther until at some point I will deserve to know myself as the perfect being that I am—that we all are. That is quite a realization to come to, for no matter whether we have supposedly found the right location, the right parents, and the other conditions to help us move through life successfully, there is still the fear, 'Can I make it?' Some place inside us is this concept that in order to return to the Godhead, we must, almost endlessly, go back and forth between these two levels of consciousness. In doing so, we hope to bring enough of this perfect state that we are coming from, to pick and choose the 'right' way to be in the present life that we are confronting. Always there is fear—a tremendous sense of fear. I am frantically asking, "Will I be able to reach back into that perfect self, that perfect state that is available to all of us, and make this life that I am stepping into, creative and enhancing to my soul, and in alignment with putting me on the 'best' path back to the Godhead? Some part of me knows beyond a shadow of a doubt that the plan is to return to the Godhead, but because of our free will it is up to us to choose the route to get from here to there. It's like knowing that we have left the most beautiful mansion in the world, where everything was perfect, where all the information we needed was available, and all of a sudden it is all deleted, like losing a huge file from your hard drive. And here I am expected to undertake a totally different existence without the necessary information files. That is the frightening place I face as I plunge into this segment of life."

OK, so how do I look at this situation in which I find myself? The place to start is that I have no choice but to travel between these two levels of consciousness and to hope to be able to bring the perfection of the transpersonal realms into my present existence. Because what I am always trying to do is find a place within myself where I make the best possible choices no matter where I find myself. I am always hoping to be overshadowed by the goodness that I have just left and apply that to whatever my life script happens to be this time around.

So I'm confronted with the distillation, or the essence, of the place I have come from, knowing that it will never leave me, but at the same time experiencing the grossness of the physical body that I have just stepped into. It is a totally new world, but I know that I have the guidance of my soul to help me make it along this road that I have chosen, or that has been chosen for me. I feel that it is a combination of the two, mutual consent. You might liken it to a counseling session before the plunge back into the earth plane, hopefully bringing enough of a feeling or knowing that we will never be alone, will never be abandoned. Since the goal is to return to the Godhead at some point, we are assured that the Divine Self will always be there to help us, to guide us to the best possible choices. That is the only way we are going to make it. As the connection between myself and this place that I have just left—known as death or the other side of life—begins to fade away, the impact of the choice that I have made, or has been made for me, suddenly hits me. I find that I'm inside this tiny, tiny embryonic form that is rapidly growing into the body that I am to have—a frightening realization. On the surface it looks as if it would be a glorious experience; yet, I realize that I am leaving behind knowledge, comfort, peace, security—all the things we long for. However, at some level I know that we are aware of these qualities after we are born. For the moment, there is a longing to return to that place of perfection, peace, harmony, and understanding; I sense that this place I have just left will soon become a big blur. I see that there is a tiny, tiny spark that settles itself into the very center of the heart. It is because of this tiny spark that we will never forget where we came from. There will always be the impulse to find a way to return to that place, not necessarily by dying but by being able to reawaken that state that we have just come from, so that we can apply those principles that are basically a part of who we are.

The goal is for us to remember that we have not been abandoned; there is no way we ever will be abandoned, and furthermore, to know that we have the courage and the clarity to make the best possible choices in this life that we have just chosen. How do we make those choices?

I feel that this is where Kundalini will make her appearance in our lives. We need to remember that even though we have left that perfect state of consciousness, we have brought the energy with us. It is at the base of the spine—Kundalini! As this Kundalini energy rises in the spine, it also opens the door to the karma that we have created. A lot of it comes from other lifetimes, but most of it comes from the present one. So as we stand in the midst of this turmoil, the assignment is to apply the spiritual principles, that some part of us knows so well, to every situation that we encounter. However, as we live out our lives in this physical world, we create a lot of psychological barriers and blockages and experience the inner confusion about how to handle a particular situation. Do we play by the rules of life, which tend to be somewhat different than the spiritual principles, or do we remember the way we handled situations in that realm where life moved so smoothly? I'm so aware of Kundalini saying, "Make the right choice! Make the right choice and you will have less pain to work through. Remember who you are, and apply the spiritual principles to the present situation. Help me to move your energy and my energy up your spine so you can begin to see worldly situations from a different perspective—a spiritual perspective"

I know that at some deep level those principles are there, but they seem so far away. At a soul level I am trying desperately not to let myself down spiritually, but at the same time survive in the world. Already I feel like a prisoner of this world I have just entered. It has become so real, so solid, and I already feel inside me that I must be very strong to be able to survive this new role that I have chosen. Already I am aware of my heart reaching out and saying, "But I just came from perfection; how can I blend these two realms? How can I do the expedient thing in the world and at the same time honor the place that I have just come from—the very Source that I am, the being that I am, that perfect being that I know has never been contaminated?"

I'm also aware of this overlay of flesh and the mind that I know must be my guide as I move through this particular role that I have chosen. This indeed is a true dilemma and has frequently been the cause of early deaths. It is like seeing a video of "This is Your Life" and knowing that you must make the right choices to have it turn out successfully in the end—a life that you can be proud of. So I am standing in that place of emptiness and loneliness wondering, "Do I have the strength, the clarity, the help to master this assignment that I have undertaken?" At that point I become extremely aware of my soul. It appears as a wonderful, angelic being that says, "But don't forget that I am here to guide you." I'm also aware that in this new existence I am called upon to be tough yet spiritual at the same time. And I'm sure that many times I am going to feel totally abandoned, as if there is no way to reach that seed in the heart that can assure me that I have not been abandoned. That is where we carry that part of the Divine Self. It never leaves us, but we have to confront so many adversities to evolve to that awareness that it seems as if the struggle never ends. Which way do we go? Do we push? Do we play by the rules of the world? We know that the goal is always to win. But what is winning? Winning in the world is the behavior that leads to survival, but always coming from a spiritual base—never forget that. We must remember that no matter how difficult the situation may become, our soul is always there to guide us. There is always that seed in the heart that says, "You have not been abandoned; it only looks that way at times.

Then I go back to Kundalini—and this is where that delicate balance must take place. Again, the goal is not to move through life as fast as we can to get back to the realm of perfection, **but to attain a state of bliss in the midst of the physical world.** We seem to have the erroneous concept that if we get our spiritual life together there will be no more pain or confusion, and we will truly know who and what we are. Although this is a very lofty goal, it is not totally true. This is the place we arrive at after we learn to balance our life problems in a logical, practical way, coming always from a spiritual base. If we can do it that way we can move through life without creating more karma, just smoothly moving along our path to enlightenment. Kundalini is very much of a taskmaster. She knows the job that should be done and she does it, because ultimately she truly cares what happens to us. She is our guide on the spiritual plane (I want to call it the Divine Plane), and as such, she has to devise a lot of ways to catch our attention, hoping that somehow we will see every situation in the most useful way. That itself is a very difficult task, based upon the conditions of the world; underlying that task is a much greater force—the Divine Energy in our spine known as Kundalini.

So I'm asking, "How do I know when Kundalini has become activated? How do I know the right choices to make so that I can honor both sides of my self at the same time—the Divine part, my identification with God, and simultaneously, the physical body that I am just entering, the vehicle through which I will combine both sources of energy?"

I am now watching Kundalini beginning to awaken, and I am going to track it from the base of the spine to the top of the head. I will be observing the process as if seen through time-lapse photography. The image that I have is a very, very tight lotus bud. I know that within that lotus bud is the totality of the Kundalini life energy, and that it is poised to open. Now I see just a tiny, tiny spark of light beginning to peek through the opening at the top of the lotus bud, and I see it moving furtively up into the first chakra—just a very fine tendril of light feeling its way upward. OK, show me clearly what you are doing. I see the energy filling the entire pelvic area, from side to side because that is our foundation, our base of operation. Kundalini needs a strong base from which to operate. Once Kundalini moves into the root chakra we get caught up in all the instincts of survival. This is where we can get lost because survival can easily become a primary issue. We are here on the earth plane and we do need to survive, but usually we go to the extreme. We begin to feel very alone, and to compensate we begin to develop all the inner strengths, the sharpness, the cleverness. The mind steps in and offers its help because it too is an entity that feels the challenge of the physical world and wants to create a place for itself. I'm seeing all these different parts of the self, like spheres of energy that awaken one at a time; however, they are not all on the same side. Some aspects of the mind are useful and some are not, so the conflict begins. With the awakening of the first chakra we really become aware of what a tough place this physical plane is. And this is where we begin to abandon the spiritual principles that are so much a part of us. We begin to devise all the strategies by which we feel we can get from here to . . . I don't know where, yet. So it is very difficult to be centered, to be aware and develop a strong base, yet not forsake the other aspect of this energy—the spiritual energy in Kundalini.

Looking then at this huge survival system that has been built up, we see that at some point the survival aspect of the mind begins to take over and create all kinds of strategies through which we can survive. Shortly the world becomes our primary domain and that very lovely tendril of Kundalini light and energy that came from the tip of the lotus bud, begins to struggle for its survival in a hostile environment. And that very gentle spiritual awakening, represented by the tendril of light from the lotus bud, is pushed back, and suddenly the physical world comes to life. At that point the spiritual side of the Kundalini energy is abandoned and it literally goes back to sleep. The energy that has been awakened is the energy on the right side of the spine which is the Kundalini of survival.

"A little review: The Kundalini energy is said to flow through the chakra system in conduits called nadis. There are said to be many thousand nadis, but only three are of primary importance to the chakra system—the Sushumna, the Ida and the Pingala. The Sushumna is said to be in the center of the spinal cord, extending from the coccyx to the Gate of Brahman in the Thousand-Petaled Lotus. The Ida and Pingala, according to ancient writings, start at the left and right sides of the Muladhara, proceed through the chakras, terminating at either nostril.) The Kundalini of survival is what fuels a powerful sex drive, conquest, war, and other aspects of survival in the world. The energy in the right-hand channel of the spine is literally the way we are in the world, our survival mode. As I observe, I see the right-hand side of the spine becoming fuller; it is coming to life. I feel that it is suddenly becoming a kind of intelligence that I have never experienced or been aware of before. It is all about how we function in the world, the strategies we create, the less-than-ethical tactics we use to get what we want or need for survival. We begin to compile a whole body of information on how to survive in this world.

The channel on the left side, the Ida, is the gentle side, the side we awaken through extensive meditation. This path is open from the base of the spine to the head centers and said to terminate at one nostril. Then when I look at the central channel, the Sushumna, I see it going from the base of the spine to the base of the skull, near or at the location of the pineal and pituitary glands, on its way to the Thousand-Petaled Lotus because one of its functions is to activate these small glands. With this information on the location of the three different channels as a basis, let's discuss how each functions in our lives.

The Sushumna, central channel, awakens the pineal and pituitary glands which generate energy in the form of a triangle of light, its base between the two glands and the apex of the triangle extending beyond the top of the head, making contact with the Sahasrara (The Thousand-Petaled Lotus). The Sushumna is between the Ida and the Pingala. The Pingala, the right-hand channel, is the warrior aspect of us. It says don't be gentle, fight—fight for what you want, take it if you can get it. It's rightfully yours if you are stronger, more clever or cunning. The other energy, the Ida, the left-hand channel, is the gentle, quiet, spiritual side that develops when we meditate and attempt to live a 'spiritual life.' So what I am aware of is this battle between these two conflicting philosophies of life—one of fight and the other saying there is a gentler way to do it. When I look at the central flow of energy, I see it as a very thin, long snake with a head pointing upward. Until these two opposing energies on the right and left can get it together, this central flow must fight all the way to the top. This central channel is the one that is continually bumping against all the psychological barriers that we have internalized, all the things we have believed or done in order to survive. For that central flow of energy to reach the head center and start bringing about some degree of illumination, it has to clear away the psychological garbage that we have accumulated through lifetimes in the survival mode.

The program to start bringing about some degree of illumination doesn't require us to give up our power in the world because we do need it; instead, we should begin to use that power in a spiritual way. When we begin to do that, the psychological barriers that we have created can begin to dissolve.

Illnesses are the conditions that carry the power to create discomfort within us. When we are afflicted with one or more, we switch our focus to it and want it healed, not realizing that the reason we have the illness is because the right and left spinal energies are not in agreement. It's just that the right side is not using the wisdom from the left side (the spiritual side) to ask for clarity and guidance so the energy that is at odds with the central channel can be dissolved.

When a healing takes place, it is as if this cute little snake is moving up the spine a little at a time heaving a sigh of relief and saying, 'I've gotten this far, but it is such a slow process to make peace between the spiritual side and the powerful survival side of this Kundalini energy.' Please note that the powerful survival aspect of Kundalini is not frowned upon—it is "an iron fist in a velvet glove." We don't give up anything; we just modify the way we do things. We honor the illness and discomfort, perhaps even thank them, as this skinny little snake moves another notch up the spine toward the pineal and pituitary glands. It really has a helluva job to do!

The survival aspect of the mind is at odds with the spiritual approach, as is almost every aspect of the body, so that little snake has a lot of resistance. Therefore, we have to choose, not one or the other, but to create a blend that will honor all the energy in the spine so that it can move up to the head centers.

I am now aware of the body of a human being, but it is like nothing I have ever seen before. It is the goal for us humans to strive toward. There is a radiance about it that is incredible. It is the radiance shown in paintings around the saints and the man Jesus, Buddha and other great spiritual teachers. For the rest of us, I'm sure we are talking about hundreds of lifetimes to reach that state. I think that this is a very fine model of an ultimate goal, something to be working toward, but what can we do in this lifetime to speed up the process? Simply honor both sides. It's just that we are so confused. We believe that if we honor one side we have to deny the other, instead of recognizing that we have both sides in our spine, and we need to honor both sides.

Let us look at power, the quality of power. There is warlike power, and there is the power to honor the God within. The latter is the use of power in a way that can eventually make all things right. And it is all the same power. Don't get hung up on using only 'spiritual power,' or power from the left side of the spine. Power is power! It is only the intention behind power that makes it useful or not useful. The goal is for the left and right-hand powers to meet in the head to activate the pineal and pituitary glands, to actually create a partnership that becomes the third energy in the spine.

Now that you have a partial understanding of the function of Kundalini in your body, how can you proceed to make the best possible use of this energy? First of all, change the model of the way you see yourself. Perceive yourself as I have discussed above with the three channels of Kundalini operating around and through your spine because this is what you look like at a spiritual level. Begin to see everything as having two sides or aspects, and two ways of being handled—the worldly way and the spiritual way. It is also useful to realize that perhaps it takes the blending of the two to create the optimum condition or outcome. We have to be sharp in the world; we have to be aware. We have to know that literally we can channel the God Power (Kundalini) within us into worldly situations, both as a solution and to add the spiritual dimension. There are always two or more ways of accomplishing a task. But what we need always to remember is to add the spiritual dimension to the situations, both large and small. We each have our own brand of power—add it to the spiritual dimension in your life. Remember, it's not either/or, it can always be a blend of the two. There are things that we need to be very practical about, but we can still add the principle of the spiritual level to them. We need to be aware of both aspects of ourselves so we can function adequately in the world; we need to be strong in the world, yet see all things through the clarity of spiritual vision.

Operating through the left channel of Kundalini, the spiritual side, doesn't mean we must be soft or stupid, it doesn't mean we have to give in and be a Mister Milktoast. It simply means that we apply different rules to the tasks before us. We don't abandon either side of our nature, a concept that many "spiritual seekers" seem to misunderstand—we simply keep them both in mind. And speaking of the mind, we have to consider it when making changes in our lives. As soon as I say that, I hear the mind beginning to laugh and say, 'I too have control, I too have power, and I can decide which way this thing is going to be acted out.' So we have to be aware of all the players, all the conditioning, for the name of the game is "win," but win while blending both sides. Never, never give up your power, it's yours; simply add the spiritual dimension and allow the mind to be logical. Use the logic of the mind but always with a spiritual base. And that is what will eventually create a perfect human being!

It's only a model, but a model that you can begin to use by being aware of what you do, why you are doing it, and what is behind it. Another way of saying it is: Be aware of everything you feel, everything you think, everything you say, and everything you do. Try it for

18 hours tomorrow. It could change your life. If you sincerely play this little game with yourself, you'll find that you are manifesting more power than you ever did before, and you will be coming from a constructive base, meaning that you don't destroy one thing to create another.

We all have a life model from which we operate, and we have the freedom to choose any model we wish. The model that has just been presented is another way of doing the same thing that we are now doing in our lives, only doing it more powerfully. When put into practice, it becomes a whole new way of being, a way that is literally built into us. You will find the plan in a seed in the heart.

Remember what I have said over and over again, we are not giving up anything when we begin to follow spiritual principles. We can still be powerful; we can be logical; we can be fair; it's only blending our attributes in a different way so that the outcome . . . OK, what should the outcome be? It is clearly "What serves in the most useful way, not serving one and destroying another." So the best way is the most logical, most productive, most creative, and the most useful way of handling anything that comes up in one's life.

Now Kundalini is saying, "If you choose to live your life this way, I will be able to flow freely from the base of your spine to the head centers with no discomfort whatsoever. The discomfort that I do create, however, is just to get your attention so you will change the focus of the way you see and do things. That is the only reason for the discomfort. The body is meant to be perfectly healthy at all times; after all, it is the vehicle for your soul. You give up nothing when you choose to work toward a properly balanced Kundalini. If you simply reframe the way you see the world, you will make my job much easier. Can you imagine the discomfort that I, Kundalini, experience as I work my way through your psychological and emotional debris? What I am looking for is a direct path from the base of the spine to the top of the head, and in this way we all win. You get healthier, I get my job done, and you will have taken another step forward on your personal path to illumination."

The Heart Chakra

No treatise on Kundalini would be complete without a philosophic discussion of the heart chakra. Beginning at the root chakra, the heart chakra is the fourth, or the first of the so-called upper chakras or spiritual chakras, the first three having been developed for use by the physical body/mind complex.

Not infrequently one of Anne's clients will be experiencing physical heart problems and asks if she has any ideas as to the cause of the problem. After a few minutes of discussion and another minute of silent probing, it becomes obvious to Anne that their Kundalini energy is, let us say, blocked between the solar plexus and heart chakras. Most people have only a meager understanding of the structure and operation of the human heart, let alone the role that Kundalini plays in its functioning. So how does one prepare the average client to receive the information that some mysterious energy that is undetectable and unmeasurable by science is being blocked between two equally non-detectable spiritual centers by some psychological trauma acquired during childhood and/or adolescence? About all Anne can do is give a crash course in "Kundalini 101," and it would sound something like this:

Close your eyes and imagine a human body with an illuminated spinal column. The illumination is from the spiritual energy contained in the vertical axis of one of our more subtle bodies. That vertical axis corresponds to the spinal column of the physical body. This energy, the Kundalini, is truly the elixir of the gods. It is our guide to, and our connection with, the higher states of consciousness. Unfortunately, Kundalini is also the direct or indirect cause of many of humanity's illnesses, including ailments of the heart, illnesses that people might not have if they had recognized and honored this Kundalini energy. It appears that the existence and purpose of this vitally important energy may have been intentionally withheld from the bulk of humanity. In ages long past it was deemed necessary by the priestly class to prevent certain esoteric wisdom from falling into the hands of the uninitiated. Now however, it seems that the time may have come to make the existence and purpose of this spinal energy known to all humanity. To persons with even a meager understanding of esoteric wisdom, it is obvious that many diseases that cannot be medically diagnosed and treated are really Kundalini energy being blocked by unawareness. I would say that at least 10 percent of my clients have problems associated with Kundalini. But if you don't know about Kundalini, you can't acknowledge it and begin to use it constructively. However, it appears that the transpersonal realms are putting a lot of energy into making this information more readily available. It is my observation that to benefit fully from any condition, especially Kundalini, one needs to be aware of its existence and modus operandi. Once it begins to become active, awareness may soon come about through numerous physical anomalies or ailments. Because of the general lack of knowledge on this subject by our professionals, unfortunately, only the symptoms get treated, with no recognition of the cause. However, it appears that some aspect of the transpersonal realm is activating the inner Kundalini in ever increasing numbers of humanity, probably because we are behind in our spiritual development. This is certainly one way to get our attention.

Again I am aware of a body in front of me with glowing Kundalini energy radiating in all directions. This is the treasure that we have within us. But if we don't know it's there, we can't assist in its development. This is the energy Moses demonstrated when he threw his cane to the ground and it turned into a serpent. Symbolically, that is the way he was made aware of his Kundalini, because at the moment he threw the cane down, there was a transmission to him from a much higher level so he would be aware of the strength he possessed.

My attention is focused upon the Muladhara Chakra or root center, and I am very much aware of how deeply this center penetrates the earth. It is definitely our foundation, our connection to the physical. The physical body and the three lower chakras are the domain of Mother Earth, and the Thousand-Petaled Lotus is the domain of the higher states of consciousness, the domain of God; and then there are all the levels in between that must be illuminated—and I'm using that word very deliberately. It's as if an illumination takes place as each chakra is touched by this God-substance—and that is truly what Kundalini is. But for the successful unfoldment of this force, we need the strength of the earth plane to give it the momentum required to move to the top of the head.

Very seldom do the higher realms interfere with the evolution of mankind, but I believe that we are at a point in our development where gaining knowledge of this energy in the spine is so important that the decision has been made to extend help to those who are ready or close to ready.

The root chakra is like a huge ballast and—considering the job it has to do—it must be massive. I'm so aware of the earth plane at one extreme and the God plane at the other, and I know that somehow these must come into alignment to bring about the inner awakening of Kundalini. There is much evidence that this transformative energy is beginning to touch many people. I know that compared to the mass ignorance that exists, the current openings seem like a drop in the ocean, but what we must remember is that this energy is so powerful that a small amount can counteract a tremendous amount of ignorance and negativity. We also need to understand that the importance of Kundalini's mission is such that if it has to bring about pain, suffering, and destruction for its accomplishment—well, then so be it. Ask the people who have resisted it. Consciousness is the ultimate reality; all else is expendable.

There is a tremendous attraction between the higher states of consciousness and the Kundalini energy that is deeply rooted in the earth plane. These two energies are being drawn together like huge magnets, and something must give. There is no doubt that Kundalini is beginning to manifest itself in many ways in millions of people. What is needed right now is for people to be empowered rather than frightened by the energy that they have within their own being. This is not something they have to acquire, rather it is something that by simply recognizing and encouraging it, it will begin to move up through the several chakras and bring about a transformation in their lives. But more than that, it's suddenly realizing that they have the key to unlock this fabulous power, this treasure within. The churches speak about goodness and transformation, but they don't give us the keys to unlock the treasure chest. They always speak of it as something "out there," very much removed from ourselves, something we have to work toward, not something that we already have within us. True, we have to put forth effort, but it would help empower us to start out with the knowledge that this energy is already within our spine, and that merely by shifting our attention we could begin to bring about the magic that releases this energy. Some part of us knows that we have this information and power within us. Do you realize how empowering it is just to know that you contain this transforming energy?

Now let's move up to the second chakra—the one that is the seat of unconditional love. In most of us this chakra is nearly inactive. Unconditional love is a state that very few people understand, and even fewer practice. This is the chakra that attempts to bring real love into the survival mode of the root chakra.

The next chakra is the solar plexus, the seat of the greatest confusion in the body, primarily because we seem to have lost sight of what's right and what's wrong, or what's useful or not useful. Maybe a better way to phrase it would be that we seem to have momentarily lost our connection to universal intelligence. Mankind in general is being bombarded by massive quantities of negativity, anger, and violence. At a personality level, many people have the feeling that there is no hope for the lifewave—no way out. I believe we must understand that nothing is irreversible. The solution, of course, is total self-responsibility. We need to take full responsibility for discovering our potential and empowering ourselves. On the one hand there is the sense of frustration and loss, but on the other hand help is being made available. How can this message be delivered en masse to the lifewave?

We are rooted in the Muladhara—the root chakra! We are so entrenched in the materialistic aspect of the world that we believe that we can fix it if we get angry and exert enough force to appease the debilitating frustration that many people feel about the state of the world. But what humanity does not realize is that within the spine is an energy that can bring about the desired transformation. It is a jewel waiting to be discovered. How can this be presented to people so that it will make sense, that it will empower them, that it will give them the impetus to at least begin to look at the possibility that the world we have created is within us and is being reflected outwardly? Now, if that frustrating world is inside of us, as well as the Kundalini energy, then we contain the solution to our problem. To acknowledge it is to give it its power.

Next, let us move up to the heart chakra, there to become involved in the battle between the heart chakra energy and the frustrations of the world. It's as if they are at opposite ends of the spectrum. It appears that enough love must be generated, not to absorb all the negative energy, but just enough to begin to understand it. Again, it is imperative that we realize that what we are talking about is inside of us; it is not "out there," so in a way it really is a condition we can do something about. That realization in itself is very empowering.

It is no accident, nor the wrath of a vengeful god, that humanity has so much heart disease. It is simply that our heart energy is not being properly used. In our ignorance we are powerless to fix it. If we could just realize that all these different levels of consciousness do exist within us, and that by focusing on that energy in the spine and in the heart, we could develop the power to bring about the desired changes. The heart energy is more than willing to cooperate.

I am now aware of the being who initiated this change in the evolution of spirituality on the earth plane, and whose energy is still behind it—the being known to the world as Jesus. His task was to awaken the heart chakra in every member of the human race and infuse us with the heart energy he represented. His task wasn't to establish a church and a religious hierarchy. The original purpose has never wavered—it's still intact. The message has always been that we must do it within ourselves. That doesn't mean that we shouldn't seek and accept help along the way. But if people would go within and use their God-given power, the negativity would have to retreat because nothing can stand against the power of unconditional love and Kundalini.

The heart chakra is the pivotal point in our spiritual development. The love generated here is the most powerful energy on the face of the earth—absolutely the most powerful. And when that heart chakra is awakened, the love force gains enough momentum to open the channel between the heart and the head chakras, and eventually to the Sahasrara, the Thousand-Petaled Lotus above the head. By the time the Kundalini gets to the heart chakra it has harnessed and incorporated the unconditional love of the second chakra, which has eliminated

245

most of our tendency to judge. This combination of forces allows us to recognize and to understand the confusion of the world, and to realize that we are not powerless——that we have the energy of the universe at our disposal—actually from within our own being. The treasure lies in really believing, in really knowing that potentially we have the power of the universe within us, and that we can individually bring about changes. We can talk about miracles and the God-within, but our finite mind needs specifics. We need to know beyond a shadow of a doubt that the power is already within us. We must know that, vehemently as we have denied it, it is still there, and that by acknowledging it we can take the energy of the earth and move it from chakra to chakra until the heart opens. We must refine our own energy until it matches the higher states of consciousness. If we don't do that we will continue to experience a sense of frustration, of being the abandoned child that has to survive on its own, not realizing that its most powerful tool is within itself.

I have come to realize, as a result of this discussion, that if we can move the Kundalini energy into the heart chakra, all the goodness of that level of consciousness can be ours to bring into manifestation. But it can't happen unless our being matches that level of consciousness, for it is at the heart level that we can truly begin to create miracles. When we reach the heart chakra the leavening takes place, and we move beyond the heaviness of the physical because the sense of inner knowing and trusting has been awakened; and, instead of looking to the past for answers, we begin to look to the future—or is it the present? It's like transcending a very dense level of consciousness to move into what we might consider to be a heavenly consciousness.

Our entire energy system moves into the heart chakra, and from there on we are working with the levels of consciousness represented by these higher realms. It's like moving from the basement of our house to the attic, except that when we are operating from that heart chakra, the attic has no ceiling. The possibilities at those higher states of consciousness are endless. I have the sense that once we move into the heart chakra we never go back. It's almost as if this is an initiation, and from this level of consciousness we are inspired to think only the highest thoughts and to act from a place of goodness. Most importantly, we have moved into a level of believing that is truly divine, so different from the way we believed when we were working our way through the lower chakras. That itself automatically opens many new pathways for us. From that point on, one is operating at a whole other level of consciousness, and furthermore, one is inspired to continue to operate from that level. Kundalini is the key—and that key is within us. It's just like it is in the physical realm, we don't make progress until we believe in ourselves. The same is true at the spiritual level—it doesn't matter what we have inside, it only becomes available when we believe in it. It is true that Kundalini can cause us a lot of difficulties as it tries to get our attention—and that is all it is. It has a message to deliver and we are reluctant to open the door. We must listen and then believe!

In a way, Kundalini divides our energy into heaven and earth, the solar plexus being the division point. The lower three chakras represent the earth, and when we move into the heart chakra we become qualified to live in the higher states of consciousness—those that might be called the heavenly realms. Once we make that transition we know that this is our domain, and we begin to see everything very differently. We begin to assess what we know and what we see from that divine level of consciousness now operating within us. The Bible even talks about inheriting the kingdom of heaven, and that the kingdom of heaven is within us. How could it be stated more clearly or more succinctly? It's just that the leaders of organized religion don't seem to believe it. We don't abandon the earth; we just view it from a higher level of consciousness.

At this moment I am feeling so totally blessed! And everyone has within himself or herself the key to feel the same—Kundalini. It has that feeling of coming Home, really and truly coming Home, and of knowing that nothing of a negative nature can ever again touch us. However, after having said that, I am painfully aware of the thrust of energy that is required to move from the root chakra to the various upper levels of consciousness. Our lives are that force. So much depends upon how we handle our lives. If we handle them in a useful way, we develop that rocket-like thrust to propel us upward through the first three chakras until the heart chakra is reached. Here the real work begins. This is where the path truly takes an upward turn. And it becomes obvious that everything that we have experienced in life is real, but what happens now is real in a totally different way. What we experience on the earth plane is real in the sense that we experience it through our five senses, but this other level is a kind of knowing and believing. I feel that the "space" between the root chakra and the heart chakra is the testing ground—groping our way along the path, and finding and organizing the information that can, hopefully, correct our course. When we reach the level of the heart chakra, we can look back at the struggle, the path, the course with its "false starts and wrong turns" and see that all of it was necessary. But I think that the most important realization that each of us must come to, is that this entire drama is taking place inside of us.

The Thousand-Petaled Lotus

During all the years that we conducted workshops and seminars, we have never had an exercise or meditation specifically associated with the Seventh Chakra, just above the physical head. People have asked us why. We have always said that if they were able to establish a smooth flow of energy through the first six chakras, they would automatically have access to the attributes of the Seventh Chakra, known in India as the Thousand-Petaled Lotus. Over the years we have accumulated a bit of information about this chakra that we would like to pass along. I don't think it is "new," just new to us, and perhaps to many of our readers.

Anne has repeatedly been made aware that the Seventh Chakra, among other things, contains the entire story of the Creation of the Universe—the physical, the celestial, the whole of Creation. The Thousand-Petaled Lotus is like tons of the most highly sophisticated microchips that can be imagined, all filled with gillions of bits of information. Let us say, e.g., that a particular petal contained all the events of the Creation of our world, each tiny cell would be found to represent some item or event of that Creation. So we begin to understand why esoteric wisdom has always stressed the proposition that everything is within us—we are complete unto ourselves.

For forty years Anne has been "taking trips" to the corners of the physical universe and to spiritual realms beyond our wildest imaginings; and at some point, she became aware, and began to verbalize, that she was not "going out" to these remote locations but that she was "going within." At some juncture along the way it seemed to her that the Seventh Chakra was her connection to these other realms, either physical or etheric. And just within the last ten years or so it has become apparent to her that this limitless wisdom which at first seemed to be "out there," and then seemed to be "within," is really contained in that Thousand-Petaled Lotus. This, of course, may again be just a metaphor. But considering what the computer industry has done with chips of silicon, a very crude, material substance compared to a cell in a petal of an etheric lotus blossom above the head that has no physical existence, it is not as far-fetched as it seems on the surface. The things science is learning about the brain today would have been laughed at less than 50 years ago. So perhaps it is figuratively and literally true that we are each a complete universe unto ourselves, containing all the wisdom, all the knowledge that has ever existed. And just maybe, when Anne obtains information about another state of consciousness or about some distant planet, it is because she has managed to illuminate (scan) some small part of that Thousand-Petaled Lotus, and it has released its information.

It would appear then, that time spent eliminating psychological blocks between the chakras may be time well spent. Just imagine having access to that kind of a hard drive!

Points to Remember

During Anne's discussion of Kundalini's basic philosophy, many salient points were made, points that are well worth remembering. It is suggested that you read through those listed below and if one (or more) catches your attention, find the quote in the text and study the context from which it was taken. Nearly every one of those quotes could be the subject of a meditation or contemplation. Don't miss this opportunity.

The Summary of: Kundalini's Dilemma

- The intellect has become very creative materially, and instead of moving upward, it has spread laterally until the foundation is immense.

- It would seem that the "committee" underestimated the willfulness of a lifewave with freewill! We appear to have lost our sense of balance and have been trapped by our own creativity, not realizing that as we developed the outer we needed to develop the inner.

- This energy that is Kundalini has been pushed aside, and to make its presence felt it has had to do some pretty dramatic things in the hope that we would become aware of its potency.

- We lost sight of the fact that there was a dual path we were to take—to glorify the earth and to find our way back to the Godhead. We have put so much energy into the physical that we have completely lost sight of the Kundalini energy that was also to have been incorporated into our sojourn upon the earth. Kundalini is the epitome of creativity. And since nearly all of us have ignored Kundalini's energy, she has devised an endless number of ingenious ways of gaining our attention—all sorts of common and exotic illnesses, many for which our medical establishment can find no cause or cure. No, she isn't being sadistic—just trying to get our attention.

- Unfortunately, pain is the most effective means of communication yet devised to get a human being's attention.

- This energy has always been confused with personal power because Kundalini energy at the root chakra level is a powerful sexual and survival force. The same energy can be used to create unbelievable havoc or the illumination of a Buddha or a Christ.

- Simply stated, Kundalini's purpose seems to be to glorify the earth, to glorify God, and eventually to return humanity to its Source. Unfortunately, it seems that it is only through pain that many of us will eventually become aware of the blessings of Kundalini.

- Our souls keep crying out, "Wake up, you have a job to do." And really all we have to do, when the time is right, is to create the proper environment inside ourselves so Kundalini can move rhythmically up the spine.

- Potentially, all these other so-called spiritual levels are within us, but it seems that we must have an awareness that they are there before we can incorporate them into our physical/ mental/emotional structure.

- The intuitive aspect of the mind says, "Don't forget that I am available and that I am an ally of the Kundalini energy. I am the part of the mind that encourages humans to open to the subtle spiritual realms of non-ordinary consciousness, the role I will continue to play during this physical existence."

- At this point in our evolution, we may not be aware that to be truly balanced we must operate at both levels at the same time. It is not an either/or choice, but realizing that they are both equally important.

- It is through love that we discover that we can be very powerful and not be destructive.

- In early adulthood the survival and the spiritual components of consciousness should begin to blend, for only in this way can humanity make the best possible choices.

- We seem to have completely lost sight of the fact that we do have a goal and that goal is returning to our Source—to the Godhead.

- Kundalini is really struggling to make us aware of her presence. Unfortunately, the most successful method of getting a human being's attention is pain. The soul has every level of illness and disease to choose from to help us become aware of Miss Kundalini's presence.

The Summary of: The Prototype Human and Rebirth

- Change the model of the way you perceive yourself. Perceive yourself as a spiritual being embodied in a physical form having thousands of energy channels, three of which conduct Kundalini energy up the spine through the several chakras to and including the Thousand-Petaled Lotus above the head.

- Start seeing every situation as having two ways of being handled or resolved—the worldly way and the spiritual or Divine Way.

- Realize that the optimum solution to any situation is a blend of the worldly and the Divine.

- We need to know that we can channel our God Power (Kundalini) into worldly affairs and still be sharp and aware.

- Another way of phrasing it is: There are always two or more ways to accomplish a task. And since we are aware, it is our responsibility to add the Divine dimension to the worldly situations, no matter how large or small.

- Add your own unique brand of power to the Divine dimensions of your life.

- Remember that it is never an either or situation. It can always be a blend of worldly power and Divine Power.

- For optimum functioning in the world we need to be aware of (and use) both aspects of our being—our worldly power, and our spiritual (Divine) vision.

- Operating through the left channel of Kundalini, the Divine side, doesn't mean that we must be soft or stupid. It simply means that we apply different rules to the tasks before us. We don't abandon either side of our nature, a concept many "spiritual seekers" seem to misunderstand.

- When we begin including the Divine aspect of our beings in everyday worldly situations, the mind really begins to flaunt its desire for control.

- Never give up your power, simply add the Divine dimension to the functioning of a logical mind.

- You give up nothing when you begin to follow spiritual principles. You can still be powerful, logical, productive, creative, and fair to all involved. This new model is only a blending of the two seemingly opposing aspects of the Kundalini energy. You don't give in to anyone; you just see all possible consequences.

The Summary of: The Heart Chakra

- The physical body and the three lower chakras are the domain of Mother Earth, and the Thousand-Petaled Lotus is the domain of the higher states of consciousness, the domain of God.

- We also need to understand that the importance of Kundalini's mission is such that if it has to bring about pain, suffering, and destruction for its accomplishment—well, then so be it. Ask the people who have resisted it. Consciousness is the ultimate reality; all else is expendable.

- They (The Churches) always speak of it as something "out there," very much removed from ourselves, something we have to work toward, not something that we already have within us. True, we could begin to bring about the magic that releases this energy.

- At a personality level, many people have the feeling that there is no hope for the lifewave—no way out. I believe we must understand that nothing is irreversible. The solution, of course, is total self-responsibility. We need to take full responsibility for discovering our potential and empowering ourselves.

- Now, if that frustrating world is inside us, as well as the Kundalini energy, then we contain the solution to our problem. To acknowledge it is to give it its power.

- His (Jesus') task wasn't to establish a church and a religious hierarchy. The original purpose has never wavered—it's still intact. The message has always been that we must do it within ourselves. That doesn't mean that we shouldn't seek and accept help along the way. But if people would go within and use their God-given power, the negativity would have to retreat because nothing can stand against the power of unconditional love and Kundalini.

- I have come to realize, as a result of this discussion, that if we can move the Kundalini energy into the heart chakra, all the goodness of that level of consciousness can be ours to bring into manifestation. But it can't happen unless our being matches that level of consciousness, for it is at the heart level that we can truly begin to create miracles.

- It is true that Kundalini can cause us a lot of difficulties trying to get our attention—and that is all it is. It has a message to deliver and we are reluctant to open the door.

- The Bible even talks about inheriting the kingdom of heaven, and that the kingdom of heaven is within us. How could it be stated more clearly or more succinctly? It's just that the leaders of organized religion don't seem to believe it.

- I am painfully aware of the thrust of energy that is required to move from the root chakra to the various upper levels of consciousness. Our lives are that force. So much depends upon how we handle our lives. If we handle them in a useful way, we develop that rocket-like thrust to propel us upward through the first three chakras until the heart chakra is reached. Here the real work begins.

- • I feel that the "space" between the root chakra and the heart chakra is the testing ground—groping our way along the path, and finding and organizing the information that can, hopefully, correct our course. When we reach the level of the heart chakra, we can look back at the struggle , the path, the course with its "false starts and wrong turns" and see that its necessity.

The Summary of: The Thousand-Petaled Lotus

- Anne has repeatedly been made aware that the Seventh Chakra, among other things, contains the entire story of the Creation of the Universe—the physical, the celestial, the whole of Creation. The Thousand-Petaled Lotus is like tons of the most highly sophisticated microchips that can be imagined, all filled with gillions of bits of information.

- For forty years Anne has been "taking trips" to the corners of the physical universe and to spiritual realms beyond our wildest imaginings; and at some point, she became aware, and began to verbalize, that she was not "going out" to these remote locations but that she was "going within."

- Just within the last ten years or so it has become apparent to her that this limitless wisdom that at first seemed to be "out there," and then seemed to be "within," is really contained in that Thousand-Petaled Lotus.

- So perhaps it is figuratively and literally true that we are each a complete universe unto ourselves, containing all the wisdom, all the knowledge that has ever existed.

- It would appear then, that time spent eliminating psychological blocks between the chakras may be time well spent. Just imagine having access to that kind of a hard drive! (The Thousand-Petaled Lotus)!

Kundalini And the Family

A Kundalini opening affects more than the person to whom it is happening. The immediate family—spouse and children—are directly affected if one of their members is partially debilitated by a "strange illness" or "malady," especially if the professionals can't diagnose or successfully treat it.

There are, however, steps to be taken that will substantially ease the pressure on everyone involved. Naturally, every situation is different, but having lived for 60 years with a person in the family having a very active Kundalini most of that time, I feel driven to pass along some suggestions to other spouses.

Anne and I know from experience that both parties have their respective responsibilities. The way we see it, the spouse having the experience should observe these guidelines:

- No matter how bad it gets, never give into physical or psychic problems, or play "poor me."

- Perform daily spousal responsibilities to the family.

- Never flaunt newly acquired skills or abilities before family, friends, or acquaintances. It can be very useful to experiment, work, or play with these abilities with a few select people.

- Maintain a small ego. You are not really that special. These experiences are being had by millions of people. If you have something that the people of the world need or want, they will find you.

The spouse of the one having the Kundalini experiences also has a long list of do's and don'ts if they want the process to be successful. As the couple moves into the Kundalini experience, they will probably find several more "do's and don'ts." To be truly successful, the Kundalini experience needs to be a shared experience. It is very difficult to do it alone. Here are a few suggestions to be considered by the other spouse:

- Be kind, understanding, patient, and loving. Your partner has enough problems to cope with.

- Be genuinely interested in your spouse's new adventures. Read books on Kundalini and related topics—preferably together.

- As new aspects of the Kundalini experience unfold, show your interest, be open-minded, and non-judgmental—and read more.

- Meditate together.

- Don't be jealous or envious of your spouse's psycho-spiritual adventures and accomplishments.

- Play with and experiment with your mate's new transpersonal skills. Encourage them to use and practice their developing skills discreetly. Discuss all aspects of the development process openly and thoroughly between yourselves.

- Encourage your spouse to develop new friendships and support systems. Be prepared to lose some existing friendships (or acquaintances), especially if you talk openly about what is transpiring.

- And for Heaven's sake, no wisecracks like, "When are you going to be able to predict the stock market?"

- Interest, patience, understanding, and love are probably the keys to a partnership surviving an extended Kundalini episode.

Be aware of self-styled gurus who want to "clean" your chakras, or "tune up" your chakras, "open" your chakras, "raise" your Kundalini, and any number of kooky ideas floating around in the workshop circuit. Also be aware of shamanic practices; many are not appropriate for the modern Westerner, especially if they are already having Kundalini experiences.

And if you have children, tell them as much as they can handle, like discussions on sex. You can't hide it from them, so keep them informed, and if possible, let them become involved in some of the fun and interesting aspects of the Kundalini opening process.

Both spouses should look upon the happening as a rare opportunity to gain a greater view of life and of the world around them, and a peek into the higher realms of consciousness. Anne's life for the last fifty years is a testament to this statement. It is by far the most important event that has happened in this lifetime for either of us, and perhaps the greatest in the last several lifetimes. So when it happens to you, don't mess it up!

Concluding Remarks

We have discussed the aspects of Kundalini about which we have some degree of firsthand knowledge and the philosophic and spiritual reasons behind the phenomenon.

We are well aware that this is a highly misunderstood subject and, as a consequence, there are a lot of confused, unhealthy people in the world. It is our belief that the best antidotes for a life made miserable by the proddings of Kundalini are knowledge, wisdom and acceptance—knowledge of the workings of the Kundalini process, the wisdom to apply the knowledge available, and the acceptance, by faith if necessary, of who and what we are and how we fit into Miss Kundalini's cosmic dance. Unfortunately, the "cure" will not happen overnight. The obvious cause of the problem is a long-standing refusal to seek a balance in our lives—a properly balanced physical and spiritual life. This didn't occur just yesterday so don't expect a cure tomorrow. It is not a matter of intellectual understanding; it is soul level knowing—this is not generally accomplished in days or months, but perhaps in years or lifetimes. We are slow learners when it comes to matters of the spirit. So study, meditate, contemplate, and pray, perhaps even write—anything that will bring about a sense of knowing, beyond a shadow of a doubt, that there is need for a physical/spiritual balance in your life. Search through your life and find examples of this kind of knowing. Analyze these areas of knowing, see what they have in common and then use that commonality to reach a level of knowing about the spiritual verities of the universe.

We all wish there were a pill or a shot that could accomplish this overnight, but the mastery of the process leading to that level of knowing is equally as important as the goal itself. So read, meditate, pray—anything that you feel will work for you—until you KNOW that you are a Divine Spark of God on your way Home, and that leading a properly balanced physical/spiritual life is the first step on the path.

In the last chapter of *Kundalini, The Evolutionary Energy In Man*, Gopi Krishna makes a plea to establish a pilot program to bring Kundalini to full bloom in a select group of humans using optimum training conditions in a scientifically controlled program, with the idea of expanding the program to include as much of the human race as possible.

I love the concept, but I'm afraid our political, religious, social, economic systems are not ready for mass produced enlightenment. What a renaissance that would be! Can you imagine a nation or a world with ten million or even one million geniuses, supermen and superwomen, world-class artists and composers, prophets and just plain highly enlightened, spiritual men and women all living and producing at the same time? Can you imagine a society with a million Michelangelos, DaVincis, Mozarts, Beethovens and Francis Bacons? That would truly be the Golden Age. Well, it's fun to dream, but it will take awhile to work out the details. In the meantime, learn as much as you can about Miss Kundalini and her goal of evolving humanity into a race of gods capable of returning to the Godhead, so our God will have the opportunity to complete Its (His or Her) development and move on to a yet higher degree of perfection.

APPENDIX I:

KUNDALINI EXERCISES

Volumes have been written about Kundalini and the chakras—the spiritual centers. If you read them all and never practiced meditation or chakra exercises, you would have a lot of information but no more spiritual growth than when you began your studies. It is a fascinating subject and hopefully this book will spark your interest so you will read more. However, it is suggested that you carry on a meditation practice along with your reading.

One method of practice would be to find a portion of an exercise that appeals to you and incorporate it into your current meditation routine. Or, you may wish to work with a complete exercise for a few weeks (or months) before moving on to another. If at any time you have indications that you are moving ahead too rapidly, back off. We suggest you always maintain a high respect for Miss Kundalini. If you do, you will significantly reduce your chances of incurring her ire.

As a group, this lifewave has been working on the heart chakra for the past two thousand years. The next major step forward in humanity's spiritual growth will be integrating the heart energy with the head energy—love with intellect. So the following exercises relate to the heart, throat, solar plexus, the second and the head centers.

These are very basic meditation concepts and it will be up to you if, or how, you wish to use them, or where you go from here.

WARNING!!

These exercises may be used in your own meditation program for your own spiritual development. And we sincerely hope you will. However, these exercises cannot under any circumstances be used with a group without explicit written permission from Azoth Institute of Spiritual Awareness; nor may they be reproduced in any form for commercial use. All material in this book is copyrighted.

It is strongly advised that these exercises not be used by persons with a history of mental disorder, or who are currently under treatment for psychological problems, i.e., schizophrenia, psychosis, severe depression, multiple personality, extreme paranoia and similar mental dysfunctions.

Heart Chakra Meditation (Fourth Center)

Always begin any meditation or spiritual exercise by getting into a comfortable sitting position and placing your total awareness on the breath. Focus your attention on the breath, to the exclusion of all other thoughts. One method to accomplish this is by placing your awareness on the tip of your nose and being fully aware of the air as it flows in and out past that point. Once the awareness of the breath is well established, and the mind and body begin to become still, advance to the next phase.

- Do this by becoming aware of a tiny spot of light in the heart. And with each breath feel or "see" that light become brighter until it fills your entire body. Visualize, imagine, feel, or just know—do whatever works for you.

- Remember, this is one of the things you are—you are this body of light. It is just that the physical body is so dense that it absorbs the light before it can emerge.

- Now think of the highest principle or force that your belief system will support—God, Buddha, Christ, the White

Light, Universal Love, etc., and allow yourself to experience that quality. Let this be the highest, most sublime feeling you are capable of experiencing. For you it might be represented by some form, such as a teacher or guru. Or it might be a sphere of light——whatever you are most comfortable with. In any case, generate a sense of reverence for something more profound than we humans; perhaps that which represents what you are striving to become. What would it feel like for your personality to merge with the highest purpose or being that you can imagine? Take a couple minutes and blend with the highest principle or force that your belief system will handle—God, Buddha, Christ, the White Light, etc. Take all the time you wish.

- Now notice that the heart and the chest area are becoming fuller—as if you are beginning to make space for a greater depth of feeling, deeper experiencing.

- Focus on your heart. Can you sense its size, its shape, its rhythm? Experience by feeling, visualizing, knowing, or imagining, depending upon your capabilities. Take all the time you wish.

- Be aware of the blood being drawn into the heart, pumped through the heart and into the lungs, back to the heart, and out again to the entire body. Experience the heart as a tremendous source of power, of energy. Take a few minutes for the experience.

- The heart is the place where we transmute the lower energies into higher energies. Now feel, see or sense a chalice in your heart: a golden chalice, capable of being filled—a receptacle to receive that which we may be given at this time. Take a minute or two for the experience.

- Continue to focus your awareness on the heart size, shape, function, and the golden chalice. Perhaps by now the chest cavity has become sensitive enough for you

- Now experience the beating of your own heart. Focus on it, turn your attention inward and listen. Take as much time as you need.

- As the energy starts to move through the body, you may feel some minor discomfort, or feel a need to move or change your posture to allow the energy to flow more freely. So be sensitive to your inner promptings and allow the body to make space for the free movement of this energy. Let your body do whatever seems necessary to allow this energy to move freely from the base of the spine to the top of the head.

- Now another dimension—let us remember special moments that we have had in our lives that have touched us at a heart level. Perhaps the most intense of these is falling in love. Spend a few minutes reaching back in time (or for some it may be happening right now), but in either case, experience the feeling of love—falling in love, knowing love in your heart, being loved. Open yourself to the deepest possible love. Let it start in the heart center like a seed that is ready to burst open. Let it radiate throughout the entire body. Feel its warmth, and notice what kind of activity is created in the heart. Don't rush it.

- Now experience moments of reverence. We have all had moments when we have been touched very deeply by what might be called divine essence, or the presence of something much greater or higher than ourselves. Let your heart re-experience that, and be totally present for it. Or perhaps experience the presence of the most divine being that you are capable of imagining. Take your time.

- Let your experience inspire you to resonate to the highest quality within you, and in that resonance experience the love of God, which includes the love of self. Let this resonate with all the moments of love that you have ever experienced in your life. It's like collecting the myriad love experiences that lie within the heart into one force. The heart is truly the organ through which we respond to love. Take as long as you wish for the experience.

- Continue to focus your awareness on the heart center, and ask that all those seeds, all those precious moments when you have been touched by love, wisdom and deep understanding—ask that all these create a huge love force within the heart center; ask that they create an energy that will intensify in feeling so that you may better experience the function of the heart center. Take time to enjoy it.

- Now holding this love force, remember the response of your heart to beautiful music. I'm sure there have been many times when the beauty and depth of feeling have been so intense that you could only respond with tears. These are the moments when the very essence within you has been touched, and you respond from a place which allows you to resonate to the highest level represented within you. These beautiful feelings that are spontaneously experienced in the heart center can become the gateway to other dimensions of you. Enjoy the process for as long as you wish.

- The Christ's mission was the opening of the heart center of mankind, so His message was love, and we are still working on that message. So to prepare the heart center to have greater capacity and depth, we need to be aware of the times when the heart was touched. As we do this, that golden chalice in the heart will become larger; it will begin to vibrate, and as it vibrates it will draw energy from the higher centers and be filled. Gold represents purity. See this shimmering golden chalice filling with magic elixir from the higher centers, elixir representing inspiration, wisdom and the highest purpose. Make no conditions about what this should feel like, or look like—just prepare a place to receive what has been promised to us, and rest in the knowledge that the purpose will be fulfilled if we create the right environment within ourselves. Continue to visualize that golden chalice in the heart center being filled with the essence of love. Take all the time you wish.

Throat Chakra Meditation (Fifth Center)

- Get into a comfortable sitting position. Place your total awareness on the breath, to the exclusion of all other thoughts. Use whatever method you have found that will allow the mind and the body to become still. Just follow the breath in and out for several cycles. Become totally relaxed. Take whatever time you need. Put your awareness on the throat chakra. Keep it there for a minute or more.

- The throat center is the energy source in each one of us from which we derive power to describe the higher realms of consciousness as well as putting into words the aspects of the self—the personality. The throat center is the vehicle through which we communicate words of love, wisdom and information. The heart speaks through the throat center. The throat center is the vehicle through which we describe ourselves to other people, and describe the world in which we live. It is our personal form of communication.

- The throat chakra (fifth center) seems to have two openings or forms of expression—one from the upper chakras, and the other from those below. If the upper centers are well activated, the channel leading to higher sources of information is available to us and we speak the truth. And as we speak the truth, more truth is revealed to us. Thus we benefit from the information we pass along.

- The highest purpose of this center is the transmission of wisdom to enlighten ourselves as well as enlighten those that might become students as we move through life. The throat chakra is one of the most precious centers, for in a sense, it can become the vehicle through which the voice of God, or the highest principle, speaks. As this happens, we experience the creative aspect of God, which is also within us. The word gives form to our imaginings, our inspirations.

- The other opening or form of expression of the fifth chakra is from the centers below it. To experience this other opening, be aware of an essence flowing up from the heart chakra—it has an aura of love about it, the essence of love as it wafts its way up into the throat center. Thus, we are inspired to speak words of love, tenderness and compassion. In so doing, the throat center reflects what is going on in another part of the body. It clothes in words what is happening at other levels of our being—feelings, inspirations, and pictures—without which there would be no completion. Take a few minutes to absorb and reflect upon this wisdom.

- The throat center is the broadcasting system of the body. This function is to be used for the highest purpose—transmitting information from the highest levels of consciousness, clothing in words that which will become realities in our physical world.

- Now put your awareness on the solar plexus center, the center through which we experience emotions. The feelings and emotions in our lives and bodies remain simply as feelings and emotions until allowed to take form through the throat center as speech. What has been experienced in the solar plexus center now becomes a reality through the spoken word—not only our individual reality but also our shared reality.

- Next move your awareness down to the second chakra and feel a resonance between it and the throat chakra. Whether or not you are aware of this resonance, it does exist, so use your creative imagination to reinforce it at a more subtle level. Work with this idea for a minute or so.

- Perhaps you can sense a thread of light, a movement of energy making its way up from the second chakra to the throat chakra.

- Now feel a sensation of love and expansion filling your body—as if you were resonating with the most beautiful

267

aspects of love—impersonal love—unconditional love—a sense of well being—unity—a feeling of appreciation for your body—a real sense of loving yourself. Feel this loving energy from this second chakra spread throughout the body. Take a few minutes to experience these feelings of love.

- Although the root chakra and the second chakra both play major roles in human sexuality, there is a vast difference in their respective energies or powers. The sexual power of the second chakra is one of sharing with others in a loving, giving way. It

- It seems to produce the fuel or the power that allows us to disseminate head center wisdom that has substance and meaning. It empowers us to create through the voice, word concepts that will touch people at a very deep level. Much of the effectiveness of vocal delivery would be lost if it were not for the power of the second chakra. From it comes an impersonal power that gives depth and clarity to information filtering down from the head center. So be aware of the interconnectedness, the interdependency of these three chakra centers—inspiration from the head center; the motivating power of the second chakra (probably a sublimation of some of the sexual energy); and the functional organ of the throat center—the voice box—from which the information is broadcast in words.

- Now take a minute or so and visualize these three centers: the head chakra (pause); the second chakra (pause); the throat chakra (pause); and the energy network that leads to the fullest use of the power they contain.

- By doing this visualization we are reinforcing an energy network that will allow us to express in words the highest, clearest information that we are capable of receiving. Return now to a full awareness of the breathing process. Breathe light, energy, and awareness into the head chakra. Don't rush—take your time.

- Now breathe light, energy, and awareness into the second chakra—several breaths with full awareness.

- Breathe light, energy, and awareness into the throat chakra. Again, several breaths.

- And now sense their interconnectedness by whatever means seems most appropriate to you. Take your time—there's no hurry.

- Now experience the greatest truth, the highest principle, like the voice of God flowing from the head center to the throat center and from there being broadcast to the universe. The prana is the vehicle through which it moves. (Prana is a Hindu term for the etheric component of air. It is not perceptible or measurable with scientific instruments.) Take a minute or two for this experience.

- Now breathe prana into the heart center on the in-breath and feel it being radiated out to the universe through the throat center on the out-breath. Continue this exercise for a minute or so.

- Now feel love, compassion, understanding, and forgiveness flowing from the heart center to the throat center, and from there being radiated into the universe. Take all the time you need.

- Now shift your awareness to the solar plexus center and start breathing prana into it on the in-breath and radiating the prana from the throat center on the out-breath. Several breaths.

- The solar plexus is the center through which we experience emotions. Take a few moments to be aware of one of the predominant, unuseful emotions influencing your life, and sense it being carried by the prana from the solar plexus to the throat center, and there being expelled. It may take several breaths.

- Now be aware of another unuseful emotion that influences your life, and feel it being carried by the prana to the throat center and being expelled. Don't rush this part of the exercise.

- Be aware of the second chakra by sensing prana being drawn into it and moving up through a thread of light, a column of prana, to the throat center. The essence from this second chakra is the fuel, the energy, the power for broadcasting love, truth, and wisdom to the universe. This connection, this resonance exists, so reinforce it by being aware of it for a minute or so.

- Now again, total awareness of the second chakra; breathe prana into it—feel the energy building up like pressure. Just allow it to accumulate for several breaths.

- Allow a sensation of love and expansion to fill your body— as if you were tuned into the most beautiful aspects of love—impersonal love, unconditional love. Don't rush it.

- Experience a sense of well-being, unity, a feeling of appreciation for your body...a real sense of loving yourself. Feel this love spread throughout the body from this second chakra. Enjoy it for a few minutes at least.

- The sexual power of the second chakra allows you to share with others in a loving, giving way. Experience this kind of unconditional love. Don't rush.

- Now be aware of the interconnectedness, the interdependency of the head chakra, the throat chakra, and the second chakra. Breathe prana into the second chakra and feel the sexual power of this center move up to the throat to supply the fuel, the energy, the motivation to disseminate the truth and wisdom of the head chakra. Relax and enjoy it.

- Again sense this network of energy between these three chakras by whatever means seems appropriate. You have all the time you need.

Head Chakra Meditation (Sixth Center)

- Get into a comfortable sitting position, eyes closed, and full awareness of the breath. Breathe a little more deeply than usual. No thoughts, just awareness of the breath. Continue breathing this way for two or three minutes.

- Now transfer your awareness to your heart chakra—the heart organ. Is your chest cavity sensitive enough to feel your heart beating? Take all the time you need.

- Now move your awareness up to the head center, that resonance between the pituitary and the pineal glands. When you begin consciously to activate the head center, you are in essence asking for the privilege of looking deeper (or higher) into the inner workings of the Universe. So become aware that this is the instrument through which you can expand your vision. Literally, this is the center through which we part the veil to look into other dimensions— dimensions that the personality is not capable of reaching. But since we are a part of the whole, a spark of Divine Essence, we have the tools to explore all the dimensions represented within us. Our task is to activate these centers, to recognize these tools, and to create the proper disciplines to make these tools available to us.

- The head center is very much like a beacon of light that penetrates these other realms. The head center is a tool through which we can reach up and out to those dimensions not available to the personality. Ask that you be given that which is relevant; that which will assist you; that which you are capable of seeing and using; and that which is consistent with the development you have created within yourself.

- The heart is a feeling center. It becomes the gateway. But activating the head center actually creates the form, the vehicle, the tool, by which you can obtain the information available to you. We are not talking about the mind. We are talking about going beyond the mind, of going through the place of inspiration to a place of knowing.

- But if we are to be connected with the information available to the head center, we must first prepare the climate, the environment, through the activity of love. Then once we have activated the head center, we can rest in that place of reverence, love and openness.

- The energy starts at the root center and moves upward—a natural flow. The grounding of the root chakra is very important in this kind of exercise. It is your anchor to Mother Earth, the "nourisher" of the physical body. So even though our attention is placed at the position of the third eye—the head center—the body will have to make certain adjustments to allow the energy to move from the root chakra through the intervening centers and finally to the head center. During this transit of energy, tension may occur at the base of the skull—the narrowest opening through which this energy must pass. So there may be some discomfort. This is a very difficult place for the energy to pass through, but do not concern yourself—just "breathe" it through—make space at this fifth or throat center by concentrating on the breath if any discomfort occurs.

- Now put your awareness on the heart chakra. Start becoming aware of the breath and the movement of energy up through the throat center. Take several conscious breaths.

- Allow the energy to move into the head chakra. As this energy moves up into the head, the pineal and pituitary glands begin to act like tuning forks—vibrating in unison. Remember, the pituitary is a few inches behind the eyebrows and the pineal is at the back of the brain stem. A triangle of energy results between the pineal, pituitary and the seventh chakra that is located just above the head—outside the physical body. The apex of this triangle is pointing upward, so in a very real sense it becomes an antenna of light through which information can flow. You may experience some eye

272

movement or other physical symptoms as the energy in this triangle becomes more intense, or you may simply experience a sense of peace and quiet. In either case, just be with it— enjoy it. Remain in this place with openness and expectancy, without striving or pushing. Ask that your perception be open to clarity, inspiration, right action, and that you be inspired to become an instrument of consciousness. It is not necessary to experience forms, inspirational messages or visions, for we are simply learning to create that bridge between the heart and the head centers. Some of you may experience various manifestations during the exercise. If this happens, simply observe, make a mental note and return to the visualization of the triangle of light between the pituitary, pineal, and the seventh center above the head. Continue to be aware that this vibrating triangle of light is an antenna capable of receiving information from outside the brain-mind system. Take all the time you want.

- It's well to remember that this head-center energy is available because it has moved up from the lower centers. So the lower centers are also important. The root chakra is your ground—your connection to the earth. The root chakra connects you to the earth, and the seventh chakra above the head connects you to the more subtle realms. They are both a part of you. The earth nourishes and maintains our body so the soul can have a suitable vehicle through which to express itself. We must never forget that without a strong physical body and without the help of the earth currents that give us vitality, we would not have a vehicle through which to experience the highest levels of ourselves. So both aspects are important. We focus on the center most appropriate to the work to be done. But that does not make one more important than the other. It simply means that for this particular moment in time, this is the center though which we can best express ourselves.

- Our assignment is to function as a total unit—to be strong physical beings walking firmly upon the ground, but reaching to the heavens for the inspiration and knowledge that will make our journey upon the earth plane more productive and more conscious. Spend a few minutes meditating on this.

- Now back to being aware of your breath.

- Again transfer your awareness to your heart chakra—the heart organ. Is your heart cavity sensitive enough to feel your heart beating? Pause and listen for a minute or so.

- Move your awareness up to the head center, and again be aware of that pulsating triangle of light between the pituitary, the pineal, and the seventh chakra above the head. Observe it for a few minutes.

- Realize that this triangle of light is a very real antenna through which information can flow. Experiment with it for a few minutes.

- Surrender to the process. Allow the breath to breathe you. Just allow it to happen. Sense the energy in the triangle becoming more intense, but remain in a place of openness, expectancy, without striving or pushing.

- Some of you may experience certain manifestations during this exercise. If this occurs, simply observe, make a mental note, and return to the visualization of the triangle of light. Continue to think of this triangle of light as an antenna capable of receiving whatever information might be available for you at any particular time. You now have all the time you need to enjoy the experience.

One-Minute Kundalini Exercise

One morning recently, before our meditation, Anne and I were discussing Kundalini and wondering what thoughts or simple exercise we could pass along to the readers of this book, as well as people in the groups that we have worked with for over twenty five years.

Our goal is to make as many people as possible aware of how useful Kundalini can be when it is accepted and welcomed into their lives. So effectively what we were asking was, "What can we do everyday of our lives that will safely awaken the Kundalini energy and make its very special properties available to us?"

After settling into a quiet receptive space, Anne answered, "Every time you think about it, visualize a full flow of Kundalini from the base of the spine to the top of the head. Don't visualize it moving up stepwise from chakra to chakra, but see it already flowing freely and smoothly from the base of the spine to the head center. See it as an accomplished fact, the way it really is at some deep level. Do this especially just prior to any creative or intuitive undertaking. Constantly ask Kundalini to participate fully in your life—expect it, know that it is already an accomplished fact—a divine reality.

"To make this visualization more effective, sense or imagine the Kundalini energy as a multi-colored, warm, sparkly fluid. Feel its warmth in the spine; see it sparkling, scintillating, as it moves through the spine. Make it as real as you can through any mental or emotional device you can conjure up. Feel, see, sense, imagine or visualize (whatever works for you) this sparkly Kundalini fluid flowing from the base of the spine, up the spine, into and around the pituitary and pineal glands in the head (the head chakra), there energizing these glands and creating that triangle of light that is capable of making contact with the Thousand-Petaled Lotus above the head.

"Kundalini can play very rough, when, in cooperation with the soul, it begins to remind the truant personality that it is time to start waking up to the God Within, and remembering who and what it really is. So take the initiative and make the first move toward an awareness of the God Within. If you don't, Miss Kundalini may decide to nudge a little."

APPENDIX II

TRANSPERSONAL DISCOURSE

I don't think a book about Anne Armstrong would be complete without a representative sample of the beautiful prose that flowed at times during Anne's spontaneous lectures. As I sat here "looking" through closed eyelids at the volumes of transpersonally inspired words that Anne has spoken during the past 50 years, I was aware of bright spots that sparkled like jewels on a sand beach. Two of these verbal jewels have been chosen to represent this segment of transmitted text.

Many times I transcribed these discourses by hand soon after they were recorded. One of the remarkable characteristics of most of these discourses is that they required practically no editing. During the initial editing I would perhaps change a word or two, then when I read it the next day I would in many cases change it back to the original wording. A few, however, required considerable editing to remove personal references to maintain the universal message. Another remarkable feature of these discourses is Anne's vocal delivery of them. To effectively deliver an inspired piece of literature, most of us need to read it through a few times to get the correct voice inflections, accentuations, pauses and cadence. But here was a person delivering a spontaneous philosophical discourse that was not only perfectly organized and technically well-constructed, but also perfectly inflected with pauses and accentuations correctly placed. It was as if the sentence or possibly the complete thought had instantly appeared in her conscious mind, giving her milliseconds to process the meaning and arrive at the proper inflections, pauses, etc.

Even now when I listen to the original recordings of these verbal jewels, I marvel at the capabilities of the human mechanism, especially when it is operating in the realm of the paranormal.

And I further realized that the most useful way to read these selections is with the thought of grasping the feeling for the Universal Plan, not an intellectual understanding of it. Gaining a meager working knowledge of The Plan may come in a lifetime, if we are one of the fortunate ones.

As I worked with the editing and formatting of the discourses that were to go into Appendix II, I kept having these "ah-ha's." I would realize that in one sentence, at most, a whole esoteric concept was espoused. Then my mind would recall where Anne had elaborated on this subject in one or several hour-long "lectures."

Yes, these Truths are very veiled at times, in allegories and cryptic phrases, but the Truth is apparent to those with a little esoteric background and the willingness to contemplate the contents.

Beyond this, I really don't know what can be said, or what needs to be said about these discourses. I just know that the profundity of these little jewels have many times brought me to tears during the editing—or reading—that's what happens when I encounter the TRUTH. Maybe all that needs to be said is, "When you need a spiritual boost, read one of these transpersonal gems."

Editor's Note

So here we are in 2010, re-reading these beautiful discourses and realizing that in 1960 the transpersonal realm was still following Funk & Wagnall's and Noah Webster's first and second definitions of "man" as a generic term for we humans, whether male or female. Changing the wording to make them acceptable to all 2010 women would destroy the rhythm and flow, and seriously detract from the cadence. So what do we do? There seem to be two options: 1) forego the inclusion of this part of Appendix II in the book, or 2) request the tolerance and forgiveness for the transpersonal realm.

A great deal of consideration and soul-searching has been given to this dilemma. We respect the feelings of those of you who wish to level the gender playing field. And we hope that in offering these words as they were originally spoken, you will accept that we have no less respect for your cause. We trust that you will simply enjoy the deep philosophical and spiritual essence behind the crude symbols writers and speakers must work with, to convey their thoughts and feelings.

My Dove Awaits

The bird of freedom sits upon my head,
and it coos as it woos my soul.
My soul kneels before this bird,
and I accept its gentle call.
The wings of this bird will enfold my soul;
I will feel the warmth
and the beating of its heart in my flight.
My mortal eyes will be closed,
and the eyes of my soul shall flutter open
as they awaken gently to the dawn of this new world.
I feel the movement as I glide through space.
I feel the gentle brush of angel wings in my flight;
and my soul leaps with anticipation
at what I am to behold.

*

And so I find myself standing
before the gates of Home.
Ceremoniously these gates are opened,
and in all my dignity,
in all my queenly beauty I walk through;
for I feel the stature of my soul.
I reflect upon the pain of many lives,
upon the harsh lessons my soul has endured
that I might be worthy to stand
at this threshold of wisdom

*

Coming forth I see the members of my court—
my heavenly family.
Intermittently I have returned to this beautiful
dwelling place—I am no stranger here.
I have returned to this place again and again,

281

but like the prodigal son, I, of my own choice,
have many times in the past closed these doors;
and even now I can feel,
I can sense the ache in my heart
as I heard the click of those beautiful doors.

*

For once more, I had set myself free
to wander through the earth in my search.
This search was led by the passions of my body,
for each passion must be thoroughly explored.
They lead us through devious avenues of expression;
they beckon to us, and the flesh,
which is weak must obey,
while the soul weeps in its solitude.

*

I can feel the battle going on
between the soul and the physical—
for it is truly a battle.
The lures of earth, the beauties of earth
that have become so real to us
call in their wicked ways.
With their melodious qualities
they ensnare, they pull,
they hold out their arms that we might enter,
and in our foolish way we listen.

*

The soul in its anguish must sit patiently,
waiting for the right moment
that once more we might
listen to that very beautiful melody within,
that hauntingly beautiful memory—
that memory of perfection.

282

And so patiently the soul awaits in its sanctuary—
but constantly it reads to us
from its book of memory,
hoping in some way to inspire us
to return to our rightful place.

*

And so like the prodigal son
I have had my day of searching.
I have followed each of these avenues
of earthly desire, of earthly emotions,
and now I have found the inner strength,
the wisdom, to turn my back upon materiality
and lift my eyes to my rightful place.
So I take up my sword of truth,
and I challenge those desires
that come to confront me,
for I have been armed with truth;
I have been shown the way,
and I am weary of the battles of earth.

*

And so, firmly, I take my sword in hand,
and clear the path to those doors
that are already open.
And thus I come to find myself within these gates.
Now I begin to feel the warmth, the hospitality,
the love that is beckoning to me,
that is drawing me in.
And so my soul has come to rest.
There are so many things to learn,
so many lessons to be reviewed;
For I have come to a point of reviewing
and not going back.

The purple robe, the crown, and the scepter are mine.
*

So, I dedicate my soul within these gates
to the avenues of service, that have been given to me,
for I know within me,
that I have already accepted this work.
My soul now knows what its mission will be,
and as the scroll,
inscribed with letters of gold and light,
begins to unroll within my heart,
the reflection of those words will become clear,
and my body shall carry out the instruction.
*

Reluctantly, my soul turns its steps
toward those beautiful gates,
and once more they are opened,
but this time I take leave with a feeling of joy,
a feeling that I have a beautiful secret within me—
a secret that is going to fill my life with beauty—
the beauty of service.
*

And so my dove awaits
and once more enfolds me in its wings,
and I make my return flight to earth
and to my earthly body.

October 1962

Behold the Land of Spirit

Let my spirit approach that place of peace,
that throne of beauty, of wisdom,
of power, of all things.
Let my spirit sit quietly within that place.
Let me assume an attitude of meditation.
For in meditation I commune with my very beingness,
and I know my beingness to be all things.
As I sit quietly in this attitude of meditation
let all wisdom pass before me.
Let me not view or try to understand this wisdom
with my mortal eyes, or my finite mind.
Let that area of feeling within me become activated,
Let its resonance remove all limitations, all barriers.
And let me become all things,
knowing at the center of my beingness
that I am all things, I am God.

*

But also let me know that the waves
or the ripples that I emit
are also a part of my beingness.
I recognize these as sound, and color, and form,
and yet I know them to be a part of myself.
My mind tries to interpret these things
that I feel and see,
for it deals in the world of form, color, and sound,
yet my search is for that stillness,
that point of stillness that has no sound,
that has no color, and that has no form.
This I know to be my goal, or purpose.
I know it to be Home,
the Home which I have never left.

285

Yet, I am weary of the travels,
for I have known them to be endless
and to take me in circles.
*

So once more I have heard the call of spirit,
and again I become quiet
and allow the stillness to reveal its message.
I have listened to the warbling of my mind,
over and over again.
I have allowed myself to step into the thought-forms
that my mind has created.
I have played with many things,
I have played with power as well as poverty.
And I have found these to be empty.
For the cup that I wish to be filled
cannot be filled with form, or sound, or color.
It can only be filled with spirit.
*

So I have finally prepared myself, my vessel.
I have emptied it of all things.
I have tested its strength and quality
through the many experiences of life.
Life I say? What is life?
Or could it be death of which I speak?
For I know this point of stillness to be more alive
than the life which I have experienced.
*

So I have finally made my choice.
And now I stand poised,
prepared to enter this moment of stillness.
But now, there is no hesitation,
for I behold a child who has played so many games.

But I know now the maturity of spirit,
for I have dared to look into the face of God,
which is my own reflection.
And I do not find it strange.
Why has it taken so long
to arrive at this point of stillness?
Was the confusion of life so attractive to me?
Was the form so enticing?
Were the pleasures of the flesh so sweet?
Yes, they must have been,
but, now, I hear the call of spirit,
and its voice is ever sweeter.

*

Yet, I know that spirit has no arms,
It has no form,
it cannot comfort me in my physical vehicle,
it cannot stroke my hair or wipe away my tears,
or increase the beating of my heart,
and yet I know spirit to be all things—
the very womb of my beingness,
the heartbeat of the Universe.
This is what I seek.
This is what all mankind seeks.
And so, we look for the path
that shall lead us to this point of union with spirit.

*

The path can be in the form of people,
in the form of books,
all distractions to woo the flesh,
to intrigue the mind, to test us.
Yet, when I look through the eyes of spirit
there are no paths,

287

for I stand in the very midst of that which I seek.
The cool water of consciousness bathes me,
Yet I feel it not,
for the flesh is not attuned to the ways of spirit.
It is attuned to the ways of materiality.
Yet, I know all things to be good.

*

Now the veils have been removed
and I feel the coolness of that water,
for my soul has thirsted long enough,
so that I now behold the drink
that is placed before me.
I look around and know myself
to be a part of all things.
But somehow my consciousness has been moved
from the physical plane to the spiritual plane.
I behold the same world, the same me.
But I behold it through the eyes of spirit.

*

I see before me a beautiful white hand
that is outstretched gently, tenderly,
its fingers curve in an enticing, inviting way.
I know this to be my own purity calling to me,
and I feel myself yielding.
For I know this to be the hand of wisdom
within myself, that shall continue to guide me.

*

I am again aware of the clamor at the physical level.
But the din no longer beats upon my eardrums.
All things have become softened.
All sharp edges have been removed,
and that which has been distorted

has become pleasing
to my eyes, to my taste, and to my senses,
because I am no longer steeped in materiality
where all things are harsh.
For I have dared to step inward
to that place of peace within myself,
and from that area of sensitivity
I view all things differently.
I realize they have not changed,
but that the change has been from within myself.
And I can now move freely
from the material state of consciousness
to the spiritual state of consciousness.
*

At the same time I know there is no movement.
But I sense the change.
I feel the dignity and the importance within me,
and yet the humility, for I am all things.
Each one of us is carrying our own torch,
looking for this place of peace,
this attitude of meditation
where we become one with all things.
But we are looking for that point of peace
outside of ourselves.
And so we create paths, we create obstacles,
we imagine a sanctuary to be just around the corner.
So man spends his lifetime in this endless search.
He lifts the candle high
to dispel the shadows before him,
he does not realize that he is the flame in that candle.
He does not realize
that the shadows

are only images his mind has projected.
He has come to accept the world of form
as being the all.
He is afraid to go beyond the world of form,
afraid to lose identity.
So the sanctuary that is within him goes unnoticed,
and the search becomes more endless,
for each thing becomes sweeter and more enticing,
and the very thing that man searches for
he carries with him.
Eventually, that candle must melt,
which is symbolic of the physical form,
for experience tears away at this vehicle
until the inner beauty is exposed.

*

Through suffering man is taught to turn inwardly,
not because the suffering is necessary,
but because it is self-imposed.
The flame within man has always burned brightly,
has always held a steady course,
but man does not see his own brightness.
For that flame is distorted through the physical form,
and man's mortal eyes
cannot show him his own inner beauty.
He beholds only the physical reflection,
and so life tears away at this physical form,
to show mankind its own inner radiance.
But each man must come to this radiance,
or this flame, in his own way.
He must follow his own imaginary path.
He must create his own sorrows,
in his search for happiness,

until one day he awakens from this dream,
which he has created,
and realizes that the flame he carries is himself.
Then all shadows, all delusions shall fall away,
and man shall blend with his inner radiance,
there to find the illumination he seeks.
*

For the physical form and the mind are shadows,
and when the inner radiance becomes bright enough
the darkness will be dispelled,
and form will cease to be,
and light shall blend with light,
The Greater Light,
yet man insists upon separation.
But as he blends with the Greater Light
he will realize that it is the same Light,
and that he is that Greater Radiance.
*

All things have value.
The tear that streams down the cheek has its value.
The pain we endure has its value.
For only by self refinement
can we enter this place of peace.
So do not cry out to be shown the way,
for it is only through stillness that it shall be found.
The infant spirit sleeps within man,
awaiting his gentle touch, that he might behold
the Land of Spirit.

July 4, 1966

GLOSSARY OF TERMS

Asana: A posture or manner of sitting (as in the practice of yoga). Many of the postures are very intricate and difficult to perform.

Astral Body: According to Rosicrucian doctrine the astral body is coincidental to the physical body but is less defined and much more etheric in nature.

Chakra: In Hinduism and Tantra, any of 88,000 focal points in the human body where psychic forces and bodily functions can merge and interact. In Hinduism there are seven and in Tantra four major chakras, each associated with a color, shape, sense organ, natural element, deity, and mantra. The most important are the heart chakra, the chakra at the base of the spine, and the chakra at the top of the head.

The Religion Book: Chakra
In the Tantric Hinduism of India, the ancient practice of yoga is a form of meditation designed to bring spiritual power through seven chakras (circles) located between the base of the spine and the top of the head. Although in the therapeutic sense chakras are viewed as the places where ch'i, or life force, is often bound up or blocked. In the religious sense, they represent psychological centers or planes of consciousness through which spiritual power flows. From first to last, chakras represent spiritual growth.

The first chakra is located at the base of the spine at the rectum. Its symbol is the serpent, coiled three and a half times, and it represents

293

the basic human need for killing and eating. The serpent, in the words of Joseph Campbell is:

> Nothing but a traveling esophagus going along just eating, eating, eating... This is the sacramental mystery of food and eating...In early mythologies (people) would thank the animal they were about to consume for having given of itself as a willing sacrifice. There's a wonderful saying in one of the Upanishads: "Oh wonderful...I am food...I am an eater of food." We don't think that way today about ourselves. But holding on to yourself and not letting yourself become food is the primary life-denying negative act. You're stopping the flow! And a yielding to the flow is the great mystery experience that goes with thanking an animal that is about to be eaten for having given of itself. You, too, will be given in time.

In short, the first chakra reminds us of our place in the universe—as part of the food chain. We don't just live in nature. We are a part of nature.

The second chakra is located at the sex organs. This represents the urge to procreate, to reproduce our species and ourselves.

The third chakra is located at the navel and represents the will to conquer, to master and subdue.

It is no accident that Sicilian dons in the Mafia, the godfathers, were referred to by a Sicilian phrase that translate to "men with a belly." From the sumo wrestler to the professional football lineman, a big belly symbolizes power and force.

These first three chakra centers represent the animal instincts of eating, procreation, and mastery. When we move up to the fourth chakra we enter a new realm, opening up to compassion and spirituality.

The fourth chakra is at the level of the heart. According to tradition, the Buddha was born from his mother's side, at the level of the heart. When you "open your heart" to someone you are elevated above the level of the animal.

The fifth chakra is located at the level of the throat and symbolizes creativity and communication.

The sixth chakra is located at the forehead—the "third eye" often pictured on the forehead of representations of Buddha. This is the eye that sees inward—the center of intuition and understanding.

The culminating, seventh chakra is the sahasrara, the thousand-petaled lotus at the top of the head. This is the chakra of spiritual maturity, exploding upward and outward into understanding and enlightenment.

When spiritual energy is brought up from the level of the animal to the level of spiritual awareness, it wakes up to the real world—the world of God-consciousness.

Occultism & Parapsychology Encyclopedia: Chakras

According to Theosophists, the sense organs of the etheric double that receive their name from their appearance, which resemble vortices. Although there are ten chakras (visible only to clairvoyants) but of these it is advisable to use only seven. They are situated not on the denser physical body, but opposite certain parts of it as follows: (1) the top of the head, (2) between the eyebrows, (3) the throat, (4) the heart, (5) the spleen (where vitality is drawn from the sun), (6) the solar plexus, and (7) the base of the spine. The remaining three chakras are situated in the lower part of the pelvis and normally are not used, but are brought into play only in black magic. It is by means of the chakras that the trained occultist can become acquainted with the astral world.

The Theosophical concept of chakras was adapted from the ancient Hindu understanding of kundalini, a cosmic energy believed to be latent in the human organism, responsible for sexual activity and also conditions of higher consciousness. The Hindu mystics pictured kundalini as a coiled serpent situated at the base of the spine in the subtle body. When aroused by spiritual disciplines, which included breath control and meditation, the energy darted up the spine in any of three channels, illuminating the seven major centers or chakras in the body.

These centers have been tentatively identified with the major nervous plexi. The seventh chakra, known as the sahasrara or "Thousand Petaled Lotus," is located in the area of the crown of the head. Many Indian yogis have described blissful conditions of mystical consciousness resulting from the arousal of kundalini and its successful culmination in the sahasrara. This supreme experience is compared with the sexual embrace of the god Siva and his consort.

Today the idea of chakras is somewhat universal in occult and New Age circles. There is some difference of opinion as to the actual nature of the chakras and the experiences associated with them but some uniformity as to their location exists. An early identification with the nervous plexi of the body was made by V.G. Rele in his book *The Mysterious Kundalini: The Physical Basis of the Kundalini-Hatha-Yoga According to our Present Knowledge of Western Anatomy and Physiology* (1939).

For comparative Chinese mysticism and meditation techniques in relation to chakras, see books of "Charles Luk" (pseudonym of K'uan yu Lu), notably *The Secrets of Chinese Meditation* (London, 1964).

• All the above discussions were taken from: Definitions From Answers.Com.

Discarnet Entity: The spirit or essence that survives the physical death of the body.

Entheogenic Substance: An entheogen (creates "god within"." en- "in, within," theo- "god, divine," -gen "creates, generates"), in the strictest sense, is a psychoactive substance used in a religious or shamanic context. Historically, entheogens are derived primarily from plant sources and have been used in a varity of traditional, religious contexts. With the advent of organic chemistry, there now exist many synthetic substances with similar properties.

More broadly, the term entheogen is used to refer to such substances when used for their religious or spiritual effects, whether or not in a formal religious or traditional structure. This terminology is often chosen to contrast with recreational use of the same substances. These spiritual effects have been demonstrated in peer-reviewed studies, though research remains difficult due to ongoing drug prohibition.

Examples of entheogens from ancient sources include: Greek: kykeon; African: Iboga; Vedic: Soma, Amrit. Entheogens have been used in ritulized context for thousands of years. Chemicals used today as entheogens, whether in pure form or as plant-derived substances, include cannabis, mescaline, DMT, LSD, psilocin, psilocybin, ibogaine, and salvinorin A.

Glamour: Alice Bailey has written an entire book on glamour, as it relates to esoteric matters. *Glamour: A World Problem.* The glamour of esoteric teachings and practice in general , has always held a fascination to a particular segment of mankind. In her book she addresses the Seventh Ray Glamours in particular:

- The Glamour of magical works.

- The Glamour of the relation of the opposite.

- The Glamour of the subterranean powers.

- The Glamour of that which brings together.

- The Glamour of the physical body.

- The Glamour of the mysterious and the secret.

- The Glamour of the sex magic.

- The Glamour of the emerging manifested forces.

For the esoteric student glamour is a serious problem. It is so easy to get trapped in psychism.

Group Spirit: An intelligent entity that is a "god" to less advanced lifewaves as ants, bees, perhaps all insects, worms, small animals, birds, etc, that have not developed a "personality" like domestic animals. The group-spirit is an "overlord" that works in the best interests of the particular species, aids in the physical as well as spiritual advancement of the groups.

Holotropic Breathwork: Holotropic Breath work is a psychotherapeutic form of breathwork developed by Stanislav Grof, M.D., Ph.D.

Kundalini: (1) In Sanskrit it means snake. In yoga, Kundalini is the latent female energy which lies coiled at the base of the spine. It is the spiritual force in every human being that lies at the base of the spine, coiled like a snake. It is also called "serpent power." Once awakened through yoga and meditation, it rises through the chakras, producing spiritual knowledge and mystical powers. (2) A mystical energy or force that exists at the base of the spine, and during a Kundalini awakening, makes its way up from the base of the spine into your forehead region.

Kundalini Opening: A person is said to be experiencing a Kundalini opening when the presence of an overactive Kundalini is readily discernable: Aware of an expanded consciousness; the presence of an unusual malady; an overwhelming sense of joy; the feeling of being one with everyone and everything.

Lifewave: A lifewave is a group of spirits with similar objectives that are injected into the world population over a reasonably short period of time.

Lingam: Sanskrit for the male sex organ.

Mantra: A sacred word, phrase, sentence or sound, used to enter a meditative, sacred, inner space.

Monad: In metaphysics, the one inseparable spirit in mankind, manifesting itself in each person; also the one inseparable spirit in nature.

Mudra: (1)During Anne's development the hands spontaneously formed gestures, movements that seemed to be expressing inner feelings and emotions. At other times she seemed to be telling a story through the postures and movements of the hands---mudras. (2) Used in the practice of Hinduism: Any of a series of arm and hand positions expressing an attitude or action of the deity. Also a series of symbolic body postures and hand movements used in East Indian classical dancing.

Psychism: The word is now used to denote every kind of mental phenomena, e.g., mediumship as well as higher forms of sensitiveness. A newly-coined word.

Psychedelics: Psychedelic drugs are psychoactive substances whose primary action is to alter the thought process of the brain, and perception of the mind.

PSI: The 23rd letter of the Greek alphabet, equivalent to (P) in the English alphabet, pronounced (SI). In parapsychology it is a collective for telepathy, clairvoyance, precognition, and psychokinesis.

Prana: In India, the etheric component, or counterpart of the air is known as prana.

Rolfing: (1) An alternative healing system developed by Ida P. Rolf (1896-1979), it is a stringent muscular realignment therapy. It is used mainly for back and neck problems and consists of deep massage therapy which "strips" the fascia. (2)It transcends chiropractic in that it is based on the notion that emotional as well as physical health depend upon being properly aligned. But in rolfing, alignment must be of much more that just the spine. To be healthy, you must align your head, ankles, hips, thorax, pelvis, knees, shoulders, ears, etc., in just the right way. By being properly aligned, gravity enhances personal energy leading to a healthy body and emotional state.

Samsara: (1) (Hinduism and Buddhism) the endless cycle of birth and suffering, and death and rebirth. (2) (In Jainism) it is the worldly life characterized by continuous rebirths and reincarnations in various realms of existence, described as mundane existence, full of suffering and misery, and hence is considered undesirable and worth renunciation.

Sesshin: A term in Zen Buddhism which means "to collect the mind". It refers to an elongated period of zazen, sometimes lasting sixteen hours a day for one or two weeks.

Shaman: A priest of Shamanism, a magician, a healer, holding that gods, demons, ancestral spirits, etc., work for the good or ill of mankind through the sole medium of the Shamans.

Soma: A "mythical" plant that the Holymen of India supposedly ingested to give them superhuman knowledge and wisdom. I know of no scientific evidence that it has ever physically existed. Also, a preported intoxicating or hallucinogenic beverage, used as an offering to the Hindu gods and consumed by participants in Vedic ritual sacrifices.

Spiritual Emergence: Expanding ones consciousness to include the non-physical aspects of the Universe.

Spiritual Intuition: (1) A clairvoyance, or knowingness resulting from a high degree of spiritual awareness. (2) Spiritual intuition is the outgrowth of healthy spiritual practice. The range of intuitive skills is a function of the person's needs and interest. A really talented spiritual intuitive can develop nearly unlimited talents, as can any enlightened individual.

Thought-form: (1) A thought form is a manifestation of mental energy, also known as a "tulpa" in Tibetan mysticism. (2) An apparition produced solely by the power of the human mind.

Thousand Petaled Lotis: (1) Identified by Yoga as the 'Crown' or "Thousand-Petaled Lotus" Chakra, this Aura-center encompasses the Crown of the Head, upper brain-mass and the ductless glands located within the brain. Associated with "Macroprospectus" in Kaballah.. and 'Cosmic Consciousness' in western Mystical traditions.. this Chakra "houses" that portion of the Self which endures unchanged through time. While the Soul (centered in the Third Eye or Crown Chakra just below the Crown of the head) evolves from Life to Life (or Phase to Phase in our development,). (2) This Chakra connects one to THE AKASHIC PLAN of 'indestructible light' of Asian Metaphysics. The Self-Identity which, lives in this dimension of Light, was called 'the Sekkem' by ancient Egyptians (meaning "the Power" and "the Form",) and may best be translated into English as "the God-Self" of Jungian Analysis. (3) The Thousand Petaled Lotus is also known as the Sahasraras. Refer to prior discussion on the chakras.

Transpersonal: The term Transpersonal is often used to refer to psychological categories that transcend the normal features of ordinary ego-functioning, that is, stages of psychological growth, or stages of consciousness, that move beyond the rational and precedes the mystical.

Transandental Experience: A spiritual experience in which the subject feels a sense of oneness with everyone and everything; has a feeling of ultimate joy; a sense that everything is perfect—just the way it ought to be, and a feeling that you are living in a tinker-toy world that just isn't quite real.

Universal Mind: Universal Mind is a generic term for Universal Higher Consciousness or Source of Being in some forms of esoteric or New age Thought, and spiritual beliefs.

Vital Body: According to Rosicrucian doctrine the vital body is an etheric, coincidental cell-for-cell reproduction of the physical body.

Yoga Breathing: Various inhalation and exhalation methods used by Holymen of the East in their meditation and other postural techniques.

Yoni: Sanskrit for the female sex organ.

Bibliography

Azoth Institute. *The Azoth Journal of Esoteric Wisdom*, Azoth Institute of Spiritual Awareness: Pine Grove, CA 95665-0537.

_____, *Meditation Training Album, Basic-Advanced-Esoteric.* Azoth Institute of Spiritual Awareness: Pine Grove, CA 95665-0537.

_____, *Twenty-Seven Esoteric Lectures*, Azoth Institute of Spiritual Awareness: Pine Grove, CA 95665-0537.

Bentov, I., *Stalking the Wild Pendulum.* New York: Bantam (1977).

Evans-Wentz, W.Y., *Tibetan Yoga and Secret Doctrines.* Oxford University Press: London, Oxford, New York, 1968.

Greenwell, Bonnie. *Energies of Transformation, a Guide to the Kundalini Process,* Shakti River Press: January 1, 1995.

Grof, S. (Editor) *Ancient Wisdom: Modern Science.* New York: State University of New York, Albany (1984).

_____, *Beyond the Brain: Birth, Death and Transcendence in Psychotherapy.* New York: State University of New York, Albany (1985).

Harman & Rheingold. *Higher Creativity.* Los Angeles: Tarcher, 1984.

Hastings, Arthur. *With the Tongues of Men and Angels.* Holt, Rinehart & Winston, Inc.: 1991.

Heindel, Max. *The Rosicrucian Cosmo-Conception, or Mystic Christianity*, Rosicrucean Fellowship, P.O. Box 713, Oceanside, CA 92049-0713, USA.

Jayakar, P. *Krishnamurti: A Biography*, San Francisco: Harper & Row (1986).

_____, Krishnamurti: *The Years of Awakening*. San Francisco, CA Harper & Row (1986).

Joy, B. *Joy's Way: A Map for the Transformational Journey*. Los Angeles: J. P. Tarcher (1979).

Jung, C.G. *Psychological Commentary on Kundalini Yoga*. New York: Spring Pub (1968).

Kaplan, Aryeh. *Jewish Meditation*. New York: Schocken Books, 1985.

Kennett, R. and MacPhillamy, R. *How to Grow a Lotus Blossom*, Mt. Shasta, CA: Shasta Abbey (1977).

Klimo, Jon. *Channeling*. Los Angeles: Tarcher, 1987.

Kripananda, Swami, *The Sacred Power, A Seekers Guide to Kundalini*. South Fallsbarg, New York: SYDA Foundation, (1994).

Krishna, Gopi. *The Awakening of Kundalini*. New York: Kundalini Research Foundation (1975).

_____, *Kundalini: The Evolutionary Energy in Man*, Boulder: Shambala (1970 rev).

_____, *Higher Consciousness: The Evolutionary Thrust of Kundalini*. New York: Julian (1974).

_____, *Kundalini, the Evolutionary Energy in Man*. Boston & London: Shambhala, (1997).

Lutyens, M. *Krishnamurti, the Years of Awakening*. New York: Farrar, Straus and Giroux (1975).

Majamdar, S. *Caitanya: His Life and Doctrine*. Bombay, Bharatiya Bhavan (1969).

Mookerjee, A. *Kundalini: The Arousal of the Inner Energy*. New York: Destiny (1983).

Motoyama, H. *Theories of the Chakras: Bridge to Higher Consciousness*. Wheaton, Ill: Theosophical Publishing House (1981).

Muktananda, S. *Kundalini, The Secret of Life*. SYDA Foundation, 371 Brickman Road, P.O. Box 600, South Fallsburg, NY 12779-0600, 1994.

_____, *Play of Consciousness: A Spiritual Autobiography*. Sidda Yoga Meditations Publications (2000).

Sannella, L., M.D. *Kundalini Experience—Psychosis or Transcendence?* Lower Lake, CA 95457, Intergal Publishing, (1992).

Shared Transformation, Sun Chariot Press. P.O. Box 5562, Oakland, CA 94605.

Tweedie, I. *Chasm of Fire*. Great Britain: Element (1979).

Yogananda, P. *Autobiography of a Yogi*. Crystal Clarity Publishers (2005).

Anne and Jim Armstrong have conducted new-age workshops for the past twenty-five years in the United States, Mexico, Canada, and Europe, at such venues as the Esalen Institute. Formerly, Anne maintained a full transpersonal counseling practice, and Jim was a chemist/rocket engineer. They currently live in California.

CPSIA information can be obtained at www.ICGtesting.com
Printed in the USA
BVOW01s0025090716

454964BV00001B/52/P